ESSAYS
HISTORICAL & LITERARY

ESSAYS

HISTORICAL & LITERARY

BY

SIR CHARLES FIRTH

OXFORD

AT THE CLARENDON PRESS

Oxford University Press, Ely House, London W. 1

GLASGOW NEW YORK TORONTO MELBOURNE WELLINGTON
CAPE TOWN SALISBURY IBADAN NAIROBI LUSAKA ADDIS ABABA
BOMBAY CALCUTTA MADRAS KARACHI LAHORE DACCA
KUALA LUMPUR HONG KONG TOKYO

FIRST PUBLISHED 1938

REPRINTED LITHOGRAPHICALLY IN GREAT BRITAIN
AT THE UNIVERSITY PRESS, OXFORD
BY VIVIAN RIDLER
PRINTER TO THE UNIVERSITY
1968

PREFACE

THE seven essays contained in this volume represent a great historian's excursions into the debatable land open to students of history and literature alike, and are admirable illustrations of the kind of contribution the historian can make towards the solution of literary problems. Though the subjects vary, there is much similarity of treatment. In most of them consideration is given to the sources on which the writer under discussion based his narrative or from which he derived his inspiration. A historian might very naturally select this approach when discussing Raleigh's *History of the World* or Milton's *History of Britain*, because to assess the value of the different kinds of evidence is fundamental. What is remarkable is the success of much the same method in literary studies. In the essay on Bunyan's *Pilgrim's Progress*, the sources of the allegory are shown to be the circumstances of the author's own life, the world at large so far as Bunyan knew it, and certain books—Firth's demonstration of the allegorist's indebtedness to medieval romances being a novel and important contribution. In the essay on *Gulliver's Travels*, it is proved that Swift often drew upon contemporary events in England for the parts of the book he first wrote; when he resumed his writing ten years later, however, his mind was more concerned with Ireland than with England, and the third and fourth voyages have many disguised references to Irish politics.

The historian's task is only half done when he has examined his sources, for there still remains the composition of his book. Similarly, the analysis of the sources was only half, if as much, of Firth's contribution in these essays. In the paper on Raleigh's *History*

of the World, the object was to show its place in the
development of historical writing in England and its
author's idea of history—that it should teach the moral
lessons that God punished evil-doers and that all events
were divinely ordained. Firth points out the effect of
these conceptions of history upon Raleigh's work and
how they influenced its proportions and made the
authority of sacred writings superior to that of profane
writings. In the essay on the *History of Britain,* Firth
holds that Milton often had a true conception of the
value of the evidence at his disposal as well as independence of judgement. Similarly, in 'Burnet as an Historian', Firth indicates that the bishop's conception of
his task was to set forth a 'true view of men and of
counsels' rather than to give a detailed narrative.
Burnet's philosophy of history is shown to be that
Providence controlled events and was on the side of
the Reformation. The lecture on Clarendon discusses
that nobleman as statesman, historian, and chancellor
of the University of Oxford. Firth had already submitted to exhaustive analysis the *History of the Rebellion*
in the *English Historical Review* for 1904; he could here
merely state his conclusions, that that part of the history which was written in the 1640's was the more
reliable, but that what was written in the 1660's was
superior artistically. In brief compass, too, the nature
of Clarendon's services to the Stuarts is judicially appreciated and the merits of his conservatism fairly
weighed.

The chapter on 'Ballads and Broadsides' contributed
to *Shakespeare's England* (1916) is here reprinted in
order that one of Firth's major interests should be
represented. All his life he had been a collector and
student of ballads, because he felt that they reproduced
the emotions and experiences of a stratum of society
otherwise inarticulate. The article is also noteworthy
inasmuch as it reveals the depth of Firth's knowledge

of an age antecedent to the Stuart period, which he had made his own.

In the editing of these essays a few small errors have been silently corrected, and all citations have been verified except about half a dozen which could not be found. In addition, fuller references have sometimes been given than were supplied in the original essays; but no attempt has been made to add footnotes to the essays their author left without annotation, though even here quotations have been checked.

GODFREY DAVIES

CONTENTS

BALLADS AND BROADSIDES[1]

SHAKESPEARE was as familiar with the English ballads of his time as Burns was with the songs of Scotland. Besides continually citing stanzas from them, he mentions their tunes or employs their language. Falstaff and Sir Toby Belch, Hamlet and Mercutio all freely echo contemporary ballad-literature. To a student of Shakespeare's plays, however, the chief value of the ballads of his time does not consist either in the light they throw on particular passages or in the explanation they supply of particular phrases. The ballads do something more than this: they supply evidence on the character of Shakespeare's audience. These remnants of the popular literature of the time show how the people lived, and what they thought, the stories with which they were familiar, and the allusions which they could understand.

Most of the ballads written in Shakespeare's days have perished, but enough survive, in one shape or another, to enable us to form general conclusions on the nature and the development of the species. Furthermore, the printers of ballads, in order to obtain copyright, were obliged to enter the titles of their productions in the register of the Stationers' Company, and the entries indicate the subjects of ballads now lost, and at times the manner in which the subjects were treated. Besides this, the date of the registration enables us to determine when a particular ballad was produced, and whether it preceded or followed others of somewhat similar title and subject.[2] Of the Elizabethan ballads

[1] Reprinted from *Shakespeare's England* (1916), chap. xxiv.
[2] Unluckily the records of the Stationers' Company are defective. Between 1570 and 1576 there is a hiatus in the register, and during a large part of the reign of James I the custom of registering ballad-titles fell into disuse.

which survive, some exist in the original broadside form, others in seventeenth-century reprints, or in 'garlands' and similar collections, while some few are preserved in manuscript.

Little is known of those who produced this mass of popular literature. Ballads are for the most part anonymous. During the early part of Elizabeth's reign the author of a ballad frequently put his name at the end: in this way we know the names of Leonard Gybson, William Fulwood, T. Ryder, Bernard Garter, Stephen Peele, and others. 'Finis, quod John Barker', or 'Finis q^d W. Elderton' are examples of signatures. It soon became usual to put initials only. William Elderton's productions are signed 'W. E.', Thomas Deloney's 'T. D'. Later it became the general practice to omit any signature, except in the case of a few men whose names had a distinct commercial value, such as Martin Parker.

Elderton and Deloney are the representative ballad-writers of the Elizabethan age, not only because they wrote more or wrote better than the rest, but because something is known about them. Elderton, according to Stow, was at one time an attorney, at another time he is said to have been master of a company of comedians. He wrote from 1559 to 1584, and died before 1592. Over twenty of his ballads have survived: the earliest are stiff and full of classical allusions; the later are vigorous and humorous, have an excellent swing and a rich vocabulary. He was frequently scurrilous, and sometimes indecent. There is extant a 'Supplication' addressed to Elderton by another ballad-writer, William Fulwood. A hosier named Leach, a simple man with no more wit than to call a spade a spade, had termed some of Elderton's verses 'filthy rhymes', and Elderton had replied with acrimony. Fulwood intervened to justify Leach, and to exercise his wit on Elderton's 'rich nose'. To this 'ale-crammed nose' Gabriel Harvey and other critics refer, and it became the tradition that

Elderton 'armed himself with ale when he ballated, as old father Ennius did with wine'.[1]

Deloney's name is better known, yet personally he is not so definite a figure as Elderton. Nashe terms him 'the ballading silkweaver'; Kemp refers to him in 1600 as 'the great ballad-maker', and as recently dead. The earliest ballad of Deloney's we possess was printed in 1586, but the most remarkable of his ballads are the three on the Spanish Armada, printed in 1588. In 1596 the Lord Mayor suppressed one of Deloney's ballads, because it made the Queen 'speak with her people in dialogue in very fond and indecent sort'. The printer was imprisoned, and the author in danger of prison; this perhaps it was that led Deloney to the safer trade of writing prose romances, such as *Jack of Newbury*, *Thomas of Reading*, and *The Gentle Craft*. Two little collections of ballads owed their existence to him, *The Garland of Good Will* and *Strange Histories*. Of the first the earliest extant edition is dated 1604, of the second 1602. Not all the ballads which these collections contain can be assumed to be Deloney's, though most of them undoubtedly are his, and it is certain that many of Deloney's ballads were not included. These ballads are for the most part simple and straightforward narratives, the best of them inspired by a patriotic fervour which lifts them above the commonplace. Deloney had also a certain power of telling a story.[2]

Ballads multiplied exceedingly as the reign of Elizabeth drew towards its close. To write them or to sing them became a profitable trade. The minstrel of the middle of the century led a hard life. One of the profession, Richard Sheale, for instance, in the curious autobiographical poem lamenting a robbery of which he had been the victim, describes his manner of living,

[1] Cf. Harvey, *Four Letters*, ed. A. B. Grosart, i. 201.

[2] H. E. Rollins, 'Notes on Thomas Deloney', *Modern Language Notes*, Feb. 1917.

and his poverty. Nevertheless, a generation or two later it had become a profitable trade both for ballad-maker and ballad-singer. Chettle, writing in 1592 his *Kinde-Hart's Dreame*, complains that 'a company of idle youths, loathing honest labour and dispising lawfull trades, betake them to a vagrant and vicious life, in every corner of cities and market townes of the realme singing and selling of ballads'. There is many a trades-man, 'of a worshipfull trade, and yet no stationer, who after a little bringing them [the apprentices] uppe to singing brokerie, takes into his shop some fresh men, and trusts his olde servantes of a two months standing with a dossen groates worth of ballads. In which, if they proove thrifty, hee makes them prety chapmen.' He goes on to mention two young men, 'the one in a squeaking treble, the other in an ale-blowen base', who bragged that they earned 'twenty shillings a day' by the exercise of these natural gifts.

Even the authors of popular ballads made money out of them. In *The Returne from Parnassus* (ed. Macray, p. 51), Luxurio, wishing to live well, scorns to be a scholar or schoolmaster, and aspires to write ballads. In one scene he is introduced with the boy he hires to sing his productions.

'Come boy', he says, 'if thou chante it finely at the fayre wee'll make a good markitt of it. . . . I am sure I have done my parte, for I am sure my pen hath sweated through a quire of paper this laste weeke; and they are noe small verses like *Captaine couragious, whome death coulde not daunte* [i.e. the first line of "Mary Ambree"], but verses full of a poeticall spirit; such that if Elderton were alive to heare . . . his blacke potts shoulde put on mourninge apparell, and his nose for verie envie departe out of the worlde.'

'I warrante youe', replies the boy, 'I'le purchase suche an auditorie of clowns that shall gape, nodd and laughe! one shall crye "a goodlie matter", another "bravely wanton", and a thirde "commende the sweet master". I'le make every hoydon bestowe a fairinge on his dore, his wall, his windowe.'

So he strikes up:

> Nowe listen all good people
> Unto a strange event,
> That did befall to two yonge men
> As they to market went.

The roguish pedlar, Autolycus, is Shakespeare's contribution to the gallery of Elizabethan ballad-mongers. Printed ballads are the most popular of his wares, and his singing of them at the sheep-shearing feast in *The Winter's Tale* is applauded ecstatically by his peasant audience. 'He sings several tunes faster than you'll tell money', says one hearer; 'he utters them as he had eaten ballads and all men's ears grew to his tunes; . . . he hath songs for man or woman, of all sizes; no milliner can so fit his customers with gloves.' 'I love a ballad but even too well', interposes the admiring clown, 'if it be doleful matter merrily set down, or a very pleasant thing indeed and sung lamentably.' The shepherdess Mopsa urges the clown to buy some ballads of the accomplished packman. 'I love a ballad', she adds, 'in print, a-life, for then we are sure they are true' (*Wint. Tale*, IV. iv. 181–263). There is another description of a 'ballad-man' and his audience in Ben Jonson's *Bartholomew Fair*. In one scene (II. i), Nightingale, 'a sweet singer of new ballads allurant', gives a list of his stock. In another (III. i) he sings to a circle of enthusiastic hearers 'A Caveat for Cutpurses'.[1] One of his auditors, Bartholomew Cokes, an esquire of Harrow, joins in the chorus:

> Youth, youth, thou hadst better been starv'd by thy nurse,
> Than live to be hanged for cutting a purse.

Squire Cokes is a lover of ballads, but demands a good picture at the head of one as well as a taking tune. 'Do you remember', he says to his sister, 'the ballads over

[1] Cf. the version in *The Roxburghe Ballads* (Ballad Society, 1871–99), iii. 491.

the nursery chimney at home o' my own pasting up—
there be brave pictures.' While he listens, eager to buy
the whole bundle of ballads, his purse is stolen. Grave
scholars like Selden and Prideaux sometimes formed
part of such an audience, for both were great collectors.
In 1600 Sir William Cornwallis, the essayist, draws the
moral which such scenes suggested to him.

'I have not beene ashamed to adventure mine eares, with a
ballad-singer, and they have come home loaden to my liking,
doubly satisfied, with profit, & with recreation. The profit, to
see earthlings satisfied with such course stuffe, to hear vice
rebuked, and to see the power of Vertue that pierceth the head
of such a base Historian, and vile Auditory.

'The recreation to see how thoroughly the standers by are
affected, what strange gestures come from them, what strained
stuffe from their Poet, what shift they make to stand to heare,
what extremities he is driven to for Rime, how they adventure
their purses, he his wits, how well both their paines are recom-
penced, they with a filthy noise, hee with a base reward.'

(Corne-waleys, *Essayes*, No. 15.)

At times more than one minstrel took part, and a
ballad developed into a duet, or a semi-dramatic performance, in which several performers united. To these
the name of 'jig' was usually given, which has been
defined as 'a dramatic ballad or a ballad drama written
to dance music, and capable of presentation by dance
action on the stage'. In one example, 'Mr. Attowell's
Jigge', the characters are 'Francis, a gentleman; Richard,
a farmer; and their wives'. In 'Rowlands Godson' there
are three characters, Bess, Bess's husband, and John,
Bess's lover. In 'Clod's Carrol' there are two characters
only: it is described as 'a proper new jigg to be sung
between a man and a woman that would need to be
married'. Some jigs extend to the length of twenty-six
or twenty-eight verses.

It is not easy to define a ballad. So far as substance
is concerned the distinction between the ballad and

various forms of lyric is not very sharply drawn. Many of the pieces included in Tottel's *Miscellany* (1557) were republished as ballads during the early years of Elizabeth's reign, and on the other hand a collection such as Clement Robinson's *Handefull of pleasant delites* (1584) contains many things originally printed as broadside ballads. Sir Edward Dyer's poem, 'My mind to me a kingdom is', was printed as a ballad in William Byrd's *Psalms, Sonets, and Songs* (1587), and Richard Barnfield's 'As it fell upon a day' became, with additions, *A Lover's Newest Coranto.*

The productions of poets and courtiers were drowned in a flood of ballads written expressly for the populace. A large proportion of these consisted of amatory ditties. 'A Newe ballade of a Lover extolling his Ladye' (1568), 'A very proper Dittie to the tune of Lightie Love', and 'Adewe, Sweete Harte' (1569), are good examples of the nature of these compositions during the earlier part of Elizabeth's reign. Mixed with them are stories of the quarrels of husbands and wives, such as 'The Pinnyng of the Basket', and 'A mery balade how a wife entreated her husband to have her own wyll', or fabliaux such as 'A mery new Song how a Bruer meant to make a Cooper cuckold, and how deere the Bruer paid for the bargaine'. Many of these ditties were immoral and indecent. A collection of songs issued about 1558 was called *The Court of Venus.* 'No filthy mind a songe can crave, but therein he may find the same', said the author of an answer to it called *The Court of Virtue.* A divine, named Thomas Brice, printed a ballad 'Against filthy writing and such like delighting', in which he asked if the English people were heathens, and whether Christ or Cupid was lord. In his *Anatomie of Abuses*, Philip Stubbes vigorously denounces the immorality of the popular ballads; and Nashe, who was not prudish, condemned some of them. 'I could hardly be perswaded', he wrote in 1592, 'that

anie professor of so excellent a science [as printing]
would be so impudent to print such ribauldrie as
Watkin's Ale, The Carman's Whistle, and sundrie such
other.' Ballads of this kind naturally lent themselves
to personal scurrilities. Falstaff threatens to avenge the
tricks which Prince Hal and his companions play upon
him by having 'ballads made on you all, and sung to filthy
tunes' (*1 Hen. IV*, ii. ii. 51). Cleopatra and her hand-
maiden are terrified by the thought that 'scald rimers'
may 'ballad us out o' tune' (*Ant. & Cleop.* v. ii. 215).

Some attempt to check these unseemly productions
was made by the Stationers' Company. On December
3, 1595, it ordered that the press and the types of Abel
Jeffes should be seized, he having printed 'divers lewd
ballads and things very offensive'. In 1597 William
Blackwell was fined 2s. 6d. for selling a ballad called
'Lusty Larrance'; in 1600 three printers were fined 5s.
apiece for selling 'a disordered ballad of "The Wife of
Bathe" '. But since their authors did not usually
attempt to register them, most ballads of this kind
escaped the Company's control. Moralists who wished
to combat this evil were driven to put their exhortations into the form of ballads in order to reach the
minds of the people. They published ballads against
particular sins, against slander, against whoredom,
against unthriftiness, and so on. Or else they produced
general exhortations to repentance and warnings of the
wrath to come:

> Good people all, repent with speede.
>
> All carefull Christians, marke my song.
>
> Awake, awake, O England.

These ballads and many others like them, as one of
their editors observes, 'discharged the functions of the
modern pulpit'.

Another way of counteracting the immorality or

frivolity of particular ballads was to moralize them. This was done upon a great scale in Scotland, where in *Ane Compendious Buik of Godly and Spirituall Sangis*, printed in 1567, a number of popular ballad tunes were wedded to new words of a religious instead of an amatory nature.[1] In England the process was not carried out on so comprehensive a scale, but there are examples of its application in particular cases. For instance, the ballad entitled 'Row well, ye Mariners', published in 1565–6, was moralized at once as 'Row well, Christ's Mariners' and 'Row well, God's Mariners', and the words of several political ballads set to this tune are extant. 'Fain would I have a prettie thing to give unto my Ladie' became next 'Fain would I have a godly thing to give unto my Ladie', and finally, 'Fain would I have a virtuous wife adorned with all modestie'. A love song with the burden, 'Dainty, come thow to me', became a devotional one with the burden, 'Jesu, come thow to mee'. Shakespeare quotes in *King Lear* (III. vi. 28), 'Come o'er the bourn, Bessy, to me', an old love song which, when Elizabeth ascended the throne, was converted into a political dialogue between the Queen's Majesty and England, and also moralized as a dialogue between Christ and mankind.

Quite apart, however, from moralization, a popular ballad was immediately answered, imitated, and continued, till air and words became familiar to everybody. Two of those referred to by Shakespeare supply good examples. In *As You Like It* (III. iii. 105) Touchstone quotes 'O sweet Oliver, leave me not behind thee'. This was the title of a ballad entered by Richard Jones on August 6, 1584, and on August 20 Henry Carr entered an answer to it. Two years later, on August 1, 1586, a third publisher registered 'O swete Olyver, altered to the Scriptures'. Still more popular were the

---

[1] Known also as *The Gude and Godlie Ballatis*, and re-edited in 1897 by A. F. Mitchell.

ballad and the tune of 'Greensleeves', mentioned by Falstaff and Mrs. Ford in *The Merry Wives of Windsor* (II. i. 64, V. v. 22). This ballad was registered on September 3, 1580, as 'a new northern dittye of the Lady Grenesleves': on the same day another publisher registered 'Ladie Greene sleeves answere to Donkyn hir frende'. 'Greene Sleves moralised to the Scripture' followed on September 15, and 'Green Sleves and Countenaunce, in Countenaunce is Greene Sleves' on September 18. On December 14 yet another version was entered, and on February 13, 1581, came 'Reprehension against Green Sleves', by Elderton. The series ended on August 24, 1581, with a ballad entitled:

> Green sleeves is worn away,
> Yellow sleeves come to decay,
> Black sleeves I hold in despite,
> But white sleeves is my delight.

At times old ballads were wholly rewritten and set to new tunes—a practice to which Armado bears witness when he proposes to have 'newly writ o'er' the ancient ditty of 'The King [Cophetua] and the Beggar', which in its original shape no longer serves 'for the writing nor the tune' (*Love's L. L.* I. ii. 115–21).

The ballads which Shakespeare quotes are always those which were most popular and best known. Amatory and religious ballads were longer lived than the rest, because they dealt with subjects of perennial interest. But a very great number of ballads were merely concerned with matters of temporary interest.[1]

---

[1] John Earle, in his *Micro-cosmographie* (1628), well described a little later in his 'character' of a 'pot poet' (No. 27) the wide range of the ballad-maker's topics: 'The death of a great man, or the fiering of a house furnish him with an Argument, and the nine muses are out strait in mourning gownes, and *Melpomine* cryes Fire, Fire. He is a man now much imploy'd in commendations of our Navy, and a bitter inveigher against the Spaniard. His frequent'st Workes goe out in single sheets, and are chanted from market to market, to a vile tune,

They filled the place of the modern newspaper, or were substitutes for prose pamphlets of news. A prose narrative of an event was often followed and sometimes accompanied by a verse narrative of the same in the shape of a ballad. For instance, on April 13, 1598, Thomas Purfoot entered a prose pamphlet called 'the true and lamentable discourse of the burning of the town of Tiverton', and on the 28th of the same month, 'The ballad of the burning of the town of Tiverton'. Sometimes the two were entered on the same day. 'Master Styrrop' entered on August 22, 1596, 'the Victorie against Rynebeck', and then 'any ballad that shall be made thereof'.

Public calamities, such as the destruction of a town, were good subjects, for at the moment every one was interested in them. The burning of the town of Beccles in Suffolk in 1586 was the subject of two ballads, both of which are still extant. One of them was the earliest known work of Thomas Deloney. In 1570 Richard Tarlton wrote a ballad on 'the fierce floods which lately flowed in Bedfordshire, in Lincolnshire and many other places'. This too has survived, but most of the many ballads printed on events of this kind have perished. Of the four ballads on the earthquake of April 6, 1580, nothing but the titles survive. One began:

> Quake, quake, 'tis tyme to quake,
> When towers and townes and all doo shake.

Another began:

> Come from the playe, come from the playe,
> The house will fall, so people say.

It is clear that the earthquake was long remembered, and that Shakespeare's allusion to it in *Romeo and Juliet*

and a worse throat, whilst the poore country wench melts like her butter to heare them. And these are the Stories of some men of Tyburne, or a strange Monster out of Germany: or sitting in a Baudy house, hee writes Gods Judgements.'

(I. iii. 23)—"'Tis since the earthquake now eleven years'
—was readily understood by playgoers. At the end of
Shakespeare's professional career, a characteristic ballad
which commemorated in detail the burning of the
Globe Playhouse in 1613 was widely circulated in manuscript versions under the title of 'Sonnet on the Pitiful
Burning of the Globe Playhouse in London'.

Few events or exploits were deemed by the mob to
be fully authentic without the ballad-maker's certifi-
cate. Falstaff desires, by way of attestation of his capture of that most furious knight, Sir John Colevile, that
the achievement should be enshrined in 'a particular
ballad with mine own picture on the top on't, Colevile
kissing my foot' (*2 Hen. IV*, iv. iii. 52–4). The sudden
surprises of the catastrophe in *The Winter's Tale* evoke
from an onlooker the regret: 'Such a deal of wonder is
broken out within this hour that ballad-makers cannot
be able to express it' (v. ii. 25–7).

Events which happened on the Continent were also
made known to the people through ballads, such as
those relating the incidents of the struggle between the
Huguenots and the Catholics in France, or of the
struggle between the Spaniards and Dutch in the Low
Countries. Most of them have perished, but half a
dozen are still extant. These are: 'A Warning to London by the fall of Antwerp' (1577); ballads on the battle
of Ivry (1590), on the capture of Calais by the Spaniards
in 1596, and on the siege of Rheinberg by Prince
Maurice in 1601; 'News from Flanders', which is an
account of the victory of Prince Maurice at Nieuport
in 1600, and 'the wofull Complaynt of France', which
laments the assassination of Henri IV by Ravaillac in
1610.

Naturally ballads on the wars in which England was
directly concerned, and on the conspiracies which
threatened to produce a civil war at home, are more
numerous. The Register of the Stationers' Company

shows that the rising in the North in 1569 was the subject of about twenty ballads, of which eight are still in existence, besides the long narrative ballad printed by Bishop Percy. Four-and-twenty ballads dealing with the struggle against the Spanish Armada and the victory over it were registered in 1588, and four of them still exist. Of this struggle Deloney was the laureate; three of the ballads are from his pen, and it is probable that he was also the author of the ballad on the capture of Cadiz by Essex in 1596.

Each of the conspiracies against Queen Elizabeth led to a series of executions, which in turn produced a crop of ballads. 'England's Lamentation for the late Treasons conspired against the Queen's Majestie by Francis Throgmorton' (1584), 'A proper new Balad breefely declaring the Death and Execution of 14 most wicked Traitors' (1586), and 'A Warning to all false Traitors' (1588), are good examples of their species. All inculcate the same moral:

> You traitors all that doo devise,
> To hurt our Queene in treacherous wise,
> And in your hartes doo still surmize
>   Which way to hurt our England,
> Consider what the ende will be
> Of traitors all in their degree,
> Hanging is still their destenye
>   That trouble the peace of England.

The most notable of these troublers of the peace of England was the Duke of Norfolk, executed in 1572, upon whom there is a curious ballad by Elderton called 'The Dekaye of the Duke'. Queen Mary Stuart's execution was celebrated in 'An Excellent Ditty made as a general rejoicing for the cutting off the Scottish Queen', but no copy of this ditty has survived. On the other hand there are two versions extant of a ballad on the murder of Lord Darnley; the first, preserved in Percy's folio MS., was probably written in Scotland; the second, printed in London about 1579, was apparently altered in order to meet some scruples raised by the licenser.

The censorship exercised by the government on all expressions of opinion about things which could be construed to be matters of State was a permanent check to the publication of ballads which touched public men or political events. No ballad on Essex's death could be registered until after the death of Elizabeth, ballads on the coronation of James I were kept back till they had been duly authorized, and those published in 1603 concerning the trial of Grey, Cobham, and Raleigh were called in and suppressed. Further, as Deloney's case showed, ballad-writers, like playwrights, might be called to account for any innocent reflections or allusions which happened to be misinterpreted or resented by persons in authority.

This minute and suspicious control was hardly necessary. Nothing could exceed the loyalty of the Elizabethan ballad-writers. 'A Prayer and also a thanksgiving unto God for his great mercy in giving and preserving our Noble Queen Elizabeth to live and reyne over us' (1577); 'A godly ditty or prayer to be song unto God for the preservation of his Church our Queene and Realme'; 'A pleasant newe ballad of the most blessed and prosperous Raigne of her Majestye' (1600), and many other productions of the same kind, attest this devotion to the Queen. A ballad, like a play, often ended with a prayer for the Queen, quite irrespective of its subject.

> Lord save our gracious soverayne,
>   Elizabeth by name,
> That long unto our comfort,
>   She may both rule and raigne,

ends the exhortation to repentance entitled 'The Belman's Good Morrow', and 'A most strange and trew ballad of a monstrous Child borne in Southampton' concludes in a similar fashion. The Queen's escape from a gun accidentally fired by a waterman while she was passing on the Thames in July 1578, her reception by the citizens of London in 1584, her visit to the camp at Tilbury in 1588, are all celebrated in ballads with a fervour and sincerity which cannot be mistaken for the expression of a conventional feeling.

The natural correlative of love for this 'peerless pearl of princes' was hatred of her enemies both at home and abroad. Popular sentiment was anti-Papal and anti-Catholic. The excommunication of Elizabeth by Pius V in 1570, and the publication in England of his bull for her deposition gave rise to four ballads, in which the Pope was denounced and derided. They supply a perfect commentary on Act III, Scene i, of Shakespeare's *King John*, and show how the scene between Pandulph and the king must have pleased the taste of an Elizabethan audience about the year 1590. Another little group of ballads written by Anthony Munday dealt with the execution of Edmund Campion, and produced by way of replication verses in favour of the sufferer written by Catholic pens. Anti-Catholic feeling was strengthened by the war with Spain, and still more by the Gunpowder Plot. But out of nine ballads entered in the Stationers' Register on the subject of the Plot, and those who suffered for it, only one has survived, and that in a very imperfect condition. It is 'The Shamefull Downefall of the Pope's Kingdome contayning the life and death of Steeven Garnet, the Pope's chiefe Priest in England'. Garnett is alluded to in *Macbeth* (II. iii. 10–13) in the Porter's speech as

'an equivocator, that could swear in both the scales against either scale; who committed treason enough for God's sake, yet could not equivocate to heaven'.

Two other ballads against the Pope, printed about the beginning of King James's reign, are preserved in the Pepysian collection.

It would not be safe to infer from the printed ballads that England was politically unanimous, and that there was neither religious nor social discontent. Only the supporters of the Government could express their opinions freely. Catholics who lamented the sufferers for their creed, or the destruction of the magnificent fabrics raised by the devotion of the faithful in earlier ages, had to lament in verses circulated in manuscript, while their opponents could answer them in print. Deloney's 'Pleasant Song between Plain Truth and Blind Ignorance', written in 1588, represents in a moderate form what the average Elizabethan Protestant thought about the controversy between the supporters of the old Church and the defenders of the Reformation.[1]

Social discontent, too, had to express itself in a general or an indirect form. 'A balade declaring how neybourhed love and trew dealyng is gone' afforded opportunity for denunciation of rack-renting landlords and rich oppressors of the poor (1561). One in praise of the Golden Age served to compare things as they were with things as they ought to be. 'The poore people's complaynt, bewayling the death of their famous benefactor, the worthy Earl of Bedford' (1585), and 'The crie of the poore for the death of the right Honourable Earle of Huntingdon' (1596), show what model noblemen were expected to be. The second Earl of Southampton, the father of Shakespeare's friend, is the subject of a ballad-epitaph praising him for his justice and liberality to the poor.

It was possible to praise good landlords individually

---

[1] *The Garland of Good Will*, Percy Society's reprint of 1851, p. 89. A more elaborate example of a controversial dialogue of the same sort is 'An Answere to a Romish Rime', reprinted in Farr's *Select Poetry, chiefly devotional, of the Reign of Queen Elizabeth* (Parker Society, 1845), ii. 267. Another instance is 'An answer to a Papisticall Byll, cast in the streetes of Northampton', reproduced in the Britwell Court collection (*Ballads and Broadsides*, 1912), edited by H. L. Collmann.

and by name, but bad landlords could only be attacked by creating imaginary types. 'A Lanthorne for Landlords' warned them neither to eject widows who could not pay their rent nor to store up corn against a dear year. The 'miserable wretch', whose story was related, turned the widow's house into a barn,

> And filled it full in harvest time
> With good red wheat and corne,
> To keep it safely from the poore
> Untill there came a yeare
> That farmers might oppress them all,
> And make all victualls deare.

Fire from heaven consumed his barn and heavy judgements fell upon his family. One is reminded of the 'farmer that hanged himself on the expectation of plenty', mentioned in *Macbeth* (ii. iii. 5). In default of an English example to serve as a warning, the balladmaker found or invented a foreign one. 'The wrathfull Judgement of God upon Bishop Hatto' was a ballad licensed on August 15, 1586, though the oldest version of it which has survived was printed about a century later. Again, in 1607, at the time of the revolt against enclosures in the midland counties, a ballad was produced entitled, 'God's judgementes showed against a covetous incloser of common pasture in Germany who was strangely trod to death of one of his own cattel'. Yet another method of attacking the enemies of society was the scriptural parallel. An attack on corruption in high places might be made by telling the story of Gehazi:

> Was not the bryber Gehazie,
> Rewarded justly of the Lord,
> Which for example verelie
> The Holie Scripture doth recorde?

His sin and his punishment are related, and the ballad closes with the hope that the Queen and her council will take care 'in this lande brybers to expell'.

Though there are a number of ballads inspired by the desire to preach a social or economic doctrine, most of the narrative ballads originated simply in the desire to tell a story. For the people ballads supplied the place of novels, and their authors derived their themes from every possible source. The Bible was continually drawn upon. The stories it contained were familiar enough to be intelligible to every one, and sufficiently interesting to attract when they were put into metre. Sometimes a number would be strung together in one ballad, as in 'A pleasant Posie or sweet Nosegay of fragrant smellyng Flowers gathered in the Garden of heavenly pleasure, the holy and blessed Bible'. Sometimes a single incident was selected for treatment. Gradually the moral became less obtrusive, and the intrinsic charm of the story the obvious motive for retelling it. A series of simple narrative ballads, dealing with the adventures of the chief characters mentioned in the Old Testament or the Apocrypha, came into existence. One of the earliest and most popular of this kind of ballads was 'The Constancy of Susanna', of which the first line is quoted by Sir Hugh Evans in the first quarto of *The Merry Wives of Windsor* (ed. Greg, l. 717), and again by Sir Toby Belch in *Twelfth Night* (ii. iii. 87).

> There dwelt a man in Babylon
> of reputation great by fame,
> He took to wife a fair woman,
> Susanna she was called by name.

Another 'pious chanson' was 'Jeptha, Judge of Israel', which Hamlet quotes to Polonius (ii. ii. 431–6). There are many more written in the same style and on the same model. When a singer began,

> In Nineve old Toby dwelt;

or

> When Samson was a tall young man;

or

> When King Nebuchadnezzar was puffed up with pride,

an Elizabethan audience settled down to hear an old story with a sound moral in nineteen or twenty stanzas. The Greek and Roman classics were used for the same purpose as the Bible. At first biblical and classical characters or incidents were often combined. Elderton, in 'The Panges and Fits of Love', leads off with the case of King Solomon:

> Was not good kyng Salamon
> Ravished in sondry wyse,
> With every livelie paragon
> That glistered before his eyes?
> If this be trewe, as trewe it was,
> Lady! lady!
> Why should not I serve you, alas,
> My deare lady?

Then come the classical examples. One verse runs:

> Knowe ye not how Troylus
> Languished and lost his joye,
> With fittes and fevers mervailous
> For Cressida that dwelt in Troye?

Another inquires:

> What say you then to Piramus
> That promised his love to mete,
> And founde by fortune mervailous
> A bloudie clothe before his feete,
> For Tysbie's sake himself he slewe,
> Ladie, ladie!
> To prove that he was a lover true,
> My deare ladie.

When Mercutio takes leave of Juliet's nurse, singing derisively, 'Lady, lady, lady' (*Rom. & Jul.* II. iv. 152), the wag doubtless has the refrain of this ballad in mind.[1] Each of the legends mentioned in 'The Panges and

---

[1] 'Lady, lady,' is however, the refrain also of the ballad of 'The Constancy of Susanna', to which reference has been made already (see p. 18).

Fits of Love' was also treated in separate ballads. One of the oldest Elizabethan ballads is that beginning 'When Troilus lived in Troy town', and one on Pyramus and Thisbe is found in Clement Robinson's *Handefull of pleasant delites*. Every Elizabethan lover knew about Troilus long before Shakespeare made a play about him, and there was nothing absurd in supposing that Elizabethan artisans were familiar with the story of Pyramus. Amongst the ballads which survive are one on Apelles and Pygmalion, another on Diana and Actaeon, and others on Aeneas, 'the wandering Prince of Troy', and 'Constant Penelope', the 'looking-glass for ladies'. But these survivors are but a tithe of the ballads on classical legends which were published during the early part of Elizabeth's reign. In the one year 1569–70, no less than seven were entered in the Stationers' Register: 'The tyranny of Judge Appius'; 'The Miserable State of King Midas'; 'The unfortunate End of Iphis'; 'The Death of Acrisius'; 'Ptolemy King of Egypt'; 'Synorix and Camma,' and one which began 'No man could get Atalanta by running'.

When the classics had been thoroughly ransacked, or classical stories had ceased to attract, English history supplied fresh materials. Fair Rosamund and Jane Shore were made heroines of romance: the downfall of the proud Spensers, the lamentable Fall of Queen Eleanor, Edward III's courtship of the Countess of Salisbury, and Edward IV's wooing of the Fair Maid of London, and many similar incidents were narrated. Deloney, who wrote a large number of these historical ballads, including all that are best known, took Holinshed, Stow, or Grafton, and turned a story into verse, sometimes adopting the very words of one of the chroniclers, sometimes altering and adding details. He did not scruple to take his subjects from very recent history, such as the May-Day riots against foreign merchants in 1517, or the wanderings of the Duchess of

Suffolk during the Marian persecution. Eight or nine of these historical ballads are contained in *The Garland of Good Will*. His *Strange Histories* contains a consecutive series of ten more, extending from the Norman Conquest to the rebellion of Wat Tyler. *The Crowne Garland of Golden Roses: Gathered out of Englands Royall Garden*, which Richard Johnson published in 1612, contained a number of additional ballads on the events of the fifteenth and sixteenth centuries, and carried the metrical history of England down to the reign of Queen Elizabeth. No doubt some of these ballad narratives were from Johnson's pen, though he is best known as the author of the prose romance entitled *The Seven Champions of Christendom*, which had appeared in 1596.

English history was not an inexhaustible source; from the first it had been supplemented by legend and romance. The Robin Hood cycle was enlarged by the addition of fresh lays, as, for instance, Robin's adventure with the Pinder of Wakefield. Adam Bell rivalled Robin in popularity, and both Mercutio and Benedick cite him as a model marksman (*Rom. & Jul.* II. i. 13; *Much Ado*, I. i. 269). The old romance of Roswall and Lilian became in 1580 the ballad of the Lord of Lorne and the false Steward. 'Guy of Warwick' was condensed into a ballad in 1592. A ballad on Patient Grissell was entered about 1566, though that we have is probably of a later date, and perhaps by Deloney. The ballad of 'The Judgement of God shewed upon one John Faustus, Doctor in Divinity', dates from 1589, or possibly 1580. Shakespeare's favourite, 'King Cophetua', which he cites five times in four different plays (*Love's L. L.* I. ii. 115, IV. i. 66; *Rom. & Jul.* II. i. 14; *Rich. II*, v. iii. 80; *2 Hen. IV*, v. iii. 103), appeared first as 'A Song of a King and a Beggar', and was doubtless written by Richard Johnson, whose *Crowne Garland* contains the oldest extant version of it. The reference to it in *Love's Labour's Lost* seems to show that it was written somewhere about 1590. Malory's *Morte d'Arthur* supplied a source for some ballads. Deloney drew from it the episode of Sir Lancelot's combat with Tarquin, and Falstaff quotes the first line of his ballad in *2 Henry IV* (II. iv. 36), 'When Arthur first in court began'. Johnson's *Seven Champions of Christendom* was another fount of inspiration. 'Why do you boast of Arthur and his knightes' began a ballad called 'Saint George's Commendation', published in 1612. On August 21 in that year there was registered 'Wonderfull Strange Newes out of Germanye of a Jewe that hath lived wanderinge ever since the passion of our Saviour Christ'.

At a pinch the ballad-writer was capable of inventing a plot instead of borrowing one. 'Maudlin, the merchants daughter of Bristow', who was called 'the touchstone of true love', is a simple love-story of the rhymer's own devising (published in 1595). The story of the fair Widow of Watling Street and her three daughters (published in 1597), the 'most sweet Song of an English merchant born at Chichester', and the 'lamentable ballad of the Lady's Fall', are good specimens of these home-made romances. Another very popular story was 'Young Bateman', one of the many ballads 'against the hard hearts of maids' who preferred rich old men to comely proper young ones, and were duly punished for the bad choice. This was originally entitled 'A godly warning for all maidens by the example of God's judgement shewed on one Jerman's wife of Clifton in the county of Nottingham', and purported to relate an event which had really happened; it was entered in the Stationers' Register, June 8, 1603. Authors discovered that the life of the time supplied better subjects than chronicles or romances, and that a recent domestic tragedy was of all topics the most attractive and the most moving. The most famous of all ballads, namely, 'The Babes in the Wood', appeared in October 1595 and was registered as 'The Norfolk Gentleman his Will and Testament, and how he committed the keeping of his children to his owne brother, who delte most wickedly with them, and howe God plagued him for it'. The murder of a husband by his wife, or a wife by her husband, if there was some story of love or jealousy behind it, was at once seized upon as a fitting theme. The murder of Mr. Page of Plymouth in 1591 furnished Deloney with the stuff of two ballads, one the Lamentation of Eulalia Page, the other that of George Strangwidge, for whose sake she consented to her husband's death. Often the same event attracted both the balladmaker and the dramatist. In 1605 Walter Calverley murdered two of his young children and stabbed his wife. 'A ballad of a lamentable Murther donne in Yorkeshire by a gent uppon two of his own Children' was registered on July 3, 1605, and on May 2, 1608, there followed the well-known drama, *A Yorkshire Tragedy*, which the publisher impudently assigned to Shakespeare's pen. At times a long interval elapsed between the event and its re-narration in ballad or play. Thomas Arden was murdered in 1551, the tragedy of *Arden of Feversham* appeared in 1592, the ballads apparently not till 1633. If there were some cases in which a popular ballad either supplied the basis of a play or suggested its composition, there were even more in which a play was popularized in the shape of a ballad. The ballad on Dr. Faustus preceded Marlowe's play by eight or nine years, since it was registered in 1580, but Kyd's *Spanish Tragedie* gave birth to the ballad of the same title; and the comedy of *Mucedorus* was printed in 1598, while the ballad is evidently much later. The play and the ballad of *Titus Andronicus* were both entered on the same day, February 6, 1594, by the same printer, John Danter. 'A newe ballad of Romeo and Juliet' was entered on August 6, 1596, a year before Shakespeare's play was printed, but probably some time after it had been put on the stage. In the case of *The Merchant of Venice*, the ballad of 'Gernutus' is no doubt older than the play, but the name given to the inexorable Jew shows that the ballad is connected with the play called *The Three Ladies of London*, rather than with Shakespeare's. So, too, the ballad of 'King Leare and his Three Daughters' is clearly later than Shakespeare's play, and was most likely suggested by it.

While players and ballad-writers often employed the same sources, the authors of the ballads made greater use of contemporary events. There are more topical ballads than there are topical plays. In the first place the communication of news was one of the chief objects of the ballad-writers; in the second place an episode was enough for him, while the dramatist needed an incident containing the elements of a plot. The dying speech of an ordinary criminal was sufficient matter for a ballad. The confession of George Sanders, the 'lamentation of Henry Adlington', a fencer, who was hanged for murder, and the lament of William Wrench, a soldier executed for desertion, are examples. One of the earliest of these laments is the 'sorrowfull Sonet made at Cambridge Castle' by George Mannington, beginning 'I waile in wo, I plunge in pain', which was entered in the Stationers' Register in 1576, and is preserved by its inclusion in the *Handefull of pleasant delites*.[1] In *Eastward Hoe* (v. i), Quicksilver, the debauched apprentice, shows his penitence for his sins against his master by singing a confession modelled on Mannington's, and earns his master's forgiveness thereby. No criminal who had any title to fame left the world without 'the meed of some melodious tear'. Luke Hutton, the highwayman, executed at York in 1595, was not only the reputed author of a poem and a prose tract, but the subject of a play and a ballad. His

[1] Ed. Edward Arber, pp. 57–9.

'Lamentation' is an autobiography in verse, reciting the robberies committed by himself, and the twelve ruffians he called his 'twelve Apostles'.

> There was no squire nor barron bold,
> Ah woe is me, woe is me, for my great folly!
> That rode that way with silver and gold,
> Be warned, young wantons, hemp passeth green holly!
> But I and my twelve Apostles gaie
> Would lighten their load ere they went away.

Nine score indictments and seventeen were read against him, and each was found felony, but he felt secure of pardon in a higher court, and ended:

> When on the ladder you shall me view
> Think I am nearer heaven than you.

There was a good deal of sympathy for criminals whose crimes had something spirited and romantic about them. John Musgrave, executed at Kendal for robbing the king's receiver, was celebrated in a ballad with the refrain, 'Farewell the flower of serving men'. We are told in another ballad that 'a thousand hearts were sorry', and 'a thousand lasses wept full sore' for the death of a 'worthy gentleman named George Stoole', executed at Newcastle for stealing sheep and horses on the Border. It is exceptional to find a ballad on a highwayman so hostile and unsympathetic as that on Philip Collins, alias 'The Devil of the West'.

Massinger introduced into his *Bondman* (v. iii) a criminal who begs that he may not be executed twice over:

> At the gallows first, and after in a ballad
> Sung to some villainous tune. There are ten groat-rhymers
> About the town, grown fat on these occasions.
> Let but a chapel fall, or street be fired,
> A foolish lover hang himself for pure love,
> Or any such like accident, and before
> They are cold in their graves some damn'd ditty's made
> Which makes their ghosts walk.

Princes and nobles suffered from rhymers in the same way. There are 'A most Royal Song of the Life and Death of our late renowned Princess Queene Elizabeth' and 'A Short and sweet Sonnet' made by one of her Maids of Honour to be sung to the tune of 'Phillida flouts me'. King James himself is said to have written a ballad on the death of his son Prince Henry, entitled 'The good Shepherd's sorrow for the Death of his beloved Son'. There are also extant funeral ballads on the Earls of Arundel, Southampton, Bedford, and Huntingdon, on Bishop Jewell, on Sir Francis Walsingham, on the Lady Mayoress, and on a foreign merchant named Benedict Spinola. The custom of actually hanging memorial verses on the tombs of the dead encouraged their production. In *Much Ado about Nothing*, Leonato bids Claudio mourn for Hero in this way:

> If your love
> Can labour aught in sad invention,
> Hang her an epitaph upon her tomb. (v. i. 295-7.)

There is a good example of these compositions amongst the *Shirburn Ballads*, one of which is headed, 'The Lover being sorrowfull for the death of his Lady E. C., writeth this Epitaph followinge'.

Another class of ballads consists of relations of prodigies and strange events. The pack of Autolycus, besides containing 'the prettiest love songs for maids', included one narrative of a fish that appeared upon the coast, and sang a ballad against the hard hearts of maids, and another telling how a usurer's wife was brought to bed of twenty money-bags at a birth (*Wint. Tale*, iv. iv. 264-84). The printers of ballads and broadsides recorded monstrous births as attentively as grave historians of the time noted meteors and comets and sights in the air.

Sometimes the event is related and the monster described entirely in verse, as in 'The true description of a monsterous Chylde' born in the Isle of Wight in October 1564, or 'The true description of two monsterous Children lawfully begotten betwene George Stevens and Margerie his wyfe', born at Swanbourne in Bucks on April 4, 1566. Pictures of the monsters are often given as illustrations to the ballads. Sometimes a prose description is preceded or followed by a verse exhortation to take heed of these warnings of the wrath of God and repent betimes. The monstrous pig with 'a head much like to a dolphin's head', born not far from Charing Cross in 1562, was a sign not difficult to interpret:

> What might these monsters to us teache
>   Which now are sent so rife,
> But that we have Goddes word well preacht
>   And will not mend our life?

So with the child born at Maidstone, October 24, 1568:

> This monstrous shape to thee, England,
>   Playn shewes thy monstrous vice,
> If thou ech part wylt understand
>   And take thereby advice.

The huge mouth typified the greediness of the English people, the fingerless hands its laziness, other deformities signified kindred vices. Occasionally a monster was treated not as a warning against vices in general, but as a manifestation of the consequences of some particular sin. 'Prides fall: or a warning to all English women by the example of a strange monster borne of late in Germany by a proud marchant's wife', is a story told to show 'England's fayre daintye dames' the result of too much devotion to new fashions in dress and other 'worldly toyes'.

Incidents of this nature were as commonly told entirely in prose as in verse. There is no rule: the choice of the form seems to have depended on the taste or capacity of the publisher. A monstrous pig born at

Mitcham in 1566, and a 'marvellous strange fish' captured between Calais and Dover in 1569 (which certain men of Captain Hawkins's called a shark), were both recorded in prose only. As a rule, however, the prose broadsides of the reigns of Elizabeth and James deal with less trivial matters. Many are official or semi-official. A large number of proclamations issued by the government have survived. Lord Crawford's elaborate catalogue enumerates 440 published during the reign of Elizabeth and 467 during that of James I, indicating in each case where the original broadside is to be found.

Akin to proclamations are the advertisements and orders issued by minor authorities, ecclesiastical or civil. Instances of this are an admonition published by the Bishop of London in 1563 about the measures to be taken in order to escape the contagion of the plague, and a notice by the Archbishop of Canterbury explaining the degrees of affinity. Instructions as to the manner of executing the laws against vagrants, an explanation of the advantage of observing fish-days, tables of the fees chargeable by watermen between London and Gravesend, or by the officials of the customs in the port of London, were printed in the same form. For calendars and ready-reckoners of every kind it was also the most convenient shape, since they could be pasted up on walls for reference. 'A Caveat for the Borrower; or a perfect Table of Usurie', and 'A Necessary Instruction to cast account by, serving for all such as are unskilful in the Art of Arithmeticke', no doubt helped to furnish London shops.

Excepting the proclamations, very few of the broadsides relate to political affairs: it is rather as illustrations of social or economic history that they are valuable. There are, however, several which relate to the foundation of new colonies. One is an offer made by Sir Thomas Smyth and his son in 1572 to adventurers willing to join in establishing a colony in Ulster. There are also four advertisements, published by the Virginia Company, stating the advantages promised to emigrants, the progress of the enterprise, and a 'declaration for the certaine time of drawing the great standing Lottery', which was intended to attract subscribers to the Company.[1]

Portraits of eminent personages were also issued as broadsides. Those of George Clifford, Earl of Cumberland, Robert Cecil, Earl of Salisbury, Prince Henry, and Queen Anne are still extant. In 1563 a portrait of Queen Elizabeth was entered in the Stationers' Register. 'Loe here the pearle whom God and Man doth love' began the verses beneath it. But Elizabeth disliked these rude representations of her features. The draft of an undated proclamation has been preserved in which 'payntors, pryntors and gravors' are forbidden to produce such pictures, until 'some cunning person mete therefor shall make a naturall representation of her Majestys person, favour, or grace', as a pattern for others to copy.[2]

Royal pedigrees were less liable to exception than royal portraits, and obviously better suited for publication in the form of broadsides than in any other shape. On the occasion of the marriage of the Princess Elizabeth with the Elector Palatine three pedigrees of the kind were published. One showed that both the Princess and the Elector were descended from Edward III, the others traced the descent of the Princess from Henry VIII, giving rude woodcuts of the sovereigns mentioned. The title of James I was set forth in a similar fashion. There is 'an excellent new ballad shew-

[1] The Virginian broadsides are printed in full in Alexander Brown's *Genesis of the United States* (1890), pp. 354, 445, 608, 797. He also gives a facsimile of that relating to the Lottery, p. 761.

[2] The portrait of Elizabeth by Hillyard, which is No. 101 of the Broadsides of the Society of Antiquaries, was apparently published after the Queen's death.

ing the petigree of our royal king James', tracing it
back to John of Gaunt. There is also as a companion
to it, a broadside representing the various branches of
the royal house of Stuart, and exhibiting the descent
of King James from Banquo. It is headed 'Regiae
Stuartorum Familiae . . . Genealogia', was evidently
published about the time of James's accession, and probably suggested the passage in Shakespeare's play in
which the witches show Macbeth the vision of the eight
kings of Banquo's issue; it is preserved in the Sutherland
Collection in the Bodleian Library.

BIBLIOGRAPHY.—Bishop Percy, who published his *Reliques of
Ancient Poetry* in 1765, devoted a portion of that collection to
ballads which in some way or other seemed to throw light on
the works of Shakespeare. 'This second book,' he wrote (vol. i,
p. 118), 'is set apart for the reception of such ballads as are
quoted by Shakespeare, or contribute in any degree to illustrate
his writings.' The Bishop made no attempt to include all the
numerous ballads quoted by Shakespeare.

The best account of the great collections of sixteenth- and
seventeenth-century ballads, many of which are entered in the
Stationers' Company Register, is contained in Mr. Chappell's
introduction to the *Roxburghe Ballads*. The Roxburghe and
other collections in the British Museum, Wood's collection in
the Bodleian Library, and the Pepysian collection in the library
of Magdalene College, Cambridge, all contain some Elizabethan
and many Jacobean ballads. But of the ballads printed during
Queen Elizabeth's reign, most of those which are still extant
are in the collections of Mr. Huth, Mr. Christie Miller, or the
Society of Antiquaries. Those in Mr. Huth's possession were
reprinted in 1870 by Joseph Lilly under the title *A Collection
of seventy-nine Black-Letter Ballads and Broadsides printed in the
reign of Queen Elizabeth*. Those in Mr. Christie Miller's possession were printed for the Roxburghe Club in 1912, under the
editorship of Mr. H. L. Collmann, and with the title, *Ballads
and Broadsides chiefly of the Elizabethan Period . . . now in the
Library at Britwell Court*. Of those in the possession of the
Society of Antiquaries, fifteen—ten belonging to Elizabeth's

reign, four to that of Mary, and one to that of Edward VI—were reprinted by Samuel Park in his edition of the *Harleian Miscellany* (vol. x), and some others by John Payne Collier in *Old Ballads from Early Printed Copies*, published by the Percy Society in 1840. Of the twenty-five ballads which Collier's collection contains, twenty were printed during the reign of Queen Elizabeth, many of which are from Mr. Christie Miller's library.

In a paper entitled 'The Ballad History of the Reigns of the Later Tudors', the present writer endeavoured to collect the ballads referring to political events from 1547 to 1603 (*Royal Hist. Soc. Trans.*, 1908–9).

Elizabethan and early Jacobean ballads derived from manuscript sources are to be found in *The Shirburn Ballads*, edited by the Rev. Andrew Clark, in 1907, from a manuscript in the possession of the Earl of Macclesfield, and in the second volume of *Ballads from MSS.*, edited by Mr. W. R. Morfill for the Ballad Society in 1873. Some ballads of this period are included in *Bishop Percy's Folio MS.*, edited by Dr. Furnivall and Mr. Hales, 1867–8, and the volume of *Songs and Ballads chiefly of the Reign of Philip and Mary*, edited by Thomas Wright, from the Ashmolean MSS., 1860, contains a few which belong to the early years of Queen Elizabeth. In 1869 there was printed for private circulation a book entitled *Twenty-five Old Ballads and Songs*, from manuscripts in the possession of J. Payne Collier. In the notes to his *Extracts from the Registers of the Stationers Company*, published by the old Shakespeare Society in 1848–9, the same editor printed a certain number of ballads from a manuscript volume said to have been written in the reign of James I (see *Extracts*, vol. ii, pp. vii, ix). As these are of very little interest and their genuineness is very doubtful, none of them are referred to in this chapter.

Since the ballads were meant to be sung, Chappell's *Popular Music of the Olden Time*, 1855–9, new edition 1893, is an indispensable companion to the reprints of the contemporary broadsides, and a necessary help in ascertaining their dates and fixing their relationship. Many tunes are hopelessly lost; those of which some record exists in printed or manuscript music-books are brought together in his pages, with notes on the various ballads sung to each air.

The ballad-maker, Thomas Deloney, is the subject of an elaborate monograph by Richard Sievers (Berlin, 1904). A collection of the works of Thomas Deloney, edited by F. O. Mann, was published by the Clarendon Press in 1912. The Percy Society reprinted Deloney's *Strange Histories* (1607), and his *Garland of Good Will* (1603), in 1841 and 1851 respectively, as well as Richard Johnson's *Crowne Garland* (1612) in 1842. Another useful contemporary collection of ballad-poetry, Clement Robinson's *Handefull of pleasant delites* (1584), was reprinted by Arber in 1878. Professor Herford's *Literary Relations of England and Germany*, 1886, and Miss P. Sheavyn's *The Literary Profession in the Elizabethan Age*, Manchester, 1909, throw occasional light on the topic of this chapter.

Of contemporary proclamations and broadsides, the chief collections are those in the British Museum, the library of the Society of Antiquaries, the Bodleian, and the library of Queen's College, Oxford. The proclamations of Queen Elizabeth were collected into a folio volume by Humphrey Dyson in 1618. Those of James I from 1603 to 1612 were similarly collected by Robert Barker, and a large number of them are reprinted at length in Rymer's *Foedera*.

For valuable lists of extant broadsides as well as proclamations see *Bibliotheca Lindesiana—Catalogue of English Broadsides, 1505–1897* (privately printed, 1898), *Tudor and Stuart Proclamations*, calendared by Robert Steele under the direction of the Earl of Crawford, Oxford, 1910, and Lemon's *Catalogue of Printed Broadsides in the possession of the Society of Antiquaries*, 1866.

Since these pages were written a flood of light has been thrown on the history of Elizabethan ballads by Dr. H. E. Rollins of New York University in a series of books and articles. His *Analytical Index to the Ballad Entries (1557–1709) in the Registers of the Company of Stationers* (University of North Carolina Press) gives titles, subjects, and first lines of 3,081 ballads, adds notes on many of them, and is indispensable for all researches in this field.

His *Old English Ballads, 1553–1625* (Cambridge University Press, 1920), consists mainly of ballads from manuscripts, dealing for the most part with religious and political subjects and including many upon Catholic and Protestant martyrs. The line,

'Some men for sudden joy do weep, and some for sorrow sing', quoted by Shakespeare in *King Lear* (I. iv. 168), is the opening of a ballad on the martyrdom of John Careless in 1556.

His *Pepysian Garland* (Cambridge University Press, 1922) consists of broadside ballads printed from 1595 to 1639, of which a dozen appeared in Shakespeare's lifetime. In its introduction he traces the development of the species of ballad drama known as a 'jig'. His edition of Robinson's *Handefull of pleasant delites*, published by the Harvard University Press in 1924, proves that most if not all its contents were broadside ballads printed before 1566. A paper on Bodleian MS. Ashmole 48 in *Modern Language Notes* for June 1919, and one on the Shirburn Ballads in the *Journal of American Folk Lore* (Sept. 1917), trace and identify in the same way the pieces contained in those collections. In addition Dr. Rollins has written lives of Thomas Deloney (*Modern Language Notes*, Feb. 1917), Martin Parker (*Modern Philology*, Jan. 1919), and William Elderton (*Studies in Philology*, April 1920), traced the development of the story of Troilus and Cressida in Elizabethan popular literature (*Modern Language Association of America*, 1917, vol. xxxii. 3), and exhaustively described in a paper on 'The Blackletter Broadside Ballad' the manner in which Elizabethan ballads were produced, registered, and circulated (ibid., 1919, vol. xxxiv. 2).

SIR WALTER RALEIGH'S 'HISTORY OF THE WORLD'[1]

MUCH has been written on Raleigh's *History of the World*. Its literary merits are admirably set forth by Mr. Stebbing[2] in his *Life* of Raleigh, while its origin, composition, and bibliography are exhaustively treated in two papers by Dr. Brushfield.[3] But there seems to be room for an attempt to estimate more precisely the place of Raleigh's work in the development of historical writing in England, and by elucidating certain aspects of the *History* it is possible to do so.

Critics agree in praising the dignity and eloquence of Raleigh's style, and praise also the vigour with which he has drawn some of his portraits, but they incline to undervalue his book as history. They judge it from too modern a standpoint; they allow the growth of a different conception of the aim of History and the demand for the scientific treatment of evidence to obscure their vision. Instead of examining what he achieved they consider rather what he failed to do.

In Matthew Arnold's inaugural lecture at Oxford he contrasted the Elizabethan age and the age of Pericles, laying down the principle that the 'supreme characteristic' of a highly developed modern age was 'the manifestation of a critical spirit, the endeavour after a rational arrangement and appreciation of facts'. To

[1] Reprinted from *Proceedings of the British Academy*, vol. viii. By permission.

[2] William Stebbing, *Sir Walter Ralegh* (Oxford, 1891). See also Hallam, *Literature of Europe* (1869), iii. 373.

[3] T. N. Brushfield, *The Bibliography of Sir Walter Ralegh* (Plymouth, 1886); 'Sir Walter Ralegh and his *History of the World*', *Trans. of the Devonshire Association*, vol. xix (1887); 'Raleghana,' Part VI, *The History of the World*, *Trans. of the Devonshire Association*, vol. xxxv (1904).

prove that the age of Pericles was more modern in spirit than the age of Elizabeth he compared the introduction which Thucydides prefixed to his *History of the Peloponnesian War* with the early chapters of Raleigh's *History of the World*. Thucydides, he said, begins by discussing the value of his authorities, Raleigh by discussing such problems as the firmament, the *primum mobile*, the influence of the stars, and the site of Paradise. There is, he complained, no critical power in Raleigh, no control of his facts, no rational appreciation of them.

Such a comparison is neither fair nor fruitful. If Arnold wished to compare the foremost historians of the two ages he should have selected Camden rather than Raleigh, and he might have remembered that Bacon was a product of the Elizabethan age as well as Raleigh.

Raleigh must not be taken as a representative of the learning or the intellectual speculations of the Elizabethan age. 'I have been a seafaring man, a soldier, and a courtier,' he said in his last speech, when he apologized for his lapses from strict rectitude, and he might also have claimed the indulgence accorded to poets.[1] He was a man of action. One of his biographers speaks of his 'invincible individuality'.[2] It found expression in the energy with which he pursued each different career that fate opened to him. The imprisonment which for eleven years debarred him from active pursuits made him an historian. Ranke undertook to write the history of the world in his old age, because he was too old to work in archives any longer;[3] Raleigh, because he was unable to explore the living world, turned to the past, and embarked on a new adventure 'in the dark backward and abysm of time'. A contemporary chronicler

[1] E. Edwards, *The Life of Sir Walter Ralegh* (1868), i. 704.
[2] Stebbing, p. 400.
[3] G. P. Gooch, *History and Historians in the Nineteenth Century* (1913), p. 97.

speaks of the 'searching and unsatisfied spirits of the English' which led our sailors to seek the confines of the East and the West, of the Arctic and the Antarctic.[1] Raleigh's enterprise was a manifestation of this spirit in another sphere. He was not prepared for his enterprise by a lifetime spent in historical studies as Ranke was, but he was always a great reader. 'Five hours he slept, four he read, two he discoursed; allowing the rest to his business and his necessities,' says one of his early biographers; another records that 'in his sea-voyages, . . . he carried always a trunke of bookes along with him'.[2] He had a number of books at his disposal whilst he was in the Tower, and borrowed from Sir Robert Cotton and other friends. However, he was widely read rather than learned. He usually cites Greek historians and poets in Latin versions, and admits that he is 'altogether ignorant' of Hebrew, and 'borrowed the interpretation' of some passages he quotes 'of some of my learned friends'.[3] To those who were surprised at his erudition he had a ready answer: that it was not to be wondered at, 'having had an eleven years leisure' to attain the knowledge of anything he desired. The amount of assistance he had has been exaggerated. 'The best wits of England were employed for making his Historie,' said Ben Jonson to Drummond. 'An ordinary man with the same helps might have performed the same thing,' wrote Algernon Sydney.[4] In any case the *History* bears throughout the impress of one mind in its style and treatment.

Two claimants there are to the honour of helping

---

[1] Stow.

[2] D. Lloyd, *State Worthies* (1670), p. 671; Aubrey, *Brief Lives*, ed. A. Clark (1898), ii. 182. Sir Robert Naunton describes him as 'the great example of industry' and 'an indefatigable reader whether by sea or land'.

[3] Bolton Corney, *Curiosities of Literature Illustrated*, p. 59.

[4] Jonson, *Works*, ed. F. Cunningham (1875), ix. 384; Sydney, *Works* (1767), p. 398.

him. Aubrey was told by the widow of Dr. Robert Burhill, D.D., that her husband had been employed by Raleigh to help him, and that 'all or the greatest part of the drudgery of his booke, for criticismes, chronology, and reading of Greek and Hebrew authors, was performed by him for Sir Walter Raleigh'. All that can be said is that Burhill was qualified to do the work in question, that Raleigh needed some help of the kind, and that there is no other evidence to support Aubrey's story.[1]

The other claimant is Ben Jonson. It is not unlikely that Raleigh had some help from Jonson in the second part of the *History*. According to Drummond, 'Ben himself had written a piece to him [i.e. Raleigh] of the Punick warre, which he altered and set in his booke.'[2] Now some of the incidents in the history of Carthage recounted in the second part of the *History of the World* are treated at disproportionate length, notably one episode which was likely to attract a dramatist, viz. the revolt of the mercenaries against Carthage.[3] The account of this episode was so little connected with the rest of the *History* that it was detached from it in 1647, and printed separately as *A Notable and Memorable story of the cruel War between the Carthaginians and their own Mercenaries*.[4]

Considering that Jonson based one of his plays on Tacitus, and another on Sallust and Cicero, there is nothing unreasonable in supposing that an episode in Polybius might have seemed to him a fitting subject for a third. The story seemed to Flaubert a good foundation for a novel. The alterations made by Raleigh in

[1] Aubrey's *Lives*, ii. 194. Anthony Wood accepted this story, and it is also found in the commonplace book of Thomas Rawlins—a compilation of no particular authority. Bolton Corney discusses, and refutes, the story, *Curiosities of Literature Illustrated*, p. 54.

[2] Cunningham, ix. 384.

[3] ii. 371–6, 386–93.

[4] 18 pp. 4to. No. 173 in Brushfield's *Bibliography*.

Jonson's contribution were, I suppose, the insertion of the discussion on mercenaries in general, and that on the habit of employing two generals of one army (p. 390).

It is uncertain when the composition of the *History* began. Raleigh became a prisoner in July 1603. During the early part of it his health was bad, and his chief recreation was chemical and medical experiments. He conducted these experiments in a little outhouse in the garden of the Bloody Tower, the upper chamber in which was his lodging, and about 1606 he was allowed to build a small room next to the outhouse, and to use it as his habitual dwelling. It is probable that he did not begin the *History of the World* till this relaxation of his confinement had taken place.

As the *History* was nominally written 'for the service' of Prince Henry, it is important to ascertain when Raleigh first came into touch with the Prince. The Prince was born on February 19, 1593–4, and we are told that about 1604 he began 'to be considered by men of learning, as a proper patron of their works, not only for his high rank, but likewise his relish for them'. Dedications to him began in 1604, and became frequent by 1609. Raleigh was certainly in communication with the Prince about 1608, and the occasion for it was afforded by the Prince's interest in ships.[1]

On October 20, 1608, the keel was laid of the first three-decker built for the English navy. Both the King and Prince Henry were greatly interested in the enterprise, and the ship was called *The Prince Royal*, in Henry's honour. The launch took place about September 1610.[2] There were great disputes amongst shipwrights about the design, material, and method of

[1] T. Birch, *Life of Henry, Prince of Wales* (1760), pp. 44, 46, 73, 158, 177, 197, 216, 236.

[2] Oppenheim, *Administration of the Royal Navy*, pp. 203–4; Birch, pp. 187, 208; John Nichols, *Progresses of James I* (1828), ii. 365.

building of the ship, and the timber from an old vessel named the *Victory* was employed. Raleigh's advice was asked by the Prince, apparently before the keel was laid, and the letter in which he gave it survives. It is undated, and was probably written in the early part of 1608.[1] This letter is reproduced almost word for word in Raleigh's *Observations concerning the Royal Navy and Sea Service*, which was addressed to Prince Henry.[2] Raleigh had also written discourses 'of a maritimal Voyage, and the Passages and Incidents therein' for the benefit of the Prince.[3] The *Discourse on the Invention of Ships*[4] was written much later.[5]

Again, 'to obey the commandment of my Lord the Prince', Raleigh wrote for him 'A Discourse touching a Match propounded by the Savoyan, between the Lady Elizabeth and the Prince of Piedmont', accompanied by another on the proposed match between Prince Henry and a daughter of the Duke of Savoy. This must have been written in 1611, as the match was proposed by the ambassador of the Duke about the end of March 1611, and was definitely rejected about December.[6]

Raleigh's own statement about the connexion between the *History of the World* and the Prince is contained in the following words. 'It was for the service of that inestimable Prince Henry . . . that I undertook this work. It pleased him to peruse some part thereof, and to pardon what was amiss.' From this passage it may be inferred that Raleigh commenced his *History* about 1608, and that he thought of dedicating it to the Prince. The design may have been suggested by the favour which the Prince had shown him by consulting him about the ship. Leave to dedicate the book to the

---

[1] Edwards, ii. 330; Raleigh, *Works* (1751), ii. 359.
[2] Ibid. ii. 91, and especially pp. 93–6.   [3] Ibid. ii. 91.
[4] Ibid. ii. 71.   [5] Ibid. ii. 88.
[6] Raleigh, op. cit. i. 249, 265; Gardiner, *History of England*, ii. 136, 137, 140.

Prince would be necessary, and accordingly when a portion of the work was completed Raleigh submitted it to him in order to obtain his permission. The entry of the title in the Stationers' Register under April 15, 1611, probably indicates that the first book of the *History* was ready for printing, or actually printed.[1] This would be the natural moment for its submission to the Prince. Something happened, as we know, to retard its publication, and it did not appear till March 1614.[2] The cause of the delay is explained by another passage in Raleigh's preface. He apologizes for a defect in the arrangement of the *History*, viz. 'the unsutable division of the bookes', which, he says, 'I could not know how to excuse, had I not been directed to inlarge the building after the foundation was laid, and the first part finished'.

The use of the word 'directed' implies a request from some superior which was equivalent to a command. I take it to mean that Prince Henry after seeing the first part made some criticism, which involved a change of plan. The first book ended with the captivity of the Jews: in it the history of other races has been subordinated to that of the chosen people. The second book began with the fall of Babylon and ended with the conquest of Greece by the Romans: in it not only was the subject changed but the scale was enlarged. It seems as if some suggestion from the Prince induced Raleigh to narrate the history of the Persians, the Greeks, and the Romans in more detail than he originally intended.

The result was that the publication of the first instalment of the *History* was delayed: the Prince died on November 6, 1612, and the *History* was not published till eighteen months after his death. Raleigh had in-

---

[1] Arber, *Stationers' Registers*, iii. 457.
[2] 'Walterus Ralegh Historiam suam universalem in lucem edit', says Camden under March 29, 1618. *Camdeni Epistolae* (1691), Appendix, p. 9.

tended to carry his *History* further. 'This Booke,' he says, 'by the title it hath, calles it selfe, The first part of the *Generall Historie* of the *World*, implying a *Second* and *Third* Volume; which I also intended, and have hewen out.'¹ This plan he now abandoned, for 'besides many other discouragements, perswading my silence; it hath pleased God to take that glorious *Prince* out of the world, to whom they were directed'.²

It has sometimes been suggested that Raleigh's first intention was to write the history of Great Britain, not the history of the world. But the sentence in the preface on which this inference is based does not bear out that conclusion. He writes simply: 'Beginning with the Creation: I have proceeded with the History of the World; and lastly purposed (some few sallies excepted) to confine my discourse, within this our renowned Iland of Great Brittaine.' What this means is simply that he proposed to continue the story till he reached the time when 'our renowned Iland' came into it, that is till the Roman Conquest and occupation of Britain, and that thenceforward he meant to make the history of England his main subject, with occasional digressions or 'sallies' on the history of Europe. In short, he meant to apply to English history in the latter part of his work the method he had applied to Jewish history in the first part.³

¹ It is supposed by some that the manuscript of Raleigh once in the possession of John Hampden may have been the materials for the part of the *History* which was 'hewen out', but never published. All that is known about these manuscripts is the following statement: 'Master Hampden a little before the Wars was at the charge of transcribing 3452 sheets of his [Sir Walter Raleigh's] Manuscripts, as the Amanuensis himself told me, who had his close chamber, his fire and candle, with an Attendant to deliver him the Originals and take his Copies as fast as he could write them.' (David Lloyd, *State Worthies*, 1670, p. 675.) Edwards was allowed to search at Hampden House, and found no trace of such papers amongst the Hampden MSS. (*Life of Raleigh*, ii, p. lvii.)   ² *History*, ii. 776.

³ There are traces of this project. In an undated letter Raleigh

Both the plan of Raleigh's book and the method of treatment were dictated by his conception of the nature of History. That conception is clearly set forth in his introduction, and in various passages of his text. His fundamental principle was that the aim of the historian was to convey moral instruction: 'It being,' says he, 'the end and scope of al Historie, to teach by example of times past, such wisdome as may guide our desires and actions.'[1]

This principle is set forth at greater length in the panegyric on History, which, 'following the common and approved custome of those who have left the memories of time past to after ages', he prefixes to the body of his book.

'True it is, that among many other benefits, for which it [History] hath beene honored; in this one it triumpheth over all humane knowledge, That it hath given us life in our understanding, since the world it selfe had life and beginning, even to this day: yea it hath triumphed over time, which besides it, nothing but eternity hath triumphed over: for it hath carried our knowledge over the vast & devouring space of so many thousands of yeares, and given so faire and peircing eies to our minde; that we plainely behould living now, as if we had lived then, that great World, *Magni Dei sapiens opus, the wise worke* (saith Hermes) *of a great God*, as it was then, when but new to it selfe. By it I say it is, that we live in the very time when it was created: we behold how it was governed: how it was covered with waters, and againe repeopled: How Kings and Kingdomes have florished and fallen; and for what vertue and piety God made prosperous; and for what vice and deformity he made wretched, both the one and the other. And it is not the least debt which we owe unto Historie, that it hath made us acquainted with our dead Ancestors; and, out of the depth

asked Cotton to lend him books or manuscripts 'wherin I cann reade any of our written antiquities . . . or any old French history wherin our nation is mentioned, or any else, in what language soever'. Edwards, ii. 322.

[1] *History*, i. 537.

and darkenesse of the earth, delivered us their memory and fame. In a word, wee may gather out of History a policy no lesse wise than eternall; by the comparison and application of other mens forepassed miseries, with our owne like errours and ill deservings.'

This conception of the nature of History and the office of the historian was held by Elizabethan writers in general. It is clearly stated by Sidney in his *Apology for Poetry*. That treatise begins with a contention between the Moral Philosopher, the Historian, and the Poet, each claiming superiority for his own art. The Historian is not sympathetically described. He will hardly let the moral philosopher finish his speech before he breaks in,

'Loden with old Mouse-eaten records, authorising himselfe (for the most part) upon other histories, whose greatest authorities are built upon the notable foundation of Heare-say, having much a-doe to accord differing Writers, and to pick trueth out of partiality; better acquainted with a thousande yeeres a goe, then with the present age, and yet better knowing how this world goeth, then how his owne wit runneth; curious for antiquities, and inquisitive of novelties; a wonder to young folkes, and a tyrant in table talke,—denieth in a great chafe, that any man for teaching of vertue, and vertuous actions, is comparable to him.'[1]

History, he argues, teaches by example, Philosophy only by precept, and in support of his claims he quotes, or rather misquotes, the famous passage in Cicero's *De Oratore* about History being *Magistra Vitae, Lux Veritatis*, and so on.[2]

Raleigh accepted and followed the Ciceronian conception of History. This is shown, not only by expressions in his book, but by the emblematic frontispiece he prefixed to it, which was certainly designed by him though executed by Renold Elstracke. In the centre

[1] Sir Philip Sidney, *An Apologie for Poetrie*, ed. E. S. Shuckburgh (1891), p. 15.
[2] Cicero, *De Oratore*, ii. 9. 36; cf. Boissier, *Tacite*, p. 55.

stands a female figure representing History: she bears up the world in her hands, and tramples on Death and Oblivion: on her robe are the words *Magistra Vitae*. Four columns at her sides bear Cicero's other phrases: *Testis Temporum, Nuncia Vetustatis, Lux Veritatis, Vita Memoriae*.

The verses which Ben Jonson prefixes to the frontispiece elucidate the meaning of the picture:

> From Death and darke Oblivion (neere the same)
>   The Mistresse of Mans life, grave Historie,
> Raising the World to good, or Evill fame,
>   Doth vindicate it to Æternitie.
>
> High Providence would so: that nor the good
>   Might be defrauded, nor the Great secur'd,
> But both might know their wayes are understood,
>   And the reward, and punishment assur'd.

Jonson ends by translating Cicero's phrases and describing History as

> Times witnesse, Herald of Antiquitie,
> The light of Truth, and life of Memorie.

Raleigh added to the Ciceronian conception of History the Christian or Puritan conception, that all the events that happened in the world were divinely ordained. Accordingly above, at the top of the frontispiece, in the centre of a cloud right over the World, there is a large, wide-opened eye labelled 'Providentia'. This symbol appears also in contemporary designs illustrating the Gunpowder Plot. In them a ray from the eye of Providence discovers Guy Fawkes as he stealthily enters the vault under Westminster Hall, and so proves by a modern instance the doctrine of providential intervention.[1]

The Elizabethans in general held this belief that

---

[1] Examples of these prints are in the British Museum. See *Catalogue of Satirical Prints*, nos. 42, 44, 45, 64, 67. Examples may also be found in the illustrated prayer-books, down to the eighteenth century.

Providence intervened in the government of the world, and most of them held that it was the business of the historian as a teacher of morality to point it out when he related the events. For instance, Edmund Bolton, in 1622, in his *Hypercritica or Rule of Judgement for writing or reading our Histories*, ends by telling the historian that four duties are imposed upon him. The first of them is, 'As a Christian Cosmopolite to discover God's Assistances, Disappointments, and Overruling in human affairs'.[1]

This conviction that it was the business of the historian to explain the working of Providence in the world led Raleigh to begin his *History* with the creation of the world, and to devote the first book to the history of the Jews. He says:

'The examples of divine providence, every where found (the first divine Histories being nothing else but a continuation of such examples) have perswaded me to fetch my beginning from the beginning of all things; to wit, Creation.'[2]

Another reason for making the history of the Jews his main subject was the greater trustworthiness of the authorities compared with those available for the history of other nations.

'All Histories do give us information of human counsels and events, as far forth as the knowledge and faith of the writers can afford; but of God's will, by which all things are ordered, they speak only at random, and many times falsely. . . . But this history of the Kings of Israel and Juda hath herein a singular prerogative above all that hath been written by the most sufficient of merely human authors; it setteth down the true and first causes of all that happened.'[3]

Besides this, the Scriptures were indubitably the oldest known historical records. 'It was the story of the Hebrewes, of all before the Olympiads, that overcame

[1] Joseph Haslewood, *Ancient Critical Essays*, ii (1815), 254.
[2] Preface. [3] *History*.

the consuming disease of time; and preserved it selfe,
from the very cradle and beginning to this day.' Accordingly, in his scheme of composition Raleigh subordinated the story of other nations to that of the Hebrews:
'The Fragments of other Stories, with the actions of
those Kings and Princes which shot up here and there
in the same time, I am driven to relate by way of
digression.'[1]

These digressions on the Greeks, the Egyptians, and
other nations are linked to the main thread of Raleigh's
narrative by purely chronological ties. Prometheus, he
tells us, lived 'in the same age together with Moses'.
'About the eleventh yeere of Gideon, was that famous
expedition of the Argonauts.' 'The Warre at Troy . . .
by most Chronologers is found in the time of Habdon,
Judge of Israel.' 'In this time of Joas, was likewise the
Raigne of Pigmalion in Tyre, and the foundation of
Carthage by Dido.' Sometimes these digressions extend
to several chapters, as those on the Phoenicians, the
Scythians, and the foundation of Rome, but throughout
the history of Israel remains the staple of the first part.[2]

In his dealings with his authorities he adopts a similar
plan, using profane writers to confirm sacred writers,
but regarding them always as inferior in value. The
ancient philosophers, poets, and historians had obscured, he said, the story of the past by their inventions,
but he would apply to their writings the method he
had learnt in the course of his chemical investigations.

'As a skilfull and learned Chymist can aswell by separation
of visible elements draw helpfull medicines out of poyson, as
poyson out of the most healthfull hearbs and plants (all things
having in themselves both life and death) so, contrarie to the
purposes and hopes of the Heathen, may those which seeke
after God and Truth finde out everywhere, and in all the
ancient Poets and Philosophers, the Storie of the first Age, with
all the works and marvailes thereof, amply and lively exprest.'[3]

[1] Preface.   [2] *History*, i.   [3] Ibid. i. 84.

It is when the modern commentators and compilers differ that he finds most difficulty. He discusses their views at length, especially when he comes to a chronological question, and decides as suits his story rather than in accordance with any principles of criticism. He states at length on one occasion the arguments of 'that worthie man' Joseph Scaliger, and at last prefers the view of Annius of Viterbo, whom he admits to be of less authority. On the other hand, he handsomely admits that Master Casaubon has convinced him that the prophecies of the Sibyl, of which he once had 'thought reverendlie', 'were no better than counterfeited peeces'.[1]

In the second part the arrangement of his matter was much easier. The Jews disappear, and other nations successively fill the foreground.

'After such time as the Persians had wrested the Empire from the Chaldaeans, and had raised a great Monarchie, producing Actions of more importance than were else-where to be found: it was agreeable to the Order of Story, to attend this Empire; whilst it so florished, that the affaires of the nations adioyning had reference there-unto. The like observance was to bee used towards the fortunes of Greece, when they againe began to get ground upon the Persians, as also towards the affaires of Rome, when the Romans grew more mighty than the Greekes.

'As for the Medes, the Macedonians, the Sicilians, the Carthaginians, and other Nations, who resisted the beginnings of the former Empires, and afterwards became but parts of their composition and enlargement; it seemed best to remember what was knowne of them from ther severall beginnings, in such times and places, as they in their flourishing estates opposed those Monarchies; which in the end swallowed them up.'[2]

The result of this improvement in the arrangement of the subject-matter is that there is a unity and cohesion in the second part which the first does not possess. The narrative proceeds with a steady and

[1] Ibid. i. 566–74; ii. 705.   [2] Preface, E3.

orderly flow, and the digressions, instead of distracting the attention of the reader, increase his interest by emphasizing important points. In these digressions Raleigh elucidates problems suggested by the events he is narrating by modern parallels, and illustrations drawn from his own experience. The importance of sea-power in the wars of the Romans and Carthaginians is shown from the struggle between England and Spain,[1] and the employment of mercenaries by Carthage gives an opportunity of discussing the question whether the Dutch would not repent their reliance upon them.[2] At one moment he illustrates a military point by recollections of what he saw during the civil wars in France, at another from his travels, and he employs indifferently examples from the history of England, France, Spain, and Italy, which his reading furnished.[3] Probably the best known of these digressions is that in which Raleigh compares Roman and English soldiers, and after reciting some of the exploits of our ancestors proudly concludes that now England and Scotland are no longer divided 'the enemie that shall dare to trie our forces, will finde cause to wish, that avoiding us, hee had rather encountred as great a puissance, as was that of the Roman Empire'.[4] If these and other references to English matters were extracted and put together in an orderly fashion they would make a very interesting pamphlet.[5]

The greater cohesion of Raleigh's narrative in this second part and its greater interest are largely due to the change in the character of his materials. He had at his disposal Herodotus, Xenophon, Thucydides, Plutarch, Polybius, and Livy, and he employs them

---

[1] *History*, ii. 351, 359–62.   [2] Ibid. ii. 381.

[3] Ibid. i. 599; ii. 196–8, 357, 364, 717, 172, 178.

[4] Ibid. ii. 311–14.

[5] Some digressions deal with abstract questions such as those on the nature of tyranny (ii. 383) and the folly of duelling (ii. 544–50).

freely. He blends them all together, but though he does not formally discuss their value, he seems to have some perception of their relative trustworthiness. Perhaps Raleigh owed most to Plutarch. While he relates the progress of events in great detail the figures of his personages stand out clearly from their background. They are drawn with a bold and vigorous touch: it is evident that they were real and living to the writer, and he makes them live for the reader. Moreover, the theological system which dominates the first part is much less in evidence in the second.

Great conquerors such as Alexander are represented as the instruments of Providence; spirits 'stirred up in sundrie Ages of the world, and in divers parts thereof, to erect and cast downe againe, to establish and to destroy, and to bring all things, Persons and States; to the same certaine ends, which the infinite spirit of the Universall, piercing, moving, and governing all thinges hath ordained'.[1] The desire of fame was their incentive. Had they realized its vanity 'they themselves would then rather have wished, to have stolne out of the world without noise; than to be put in minde, that they have purchased the report of their actions in the world, by rapine, oppression, and crueltie, by giving in spoile the innocent and labouring soule to the idle and insolent, and by having emptied the Cities of the world of their ancient Inhabitants, and filled them againe with so many and so variable sorts of Sorrowes'.[2] So, too, if other monarchs had realized 'the Variable successe of worldly things, and Instabilitie of Fortune', they would have been just and merciful in the days of their greatness.

'If Perseus had knowne it before, that his owne sonne should one day bee compelled to earne his living by handie-work, in a painefull Occupation; it is like, that he would not, as in a wantonnesse of Soveraignetie, have commaunded those poore

[1] *History*, ii. 174; cf. 485; i. 508.   [2] Ibid. ii. 775.

men to be slaine. . . . He would rather have been verie gentle, and would have considered, that the greatest oppressors, and the most undertroden wretches, are all subject unto One high Power, governing all alike with absolute command.'[1]

In relating the falls of princes, Raleigh insists on what he termed 'second causes', and dwells more on the influence of their characters on their fate, the defects which led to their failure, and the vices which became instruments to scourge them. The moral lesson he conveys becomes that taught by the poets and dramatists of his own time, and the *History* gains in human interest.

For these various reasons the second part of Raleigh's *History* continued to please when the first part had ceased to attract. Hume reflected the opinion of eighteenth-century readers when he said, 'If the reader of Raleigh's history can have the patience to wade through the Jewish and Rabbinical learning which compose the half of the volume, he will find, when he comes to the Greek and Roman story, that his pains are not unrewarded. Raleigh is the best model of that ancient style, which some writers would affect to revive at present.'[2]

Even people who rejected or doubted his belief in the direct intervention of providence in the government of the world found an inclination, or a desire, to believe his doctrine of historical justice. 'I shall not, I trust, be accused of superstition,' wrote Gibbon, 'but I must remark that, even in this world, the natural order of events will sometimes afford the strong appearances of moral retribution.'[3]

In his own day the success of Raleigh's *History* was immediate, general, and lasting. Ten distinct editions were published between 1614 and 1687, and it was reprinted once in the eighteenth century, and twice in the nineteenth. Two continuations of it were compiled

[1] *History*, ii. 773.   [2] *History of England* (1871), iii. 113.
[3] *Decline and Fall*, ed. Bury, vi. 479.

by different hands, one bringing the narrative down to 1640, the other to 1708. Three abridgements were also issued, in 1650, 1698, and 1708.[1] Some contemporary critics praised its style. Edmund Bolton characterized it as 'full of proper, clear, and Courtly graces of Speech'.[2] Historical scholars recommended it as an authority. Degory Whear, the first Camden Professor of Ancient History at Oxford, gave Raleigh, according to Aubrey, 'an admirable encomium', and preferred him before all other historians,[3] while the learned Dr. Peter Heylyn termed the book 'Primus in Historia' for its worthiness.[4]

Amongst the notable readers of the *History* were Elizabeth of Bohemia, Montrose, Milton, and Cromwell. The Queen took with her to Bohemia a copy of the *History*, which fell into the hands of a Spanish general on her flight from Prague, but was finally restored to one of Elizabeth's sons, and is now in the British Museum. It was doubtless a presentation copy offered by the author to the sister of his dead patron.[5] Montrose had a copy of Raleigh's *History* on which he set great value: he took it with him to the University of St. Andrews when he began his studies there.[6] There are many indications of Milton's interest in the *History* and its author. He published himself in 1658 one of the posthumous works of that 'Ever-renowned Knight, Sir

[1] For a complete list see Brushfield's *Bibliography*, pp. 19-23. The best-known compendium was Alexander Ross's *Marrow of History*, published in 1650. 'Divers,' said Ross, 'have three or four shillings to bestow on this, which have not twenty or thirty to impend upon the great book.' It was popular with undergraduates. Daniel Fleming bought a copy for 1*s*. 6*d*. when he came up to Oxford in 1653 (*The Flemings at Oxford*, i. 39). The folio edition of the *History* cost 30*s*. in 1676. See Arber, *Term Catalogues*, i. 258.

[2] 'Hypercritica', Haslewood, *Ancient Critical Essays*, ii. 249.

[3] Aubrey, ii. 191.   [4] W. Winstanley, *England's Worthies*, p. 255.

[5] See Brushfield, *Bibliography*, p. 20; and *British Museum Catalogue of Early Printed Books*, p. 820.

[6] M. Napier, *Memoirs of the Marquis of Montrose* (1856), Appendix, pp. 21, 28.

Walter Raleigh'.[1] In his *Common-Place Book* he extracts
a long passage from the *History*, doubtless for use in
his controversy about Divorce, since it is an argument
for not forbidding too rigorously 'plurality of wives'.[2]
Milton's descriptions of the site and the topography of
Paradise are worth comparing with the corresponding
chapters in the *History of the World*. On many points
they agree, and even their differences of opinion show
that Milton had read Raleigh. For instance, Raleigh
devotes a section to the questions whether the tree of
knowledge was the Indian fig-tree, and whether Adam
and Eve did not clothe themselves in its leaves. 'These
leaves of all other were most commodious . . . which
Plinie avoweth in these wordes; *Latitudo foliorum peltae
effigiem Amazoniae habet*, The breadth of the leaves
hath the shape of an Amazonian shield.' Raleigh describes the tree at length, but disbelieves the theory.
Milton adopts it, and follows Raleigh's description:

> The Figtree, not that kind for Fruit renown'd,
> But such as at this day to *Indians* known
>
> .   .   .   .
>
> Those Leaves
> They gatherd, broad as *Amazonian* Targe,
> And with what skill they had, together sowd.[3]

The first map in Raleigh's *History of the World* would
form an admirable illustration for *Paradise Lost*.

There is another allusion to Raleigh in the list of
famous cities which Michael shows to Adam. It includes:

> Yet unspoil'd
> *Guiana*, whose great Citie *Geryons* Sons
> Call *El Dorado*.[4]

---

[1] D. Masson, *Life of Milton*, v. 405; Brushfield, *Bibliography*, p. 29.
It was *The Cabinet Council*.

[2] Milton's *Common-Place Book*, section 114.

[3] *History of the World*, i. 67; *Paradise Lost*, ix. 1101-12.

[4] *Paradise Lost*, xi. 409-11. Perhaps also in *Paradise Lost*, ii. 945,
Milton takes the story of the Gryphon and the Arimaspian from
Raleigh, i. 176.

Other poets, too, probably drew stories and illustrations from the mass of miscellaneous information Raleigh brought together in his *History*.[1]

Political reasons increased Raleigh's popularity and the popularity of his book. As a victim to the Stuarts he became a hero to the Opposition. Republicans imagined that he was a republican. There was a rumour abroad that in some secret consultations after Queen Elizabeth's death he had declared against a Scottish monarch; saying, "twas the wisest way for them to keep the government in their owne hands, and sett up a commonwealth, and not be subject to a needy beggerly nation'. Andrew Marvell, referring to this story, entitled one of his satires a *Dialogue between Britannia and Raleigh*, and a popular life of Shaftesbury was entitled *Rawleigh Redivivus* (1683).[2]

With Puritans in general his popularity had a sounder basis. His theological conception of History agreed with theirs: it was a belief in which the events of the Civil War confirmed them; they saw in their initial defeats and their final triumph the working of the same power.[3]

When Cromwell recommended his son Richard to read Raleigh's *History of the World* he specified it, rather than other books, because of its comprehensiveness. 'It's a body of History, and will add much more to your understanding than fragments of story.'[4] But Oliver's choice must have been dictated also by the spirit which inspired that 'body of history'. For he complained that the histories which were written of his own time gave only 'narratives of matters of fact', and

---

[1] Cf. Massinger, *The Bondman*, Act iv, sc. ii, and Raleigh's *History*, i. 643. Shelley's sonnet on Ozymandias was perhaps suggested by *History*, i. 603. Steele quotes the *History* in the *Spectator*, no. 510.

[2] Aubrey's *Lives*, ii. 186; Marvell's *Poetical Works*, ed. Aitken, ii. 82.

[3] Compare Stephen Marshall's sermon before the House of Commons, on the day of Thanksgiving for the victory of Naseby.

[4] Carlyle's *Cromwell*, Letter cxxxii.

omitted the 'strange windings and turnings of Providence' and the 'very great appearances of God' which he desired to find recorded there, as Raleigh had set them forth in his story of the past.[1]

There was one exception to this general applause, namely King James. Soon after its publication he threatened to suppress the book. On December 22, 1614, Abbot, the Archbishop of Canterbury, wrote to the Stationers' Company, saying: 'I have received expresse directions from his Majestie that the booke latelie published by Sir Walter Rawleigh, nowe prisoner in the Tower, should be suppressed, and not suffered for hereafter to be sould.' All copies of it were to be brought to the Archbishop or to the Lord Mayor.[2]

The letter of the Archbishop gave no reasons for the suppression, but a letter from John Chamberlain to Sir Dudley Carleton, on January 5, 1615, supplies an explanation.[3] It says that Sir Walter Raleigh's book is called in 'for divers exceptions, but specially for being too saucy in censuring princes'. Later authorities add, from tradition, further particulars. 'It is well known,' wrote a pamphleteer in 1656, 'King James forbad the book for some passages in it which offended the Spaniards, and for being too plain with the faults of princes in his preface.'[4] A story recorded by Francis Osborne is, that after much scorn cast on Raleigh's *History*, the King, 'being modestly demanded what fault he found, he answered, as one surprised, that he spake irreverently of King Henry the Eighth'.[5] However, in spite of these objections to the *History*, the

[1] Carlyle's *Cromwell*, Speech I.

[2] Arber, *Stationers' Registers*, v, p. lxxvii.

[3] First printed by John Nichols, *Progresses of . . . James I* (1828), iii. 27. See also Stebbing, p. 280.

[4] Quoted by Stebbing, p. 280, from *Observations on Sanderson's History of James I* (1656).

[5] Osborne's *Traditional Memoirs*, reprinted in *Secret History of the Court of James I* (Edinburgh, 1811), i. 168.

suppression was merely temporary. The government contented itself with the removal of the title-page, which contained the author's portrait as well as his name, and no alterations or omissions in the text were ordered.

This excision is not difficult to explain. Raleigh was a state prisoner condemned to death for high treason, owing his life to the King's mercy; respited, not pardoned. He was a man 'civilly dead', as it was alleged.[1] Yet he had the impudence to show that he was very much alive, not only by writing a great book, which might have been winked at, but by putting his name and even his portrait on the title-page. There is a fragment of an undated letter from Raleigh to James I, written probably about 1616, which proves that his offence was of this nature.

'There have bene, in all ages, some that have risen againe after a civill death; yea, we have of them now liveing which take themselves to be honest men. . . . Why they may not write while they lyve in nature, I know not. If by writing they may serve their countrie and be profitable to others, *they* are dead, in charitie that thinke the contrary, and [are] to be numbred amongst those *qui gloriantur in malitia*.'[2]

The difficulty is not to explain why the sale of the *History* was suspended, but why the order was rescinded. There would have been nothing surprising in either the prohibition of the book, or in far more drastic expurgation.

Under the Tudors and the Stuarts historians were subjected to a severe censorship, and wrote under many restrictions. Anything which might give offence to foreign potentates, and so hamper the foreign policy of the sovereign, was liable to suppression, either if complaint were made, or to avoid complaint being made. At the moment when Raleigh's *History* was published

[1] Cf. Edwards, i. 689-91; and Bacon's *Works*, ed. J. Spedding, vi. 412.   [2] Edwards, ii, p. lxiii.

the long negotiations about the Spanish match were beginning, and there were certainly passages in the book which might have called forth a protest from the Spanish ambassador. While Raleigh praised in one of his digressions the 'patient virtue' and the 'invincible constancy' of the Spanish explorers, he condemned in unsparing language the crimes of the Spanish kings from Pedro the Cruel to Philip II, and devoted about four pages of his preface to this indictment. He wound up the *History* itself by an attack on Spanish policy.

'Since the fall of the Roman Empire (omitting that of the Germaines, which had neither greatnesse nor continuance) there hath been no State fearfull in the East, but that of the Turke; nor in the West any Prince that hath spred his wings farre over his nest, but the Spaniard. . . . These two Nations . . . are at this day the most eminent, and to be regarded; the one seeking to roote out the Christian Religion altogether, the other the truth and sincere profession thereof, the one to joyne all Europe to Asia, the other the rest of all Europe to Spaine.'[1]

If an author touched English history he was still more liable to give offence and to incur suspicion. Raleigh realized and regretted the impossibility of writing contemporary history.

'I know,' said he, 'that it will bee said by many, That I might have beene more pleasing to the Reader, if I had written the Story of mine owne times; having beene permitted to draw water as near the Well-head as another. To this I answere, that who-so-ever in writing a moderne Historie, shall follow truth too neare the heeles, it may happily strike out his teeth. There is no Mistresse or Guide, that hath led her followers and servants into greater miseries.'[2]

Supposing that an historian, to avoid this peril, confined himself to the story of less recent times, he might be charged with referring to modern events and living rulers by insinuating criticisms and suggesting comparisons. Thus in 1599 Sir John Hayward was called in

[1] *History*, ii. 367, 775, and Preface, B4.   [2] Preface, E4.

question for his account of the deposition of Richard II
and the accession of Henry IV, which was alleged to be
a veiled attack on the government of Queen Elizabeth.
'I am Richard the Second; know ye not that?' said
Elizabeth.[1] In the same way, in 1627, Sir Robert
Cotton's *Short View of the Life and Reign of Henry III*
was suppressed, as being an attack on the government
of Charles I. Raleigh seems to have been conscious that
some of the characters he drew in his *History* might
have been interpreted as libels on contemporary statesmen. 'Why may it not be said', he asked, 'that in speaking of the past, I point at the present, and taxe the
vices of those that are yet lyving, in their persons that
are long since dead.' He answered that there was no
way of avoiding this charge. 'But this I cannot helpe
. . . if there be any, that finding themselves spotted like
the Tigers of old time, shall finde fault with me for
painting them over anew; they shall therein accuse
themselves justly, and me falsly.'[2] But this was a very
inadequate defence. Any attack upon the King's ministers was equivalent to an attack upon the King, and
classical parallels were a familiar weapon in political
controversy. When Sir John Eliot, in 1626, compared
Buckingham to Sejanus, Charles I at once demanded
his punishment. 'Implicitly', said Charles, 'he must
intend me for Tiberius.'[3] Ancient history was a storehouse of examples, and Tacitus was an author whom the
Stuarts, like Napoleon, regarded as the most dangerous
of all historians.[4] The first teacher of History at Cambridge, Dr. Dorislaus, was silenced in 1627 for lecturing

[1] D. Hume, *History of England* (1841), iv. 195. See also Bacon's
Works, vii. 133, and *Index Expurgatorius Anglicanus*, p. 35.
[2] Preface. Cf. Sir J. Hayward's *Annals of Queen Elizabeth*, ed. J.
Bruce, p. xviii.
[3] Forster, *Sir John Eliot* (1864).
[4] See Boissier, *Tacite*, p. 112; Welschinger, *La Censure sous le
Premier Empire*, p. 149; Sainte-Beuve, *Chateaubriand et son groupe
littéraire*, ii. 99; Lanfrey, *Napoléon*, iv. 192.

E

on the *Annals*.[1] A few years later a more courtly historian wrote a commentary on the *Annals*, intended 'to preserve the noble and other the ingenuous youth of this monarchy from taking harm by their unwary reading that historian (who is no friend to regality)'.[2]

Raleigh's *History* never reached the most perilous period of Roman history, but it is interesting to observe the extreme caution with which he felt bound to treat certain episodes in Hebrew history, such as the establishment of kingship and the rebellions against the kings of Judah and Israel. To make sure of his ground he refers to King James's book on *The true Law of free Monarchies*, as containing the orthodox doctrine about the nature of kingship, and when he has to explain the nature of tyrants and tyranny inserts as a contrast the description of a virtuous king, taking King James as an example.[3]

Neither precautions nor compliments could prevent such a sovereign as James from thinking the preface objectionable. History, according to Raleigh, must teach a moral lesson, and the lesson was that God punished wrongdoers. This truth was best proved by the lives of the great, not the small. 'Gods judgments upon the greater and greatest, have beene left to posterity. . . . Who hath not observed, what labour, practise, perill, bloudshed, and cruelty, the Kings and Princes of the world have undergone, exercised, taken on them, and committed; to make them-selves and their issues maisters of the world?' All that remained of the empires which ancient kings had raised in this way was hardly the ruins. Yet modern kings imitated their example. 'I will,' says Raleigh, 'for the present, examine what profit hath beene gathered by our owne Kings,

---

[1] J. B. Mullinger, *The University of Cambridge*, iii. 81–8.
[2] Edmund Bolton. See *Report on the MSS. of Earl Cowper*, ii (1888), 66. Cf. Jonson, *Works*, ed. Cunningham, iii. 243.
[3] *History*, i. 464, 514; ii. 385.

and their Neighbour Princes: who having beheld, both in divine and humane letters, the successe of infidelitie, injustice, and crueltie, have (notwithstanding) planted after the same patterne.' To prove his case he takes in succession the royal lines of England, France, and Spain: 'Let us now see if God be not the same God in Spaine, as in England and France.' Then he enumerates in succession the crimes of one king after another and the judgements which fell upon him and his house. 'Oh by what plots, by what forswearings, betrayings, oppressions, imprisonments, tortures, poysonings, and under what reasons of State, and politique subteltie, have these forenamed Kings, both strangers, and of our owne Nation, pulled the vengeance of God upon them selves, upon theirs, and upon their prudent ministers!'[1] Retribution came to all of them, says Raleigh, 'They were the lovers of other men's misery, and misery found them out.'

This was what Chamberlain meant when he said that Raleigh was 'too saucy in censuring princes'. Criticism of any English monarch was objectionable to the Stuarts and their courtiers. In 1627, when Samuel Daniel published his narrative of the reign of the Norman kings, he thought it necessary to write an apologetic preface.

'Yet will it bee much to the glory of his Reigne', he said (speaking of Charles I), 'that in his daies there was a true History written: a liberty proper onely to Common-wealths, and never permitted to Kingdomes, but under good Princes. Upon which liberty notwithstanding I will not usurpe, but tread as tenderly on the graves of his magnificent Progenitors as possibly I can: Knowing there may (in a kind) be *Laesa Maiestas*, even against dead Princes.'[2]

Instead of speaking of the King's 'magnificent Progenitors' with bated breath, Raleigh had handled them

[1] Preface.
[2] *Complete Works . . . of Samuel Daniel*, ed. Grosart (1896), iv. 78.

without reticence or reverence. Of Henry VIII, for instance, he said: 'If all the pictures and Patternes of a mercilesse Prince were lost in the World, they might all againe be painted to the life, out of the story of this King.' Moreover, it was not only the censure of his predecessors James disliked; he felt that sovereigns as a class were sacred beings. 'I have said ye are gods' was a text on which he loved to enlarge when he discussed monarchy. Hence, while he agreed in theory that the world was divinely governed, he objected to the method in which Raleigh proved it.

The characteristic of Raleigh's *History* which offended James earned Raleigh the praise of a modern historian, who was a member of this body.[1] 'I venerate', said Lord Acton, in one of his letters, 'that villainous adventurer, for his views on universal history.'[2] Acton was revolted by the manner in which modern historians, in their judgements of men and things, eliminated morality from History, writing as if evil acts were to be attributed to the times, not to the men, or as if there were one law for the great figures of the past and another for ordinary men. 'It is the office of historical science', he said in one of his reviews, 'to maintain morality as the sole impartial criterion of men and things.' He told his pupils at Cambridge 'Never to debase the moral currency or to lower the standard of rectitude, but to try others by the final maxim that governs your own lives, and to suffer no man and no cause to escape the undying penalty which history has the power to inflict on wrong.'[3]

Is not this the very doctrine which Raleigh expressed in his *History* more than two centuries earlier?

[1] i.e. The British Academy.
[2] Letter dated May 21, 1869, printed in Gasquet, *Lord Acton and his Circle*, p. 353.
[3] *Historical Essays and Studies* (1908), p. 437; *Lectures on Modern History* (1906), pp. 24–7.

MILTON AS AN HISTORIAN[1]

FEW people ever think of Milton as an historian. His interest in history is revealed to his readers by some similes in *Paradise Lost*,[2] and by those great passages in *Paradise Regained* embodying his conception of Roman rule and Athenian culture,[3] but his historical writings are of such slight importance compared to his pamphlets and his poetry, that they are almost forgotten. Yet Milton's *History of Britain* is worth studying. It elucidates both his political writings and his poems; like all that he wrote, it bears the impress of his character, and is, therefore, of some biographical value; finally, the book in itself is a work of learning and originality, worthy to be remembered in any account of the development of historical writing in England.

The full title of the book is 'The History of Britain, That part especially now call'd England. From the first Traditional Beginning, continu'd to the Norman Conquest. Collected out of the antientest and best Authours thereof by John Milton.'[4] It was published in 1670 by James Allestry, as a quarto volume of about 350 pages, costing five shillings. Eleven years later, in 1681, appeared a little pamphlet of twelve pages, entitled 'Mr John Miltons Character of the Long Parliament and Assembly of Divines', which purported to be a passage of the *History* suppressed by the licenser when the book was published, and is usually inserted

[1] Reprinted from *Proceedings of the British Academy*, vol. iii. By permission.

[2] *Paradise Lost*, i. 351–5; x. 306–11.

[3] *Paradise Regained*, Book iv.

[4] See Masson's *Life of Milton*, vi. 642–8; Arber, *The Term Catalogues*, i. 277, 443.

in modern editions at the beginning of the third part of the *History*.[1]

The early history of Britain had long occupied Milton's mind. We can trace the progress of his studies and the growth of his schemes up to the moment when he began to write the book which some four-and-twenty years later he gave to the world. The notes contained in his *Common-place Book* (written apparently in the interval between leaving Cambridge in 1632 and visiting Italy in 1638) prove that he had carefully read the Chronicles of Holinshed, Stow, and Speed,[2] as well as several foreign historians.[3] It is clear that at that time the 'first Traditional Beginning' of British history attracted him most, and twice in the Latin verses written during the year 1639 he expressed his resolve to make these legends the subject of an epic poem. In the *Epitaphium Damonis* he declared that his future theme should be the coming of the Trojans, and the fortunes of the line of Brutus:

> Ipse ego *Dardanias Rutupina* per æquora puppes
> Dicam, & *Pandrasidos* regnum vetus Inogeniæ,
> *Brennùm*que *Arviragúm*que duces, priscùmque *Belinum*,
> Et tandem *Armoricos Britonum* sub lege colonos;
> Tum gravidam *Arturo* fatali fraude *Jögernen*
> Mendaces vultus, assumptáque *Gorlöis* arma,
> *Merlini* dolus.[4]

---

[1] *The Works of John Milton*, ed. John Mitford, v. 94–101; Masson, vi. 806–12.

[2] *A Common-place Book of John Milton*, ed. A. H. Horwood, pp. 9, 10, 22, 25, 27, 31; cf. Masson, i. 303, 645, 736; vi. 790.

[3] In Milton's *Apology for Smectymnuus*, published in 1642, he speaks of his early historical reading: '. . . some years I had spent in the stories of those Greek and Roman exploits, wherein I found many things both nobly done, and worthily spoken.' He explains that when he came to the period of Constantine the Great the history of the Church proved intolerably repulsive. *Works*, iii. 269, 318.

[4] *Epitaphium Damonis*, ll. 162–8; Masson, ii. 84–94. Dated by Masson about October 1639.

In the *Epistle to Mansus*, written a few months earlier, his chosen theme was to be the life of King Arthur:

Si quando indigenas revocabo in carmina reges,
Arturumque etiam sub terris bella moventem;
Aut dicam invictæ sociali fœdere mensæ,
Magnanimos Heroas, & (O modo spiritus ad sit)
Frangam *Saxonicas Britonum* sub *Marte* phalanges.[1]

Once more, in 1642, in his fourth pamphlet, he returned to his project. It was his purpose, he declared, to add to the fame of his native country by his writings. Hitherto its history had been meanly written. 'If the Athenians . . . made their small deeds great and renowned by their eloquent writers, *England* hath had her noble atchievments made small by the unskilfull handling of monks and mechanicks.'[2] To him it appeared that 'our own ancient stories' supplied fit matter for a poem, and he was deliberating over the question 'what K[ing] or Knight before the conquest might be chosen in whom to lay the pattern of a Christian *Heroe*'.[3]

One doubt, however, was still unresolved: whether it was best to adopt for his poem the epic or the dramatic form, and which of the two would be 'more doctrinal and exemplary' to his countrymen. For some time a tragedy with a chorus, after the antique model, had seemed the form best suited for his purpose, and about 1640 he jotted down on paper a long list of possible subjects, with brief notes as to the way of treating them. Of these subjects, numbering ninety-nine in all, sixty-one were scriptural and thirty-eight

[1] *Mansus*, ll. 80–4; Masson, i. 524.

[2] Milton is here referring to an observation made by Sallust: 'Atheniensium res gestae, sicuti ego aestumo, satis amplae magnificaeque fuere, verum aliquanto minores tamen quam fama feruntur, sed quia provenere ibi scriptorum magna ingenia, per terrarum orbem Atheniensium facta pro maxumis celebrantur.'—Sallust, *Catiline*, 8.

[3] Masson, ii. 361, 385; *The Reason of Church-government urg'd against Prelaty*, in *Works*, iii. 145.

from British history, and it is noticeable that the subjects of the British tragedies were chosen not from the legendary period, but the times between the Roman Conquest and the year 1066.[1]

None of these various schemes was realized in the form in which it was first conceived. The tragedy of 'Adam Unparadised' became ultimately the epic of *Paradise Lost*; the epic on Arthur and the 'British Tragedies' developed into the prose *History of Britain*.

We can trace with tolerable accuracy the progress of the *History of Britain*. Milton began to write it after the conclusion of the series of pamphlets on divorce (March 1645), and after the close of the first Civil War (June 1646). It is probable that by the end of 1647 he had completed the first and second books, since the original introduction to the third book must have been written, judging from its tone, about the close of 1647 or the beginning of 1648. It is certain, on Milton's own evidence, that by March 1649, when he became Secretary to the Council of State, he had finished four out of the six books, and had brought the story down to the union of England under the rule of Egbert. He tells us that he then intended to relate the history of England from its first beginnings to his own day.[2] But this intention was never fulfilled. At some period after 1649 Milton wrote the fifth and sixth books, which contain the story of the Danish invasions and the Norman Conquest, but he proceeded no further. His blindness proved no doubt too great an obstacle.[3]

[1] Masson, ii. 106; Aldis Wright, *Facsimile* (1899), pp. 35, 36.

[2] He says: '. . . ad historiam gentis, ab ultima origine repetitam, ad hæc usque tempora, si possem, perpetuo filo deducendam me converti.' *Defensio Secunda*, in *Works*, vi. 293.

[3] Milton probably resumed the *History of Britain* about the end of 1655, since he published his *Pro Se Defensio* in August 1655, and, having completed the Salmasius controversy, had time at his disposal. 'Being now quiet from State adversaries and public contests', says Phillips, 'he had leisure again for his own studies and private designs.'

The purpose which Milton set before himself when he began to write is clearly explained in the exordium to his *History*:

'The beginning of Nations, those excepted of whom sacred Books have spok'n, is to this day unknown. Nor only the beginning, but the deeds also of many succeeding Ages, yea periods of Ages, either wholly unknown, or obscur'd and blemisht with Fables. . . . Of *British affairs*, from the first peopling of the Iland to the coming of *Julius Cæsar*, nothing certain, either by Tradition, History, or Ancient Fame hath hitherto bin left us. That which we have of oldest seeming, hath by the greater part of judicious Antiquaries bin long rejected for a modern Fable.

'Nevertheless there being others besides the first suppos'd Author, men not unread, nor unlerned in Antiquitie, who admitt that for approved story, which the former explode for fiction, and seeing that oft-times relations heertofore accounted fabulous have bin after found to contain in them many footsteps, and reliques of somthing true, as what we read in Poets of the Flood, and Giants little beleev'd, till undoubted witnesses taught us, that all was not fain'd; I have therfore determin'd to bestow the telling over ev'n of these reputed Tales; be it for nothing else but in favour of our English Poets, and Rhetoricians, who by thir Art will know, how to use them judiciously.

'. . . I intend not with controversies and quotations to delay or interrupt the smooth course of History; much less to argue and debate long who were the first Inhabitants, with what probabilities, what authorities each opinion hath bin upheld, but shall endevor that which hitherto hath bin needed most, with plain, and lightsom brevity, to relate well and orderly

In March 1657 he was inquiring about the cost of editions of Byzantine historians, which is evidence that his mind was once more turned to historical studies (see Masson, v. 225, 284).

There is also another piece of evidence. On pp. 273, 287 of his *History* he refers to 'the Chronicle attributed to *John Bromton* a *Yorkshire* Abbot, but rather of some nameless Author living under *Edward* the 3*d*. or later'. This chronicle was first published in Twysden's *Decem Scriptores* in 1652 as 'Chronicon Johannis Brompton Abbatis Jorvalensis'. Milton no doubt used the edition of Simeon of Durham included in the same collection. He often refers to that author in the two latter books of the *History* and towards the end of Book IV.

things worth the noting, so as may best instruct and benefit them that read.'[1]

It is evident that for the moment the truth of the facts related was less important in Milton's eyes than the manner in which they were related. History meant to him, when he began, merely the art of story-telling. As he hinted, the early history of England had been lengthily and tediously told in the ponderous volumes of his predecessors. In Holinshed's *Chronicle* 202 pages are required to reach the Battle of Hastings, out of which 22 pages are devoted to the legendary period before the landing of Caesar. Speed expends 411 pages and 41 pages respectively on those two divisions of his subject.[2] Milton, on the other hand, contrives to cover the legendary period in 30 pages, and to complete his whole story in 308 pages, and these are quarto pages containing not much more than three hundred words, while the pages of Holinshed and Speed are folios printed in double columns. One page of Holinshed contains as many words as four pages of Milton, and in lightness of touch, as well as brevity, Milton as a story-teller exceeds either Holinshed, Speed, or Stow.

The legends which formed the staple of early British history had already been told and retold by many Elizabethan and Jacobean poets. Spenser in the second book of the *Faerie Queene* had versified in some six hundred lines the story of the landing of Brutus and the fortunes of his descendants up to Uther Pendragon.[3] Milton quotes a stanza from his version.[4] Drayton interspersed the thirty 'Songs' of his *Polyolbion*, wherever a legend could be localized, with narratives of British or Saxon

---

[1] *History of Britain* (1670), pp. 1–3.

[2] The computation is based on the edition of Holinshed of 1586, and the 1632 edition of Speed. Milton, as his *Common-place Book* shows, used this edition of Holinshed and the 1631 edition of Stow.

[3] Book II, canto x.

[4] Ibid. x, l. 212; *History of Britain*, p. 16.

monarchs which hill tells to hill and river certifies to river. In the first song of all the Dart claims the royalty of all the streams in the West because Brutus landed at her mouth, 'which now the envious world doth slander for a dreame'.[1] It is to Drayton and Spenser that Milton alludes when he recites his story of the wrestling match between Corineus and the giant Goemagog, terming it 'a grand Fable, though dignify'd by our best Poets'.[2]

Minor poets, too, had sought the same inexhaustible storehouse. Higgins, in his additions to *The Mirror for Magistrates* (1574), Warner in *Albion's England* (1586), Heywood in *Troja Britannica* (1609), and Slatyer in *Palaeo-Albion* (1621), all had found material for their art in the mythical history of Britain. Nor had the dramatists, from the author of *Gorboduc* to the author of *Lear* and *Cymbeline*, been behindhand in employing plots from the same source in tragedies or chronicle plays. Whether Milton believed these stories or not, their familiarity and their attractiveness made it impossible for him to pass them over in silence.

Moreover, they had a great attraction for Milton himself, even if his judgement rejected them as fictitious. In *Comus* he had already utilized the story of Sabrina, the 'virgin daughter of Locrine', who gave her name to the Severn, and he now told it once more in prose.[3] The space devoted in the *History of Britain* to the story of Lear and Cordelia is probably a tribute to Shakespeare, but the two pages devoted to kings Brennus and Belinus must be explained by the fact that they were to have been personages in the intended epic.[4]

[1] *Polyolbion* (1613), p. 8. Drayton is a convinced believer in the Brutus legend. Selden, in the notes, argues for it 'as an Advocat for the Muse', but not 'if alledg'd for my own Opinion'. See pp. 17, 93, 162, and the address 'from the author of the Illustrations' prefixed.

[2] *History of Britain*, p. 13; *Faerie Queene*, II. x. 92; *Polyolbion*, p. 12.

[3] *Comus*, ll. 824–937; *History of Britain*, p. 15.

[4] Ibid., pp. 17, 23.

It is not only by his treatment of the mythical period of English history that Milton's interest in the legendary and anecdotic side of history is revealed. It appears in the later books as well as the earlier, and the introduction of certain episodes or the space devoted to them may often be explained by their inclusion in the list of suggested subjects for his 'British Tragedies'. The story of Queen Eadburga, the vision of King Edwin, Athelstan's murder of his brother and his repentance, are cases in point.[1] But the most remarkable instance is the narrative of King Edgar's marriage with Elfrida, and of another love adventure of that king's which Milton himself styles 'fitter for a Novel then a History'.[2] 'Edgar slaying Ethelwold for false play in wooing' had once seemed a good plot for a tragedy. 'Wherein', noted Milton, 'may be set out his pride [and] lust, which he thought to cloak by favouring monks and building monasteries; also the disposition of woman, in Elfrida toward her husband.'[3]

Another episode treated at somewhat disproportionate length is that of the murder of Ælfred, the second son of Ethelred the Unready, which some authorities attributed to the treachery of Earl Godwin. The explanation of the space given to the story, and of the elaboration with which the statements of conflicting authors about it are set forth, appears to be that Milton once intended to make it the starting-point of a classical tragedy. The first scene of the tragedy of Harold, he had noted, 'may begin with the ghost of Alfred . . . slain in cruel manner by Godwin, Harold's father, his mother and brother dissuading him'.[4]

Here and elsewhere throughout the *History of Britain* the influence of Holinshed's *Chronicle* is plainly perceptible. Alike in the anecdotes inserted and the anec-

---

[1] *History of Britain*, pp. 184, 224, 289.   [2] Ibid., p. 239.
[3] Masson, ii. 114.
[4] Ibid., p. 114; *History of Britain*, p. 274.

dotes omitted, Milton usually follows in the track of Holinshed (or rather of Abraham Fleming, who wrote that part of Holinshed's compilation). For instance, under the reign of Edward the Confessor Milton relates the stories of the divine judgement upon Godwin, the soldierly death of Siward, and the prophetic vision of Edward the Confessor;[1] all these are to be found in Holinshed, but none of them in Speed or Stow. Similarly, Milton omits the story of Alfred and the cakes, which is omitted by Holinshed though it is told by Stow and Speed. In the first book of the *History of Britain* the author's obligations to Holinshed are still more evident, nor is it by a mere coincidence that the first sentence of one is an echo of the second sentence in the other. 'The beginning of Nations, those excepted of whom sacred Books have spok'n, is to this day unknown', writes Milton. 'The originall in maner of all nations is doubtfull,' wrote the chronicler, 'and even the same for the more part fabulous (that alwaies excepted which we find in the holie scriptures).'[2]

On the other hand, Milton's was too vigorous and too independent a mind to adopt implicitly the conclusions of any previous writer. He had read Stow and Speed as well as Holinshed, and seems from his notes to have compared their narratives. At a later stage he read what original authorities he could obtain for the period from the coming of the Romans to the Norman Conquest, and tested the statements of the chroniclers by their aid. Many statements and theories which the chroniclers had accepted he dismissed as unfounded or improbable when he came to write.

Holinshed (or rather Abraham Fleming) begins the history of Britain, about the time of the flood, with the rule of Samothes, the sixth son of Japhet, and his sons, and the subjugation of the island about three hundred

[1] *History of Britain*, pp. 290, 291, 298.
[2] Ibid., p. 1; Holinshed (1587), Bk. I, p. 1.

years later by the giant Albion, the son of Neptune.
Milton, with Stow and Speed, rejects this story, calling
it an 'outlandish figment', and condemning those 'of
our own Writers, who thought they had don nothing,
unless with all circumstance they tell us when, and who
first set foot upon this Iland'.[1]

Holinshed and Stow both accept with implicit faith
the Brutus legend. The latter intercalates in his narrative 'A briefe Proofe of Brute', showing how many
learned men affirm this history, and denounced Poly-
dore Vergil for denying it. This man, he complains,
'with one dash of a pen cashireth threescore Princes
together, with all their histories and Historians, yea, and
some ancient Lawes also'.[2] On the other hand, Speed
states, with convincing clearness and great elaboration,
the arguments against the legend. 'As *France*', he concludes, 'hath cast off their *Francio* King *Priamus* his
sonne, *Scotland* their *Scotia* King *Pharoes* daughter,
Denmarke their *Danus*, *Ireland* their *Hiberus*, and other
Countries their Demi-gods, so let Britaines likewise
with them disclaime their Brute.'[3]

Milton endeavours to hold the balance between absolute credulity and complete rejection. He will not follow
Speed the whole way:

'. . . of *Brutus* and his Line, with the whole Progeny of Kings,
to the entrance of *Julius Cæsar*, we cannot so easily be dis-
charg'd; Descents of Ancestry, long continu'd, laws and exploits not plainly seeming to be borrow'd, or devis'd, which on
the common beleif have wrought no small impression: defended by many, deny'd utterly by few. For what though
Brutus, and the whole *Trojan* pretence were yeelded up, . . . yet
those old and inborn names of successive Kings, never any to
have bin real persons, or don in thir lives at least som part of
what so long hath bin remember'd, cannot be thought without
too strict an incredulity.

[1] *History of Britain*, p. 4.
[2] Stow's *Chronicle* (1631), pp. 6, 7, and preface.   [3] Speed, pp. 14–20.

'For these, and those causes above mention'd, that which hath receav'd approbation from so many, I have chos'n not to omitt. Certain or uncertain, be that upon the credit of those whom I must follow; so far as keeps alooff from impossible and absurd, attested by ancient Writers from Books more ancient I refuse not, as the due and proper subject of Story.'[1]

Another series of legends clustered round the introduction of Christianity into Britain. It was said that Simon Zelotes or Joseph of Arimathaea had preached Christianity in this country during the reign of Nero, and that about the year 177, when Lucius was king of Britain, the whole island accepted the faith. A letter of Pope Eleutherius to the king was quoted in support of the facts; Lucius was canonized as the first British saint, and it became the accepted belief of English historians that the British nation was the first to make public profession of Christianity. Holinshed, Stow, and even the critical Speed, with some differences as to the details, all accepted these stories. Milton relates them, but he does so with obvious scepticism, and concludes: 'Of these matters, variously written and believ'd, Ecclesiastic Historians can best determin: as the best of them do, with little credit giv'n to . . . such uncertain relations.'[2]

Milton shows the same scepticism about the popular belief that Constantine the Great was of British descent. 'There goes a fame,' he says, 'and that seconded by most of our own Historians, though not those the ancientest,

[1] *History of Britain*, p. 6.

[2] Ibid., p. 80; Holinshed, i. 37. 51; Speed, pp. 73–81, 103; Stow, p. 38. Fuller, *Church History* (1655), p. 9. Milton was indifferent to this claim, holding it a greater glory that Wicliffe, the beginner of the Reformation, was an Englishman: England 'having had this *grace* and *honour* from God to bee the first that should set up a Standard for the recovery of *lost Truth*, and blow the first *Evangelick Trumpet* to the *Nations*'. *Of Reformation, The Works of John Milton*, iii. 5. Archbishop Parker firmly believed in the Lucius legend, and also did Cardinal Pole; Strype's *Parker*, i. 139, 467; iii. 247.

that *Constantine* was born in this Iland, his Mother
Helena the Daughter of *Coilus* a *British* Prince.' He
proceeds to point out a few improbabilities, and to
summarize the evidence of the Roman authorities
against it. Here again he is more difficult to satisfy
than Speed, who accepts the tradition, quoting, in
answer to unbelievers, the opinion of '*Times chiefe
Secretary*, the learned *Cambden*' in its favour.[1]

Milton's treatment of the Arthurian legend is a still
more interesting example of the progress of scepticism.
The three chroniclers who were the standard historians
of Milton's time all doubted the details of the legend,
but believed that Arthur was a real king who gained
genuine victories. 'Of this Arthur,' says Holinshed's
Chronicle, 'manie things are written beyond credit, for
that there is no ancient author of authoritie that con-
firmeth the same: but surelie as may be thought he was
some worthie man, and by all likelihood a great enimie
to the Saxons, by reason whereof the Welshmen which
are the verie Britains in deed, have him in famous
remembrance.' Then at length he relates the legendary
life and exploits of the hero.[2]

Stow is briefer, but adopts much the same position.
'Of this King Arthur there be many fabulous reports:
but certaine he was (saith Will. of Malmesbury) a Prince
more worthy to have advancement by true Histories
then false fables, being the onely prop and up-holder
of this his country.' He supports the truth of the
story by identifying the sites of Mon Badonicus and the

[1] *History of Britain*, p. 89; Speed, p. 156; Holinshed, pp. 62, 63.
Gibbon summarizes the question in a sentence: 'This tradition, unknown to the contemporaries of Constantine, was invented in the
darkness of monasteries, was embellished by Jeffrey of Monmouth and
the writers of the xiith century, has been defended by our antiquarians
of the last age, and is seriously related in the ponderous history of
England, compiled by Mr. Carte (vol. i, p. 147).'—*Decline and Fall*,
ed. Bury (1896), i. 397, n. 10.

[2] Holinshed, i. 90-3.

Castle of Camelot, and describing the remains found there.[1] The critical Speed quotes Malmesbury too, and condemns Geoffrey of Monmouth for discrediting the truth about Arthur by his toys and tales. 'Of his person', he concludes, 'wee make no doubt, though his acts have bin written with too lavish a pen.'[2]

Milton is much more thoroughgoing. All that happened about that time is doubtful. 'The age whereof we now write, hath had the ill hap, more then any since the first fabulous times, to be surcharg'd with all the idle fancies of posterity.' He introduces Arthur by describing him as a British leader, 'more renown'd in Songs and Romances, then in true stories'. With real insight he dismisses at once the medieval fictions and examines the account of Nennius as the only evidence of any real value:

'. . . who *Arthur* was, and whether ever any such reign'd in *Britain*, hath bin doubted heertofore, and may again with good reason. For the Monk of *Malmsbury*, and others whose credit hath sway'd most with the learneder sort, we may well perceave to have known no more of this *Arthur* 500 years past, nor of his doeings, then we now living; And what they had to say, transcrib'd out of *Nennius*, a very trivial writer yet extant, which hath already bin related. Or out of a *British* Book, the same which he of *Monmouth* set forth, utterly unknown to the World, till more then 600 years after the dayes of *Arthur*, of whom (as *Sigebert* in his Chronicle confesses) all other Histories were silent, both Foren and Domestic, except only that fabulous Book. Others of later time have sought to assert him by old legends and Cathedrall regests. But he who can accept of Legends for good story, may quickly swell a volume with trash, and had need be furnish'd with two only necessaries, leasure, and beleif, whether it be the writer, or he that shall read.'[3]

'As to *Artur*,' he continues, 'no less is in doubt who was his Father,' and then proceeds to demolish Uther

[1] Stow, pp. 53–5.   [2] Speed, p. 271.
[3] *History of Britain*, pp. 122–3.

Pendragon: 'And as we doubted of his parentage, so may we also of his puissance; for whether that Victory at *Badon* Hill were his or no, is uncertain.' All he will concede is that, 'whether by *Artur* won, or whensoever,' that battle 'seems indeed to have giv'n a most undoubted and important blow to the *Saxons*, and to have stop'd thir proceedings for a good while after'.[1]

When we compare Milton's treatment of this with that of Holinshed, Stow, and Speed, his superiority is evident. Alter the phraseology, and he might have been writing in the nineteenth rather than in the seventeenth century. For his conclusions are roughly those of modern scholars, and his reasoning practically that of a scientific historian.[2]

Here, as in many other places, Milton's *History* helps to explain his poetry. One of the reasons for the abandonment of the intended epic on the story of Arthur was that his studies had convinced him there was no more truth in it than there was in the story of Brutus. When he referred later to the Arthurian legends he was careful to emphasize their fictitious character. He speaks of

> . . . what resounds
> In Fable or *Romance* of *Uthers* Son
> Begirt with *British* and *Armoric* Knights;

or of ladies

> . . . that seem'd
> Fairer then feign'd of old, or fabl'd since
> Of Fairy Damsels met in Forest wide
> By Knights of *Logres*, or of *Lyones*,
> *Lancelot* or *Pelleas*, or *Pellenore*.[3]

It was not in these legends of 'fabl'd Knights' and 'Battels feign'd' that he could find the substance of his

[1] *History of Britain*, pp. 119, 122, 124.
[2] Hodgkin, *Political History of England*, i. 104–5, 107; Ramsay, *Foundations of England*, i. 124–5, 135.
[3] *Paradise Lost*, i. 579; *Paradise Regained*, ii. 357.

'Heroic Song',[1] nor was it through them that he could convey the ethical teaching which it was the office of the poet to give.

As we have already pointed out, Milton's *History* is not entirely a compilation from the standard historians of his day, but is also based upon a considerable study of the original sources accessible when he wrote. He begins by endeavouring to form an opinion of the value of the authorities for each particular period taken collectively, and supplements this by incidental estimates of individual authors.

For the legends of the prae-Roman period he says at the outset: 'The principal Author is well know'n to be *Geoffrey of Monmouth*; what he was, and whence his authority, who in his age or before him have deliver'd the same matter, and such like general discourses, will better stand in a Treatise by themselves.'[2] The treatise was never written, but we can gather Milton's opinion of Geoffrey's credibility from his rejection of his statements, and from disparaging references to his fables and untruths.[3] Authentic history, Milton declares at the close of his first book, begins with the coming of the Romans.

'*By this time, like one who had set out on his way by night, and travail'd through a Region of smooth or idle Dreams, our History now arrivs on the Confines, where day-light and truth meet us with a cleer dawn, representing to our view, though at a farr distance, true colours and shapes.* For albeit, *Cæsar*, whose Autority we are now first to follow, wanted not who tax'd him of misreporting in his Commentaries, yea in his Civil Warrs against *Pompey*, much more, may wee think, in the *British affairs*, of whose little skill in writing he did not easily hope to be contradicted, yet now in such variety of good Authors, we hardly can miss from one hand or other to be sufficiently inform'd as of things past so long agoe.'[4]

---

[1] *Paradise Lost*, ix. 27–40.   [2] *History of Britain*, p. 6.
[3] Ibid., pp. 24, 28, 47, 54, 79, 84, 103, 144.   [4] Ibid., p. 29.

'. . . The only Authors wee have of *Brittish* matters, while the power of *Rome* reach'd hither' are Roman authors 'who in the English Tongue have laid together, as much, and perhaps more then was requisite to a History of *Britain*'. The story they tell is 'a story of much truth', and for the first hundred years and more it may be 'collected without much labour'. For the most part 'little seems to be requir'd above transcription', although something may be added by diligence and explained by the arrangement of the facts. Towards the end of the period, however, 'the *Roman* Empire declining apace, good Historians growing scarce, or lost, have left us little else but fragments for many years ensuing'.[1]

When the Roman Empire fell, darkness settled down again; learning and history, and even language itself, decayed with it:

'Henceforth we are to stear by another sort of Authors; neer anough to the things they write, as in thir own Countrie, if that would serve; in time not much belated, some of equal age; in expression barbarous; and to say how judicious, I suspend a while: this we must expect; in civil matters to find them dubious Relaters, and still to the best advantage of what they term holy Church, meaning indeed themselves: in most other matters of Religion, blind, astonish'd, and strook with superstition as with a Planet; in one word, Monks. Yet these Guides, where can be had no better, must be follow'd; in gross, it may be true anough; in circumstance each man as his judgment gives him, may reserve his Faith, or bestow it.'[2]

One of these monks was Bede, the chief authority, says Milton, for the period from the coming of the Saxons to 731, but even he could not make it intelligible:

'. . . *Beda* surceas'd to write. Out of whom cheifly hath bin gatherd, since the *Saxons* arrival, such as hath bin deliverd, a scatterd story pickt out heer and there, with some trouble and

---

[1] *History of Britain*, pp. 31, 33, 84.   [2] Ibid., p. 97.

tedious work from among his many Legends of Visions and Miracles; toward the latter end so bare of civill matters, as what can be thence collected may seem a Calendar rather then a History, tak'n up for the most part with succession of Kings, and computation of years, yet those hard to be reconcil'd with the *Saxon Annals*. Thir actions we read of, were most commonly Wars, but for what cause wag'd, or by what Councells carried on, no care was had to let us know: wherby thir strength and violence we understand, of thir wisedom, reason, or justice, little or nothing, the rest superstition and monastical affectation; Kings one after another leaving thir Kingly Charge, to run thir heads fondly into a Monks Cowle: which leaves us uncertain, whether *Beda* was wanting to his matter, or his matter to him.'[1]

Yet whatever Bede's defects might be he was a better guide than the authors on whom it was necessary to depend for the following period:

'. . . From hence to the *Danish* Invasion it will be worse with us, destitute of *Beda*. Left only to obscure and blockish Chronicles; whom *Malmsbury*, and *Huntingdon*, (for neither they then we had better Authors of those times) ambitious to adorn the History, make no scruple oft-times, I doubt to inter-line with conjectures and surmises of thir own: them rather then imitate, I shall choose to represent the truth naked, though as lean as a plain Journal. Yet *William* of *Malmsbury* must be acknowledg'd, both for stile and judgment, to be by far the best Writer of them all: but what labour is to be endur'd, turning over Volumes of Rubbish in the rest, *Florence* of *Worster*, *Huntingdon*, *Simeon* of *Durham*, *Hoveden*, *Mathew* of *West-minster*, and many others of obscurer note, with all thir monachisms, is a penance to think. Yet these are our only Registers, transcribers one after another for the most part, and somtimes worthy enough for the things they register. This travail rather then not know at once what may be known of our antient story, sifted from Fables and impertinences, I volun-tarily undergo; and to save others, if they please the like un-pleasing labour.'[2]

At intervals during the later part of his narrative

---

[1] Ibid., p. 172–3. [2] Ibid.

Milton characterizes or criticizes particular authors more fully. Malmesbury, though the best, had other defects besides those mentioned. 'He refus'd not the autority of Ballats for want of better' and inserted stories he confessed 'to be sung in old Songs, not read in warrantable Authors'.[1] Besides, he was too much biased in favour of monks and kings who loved monks, and against the secular clergy. Henry of Huntingdon was not to be trusted unless he was confirmed by some other authority: 'little credit is to be plac'd in *Huntingdon* single.' He was too imaginative. 'His manner is to comment upon the annal Text' (that is, the *Saxon Chronicle*) and to add fictitious details of the events recorded, describing 'the manner of those Battels and Encounters, which they who compare, and can judge of Books, may be confident he never found in any current Author whom he had to follow'.[2]

Of the value of the 'Saxon Annals', as Milton terms the *Anglo-Saxon Chronicle*, he has a very just conception. 'These I take . . . to be the Chief Fountain of our story, the ground and basis upon which the Monks later in time gloss and comment at thir pleasure.' But to understand them and make out the real significance of the Annals was a very difficult task. Sometimes their record of events was 'without coherence of sense or story'. Alfred's wars with the Danes are 'set down so perplexly by the *Saxon* Annalist, ill-guifted with utterance, as with much ado can be understood sometimes what is spok'n, whether meant of the *Danes*, or of the *Saxons*'. For instance, it is impossible to say who won the battle of Merton, 'so darkly do the *Saxon Annals* deliver thir meaning with more then wonted infancy'. Poetical passages, such as the ballads on the battles of Brunanburh and Maldon completely baffled and somewhat enraged Milton. Of the former he says: '. . . the *Saxon* Annalist wont to be sober and succinct, whether the

[1] *History of Britain*, pp. 224, 229.   [2] Ibid., pp. 122, 175, 211.

same or another writer, now labouring under the weight of his Argument, and over-charg'd, runs on a sudden into such extravagant fansies and metaphors, as bare him quite beside the scope of being understood. . . . I shall only summe up what of him I can attain, in usuall language.'[1]

Milton endeavoured to supplement the scantiness of the English sources by the help of foreign historians, but got little satisfaction from them. He searched the *Rerum Danicarum Historia* of J. J. Pontanus for information about the Danish invasion, but found nothing of any value. As to the ninth century 'of all these terrible landings and devastations by the *Danes* . . . or of thir Leaders, whether Kings, Dukes, or Earls, the *Danish* History of best credit saith nothing; So little Wit or Conscience it seems they had to leave any memory of thir brutish, rather then manly actions'. As to the tenth century: '. . . the *Danish* History, at least thir latest and diligentest Historian, as neither from the first landing of *Danes*, in the Reign of *West-Saxon Brithric*, so now again from first to last, contributes nothing; busied more then anough to make out the bare names and successions of thir uncertain Kings, and thir small actions at home: unless out of him I should transcribe what hee takes, and I better may, from our own Annals.'[2]

When Milton turned to the Scottish historians for facts about the invasion of the Picts and Scots the result was still more disappointing, for he found nothing but pure fiction. George Buchanan, he complains, in his *Rerum Scoticarum Historia*,

'Departs not much from the Fables of his Predecessor *Boethius*' [i.e. Hector Boece]; 'with no less exactness of particular circumstances, he takes upon him to relate all those tumultuarie inrodes of the *Scots* and *Picts* into *Britain*, as if they had but yesterday

---

[1] Ibid., pp. 203, 211, 212, 225.
[2] Ibid., pp. 179, 192, 203, 244.

happen'd, thir order of Battel, manner of fight, number of slain, Articles of Peace, things whereof *Gildas* and *Beda* are utterly silent, Authors to whom the *Scotch* Writers have none to cite comparable in Antiquity; no more therefore to be believ'd for bare assertions, however quaintlie drest, than our *Geofry* of *Monmouth* when he varies most from authentick storie. But either the inbred vanity of some, in that respect unworthily call'd Historians, or the fond zeal of praising thir Nations above truth hath so far transported them, that where they find nothing faithfully to relate, they fall confidently to invent what they think may either best set off thir Historie, or magnifie thir Countrie.'

It was amusing when 'our Neighbour Historian' gravely reprehended Geoffrey of Monmouth and others 'for fabling in the deeds of Arms, yet what he writes thereof himself, as of better credit, shews not whence he had but from those Fables; which he seems content to believe in part, on condition that the *Scots* and *Picts* may be thought to have assisted *Arthur* in all his Wars and atchievements; whereof appears as little grownd by any credible story, as of that which he most counts Fabulous'.[1]

Another modern author of whom Milton made constant use was Camden. Whenever the locality of a battle had to be fixed, or the modern name of a place given, it was naturally to Camden's *Britannia* that he turned. The spot where Caesar landed, the ford by which he crossed the Thames, the site of the camp of Caractacus, the position of the Roman wall, and other topographical facts mentioned were all derived from the same source. These questions of identification did not interest Milton much; he contented himself with briefly giving the necessary minimum of information on such points without interrupting the narrative by discussions. If they could not be identified he preferred to omit them. He did not care, he said, 'to wrincle the

[1] *History of Britain*, pp. 102–3, 126, 185.

smoothness of History with rugged names of places unknown, better harp'd at in *Camden*, and other Chorographers'.[1]

Milton's method of combining and comparing the statements he found in the various authorities he used deserves notice. At the outset he had declared 'I intend not with controversies and quotations to delay or interrupt the smooth course of History'.[2] But these words referred, as the context shows and his later practice proves, merely to the legendary period covered in the first book. He declined to waste labour 'computing, or collating years and Chronologies', when he was dealing with the reigns of the progeny of Brutus, because it was absurd to 'be vainly curious about the time and circumstance of things wherof the substance is so much in doubt'.[3] In the later books where his authorities were more trustworthy and he was dealing with historical events, it was worth while to discuss dates, to point out discrepancies, and to attempt to reconcile statements. The task, he admitted, was laborious, but he did not shrink from it. 'This travail rather then not know at once what may be known of our antient story, sifted from Fables and impertinences, I voluntarily undergo; and to save others, if they please the like unpleasing labour.'[4]

Milton's favourite method, in the later books, is to place the different stories of his authorities side by side, and conclude by saying which account seems most probable. For instance, in relating the division of England between Canute and Edmund Ironside, he summarizes first Malmesbury's account, then that of Huntingdon, finally that of Matthew of Westminster. As to the accession of Edward the Confessor he gives the versions of Huntingdon, Malmesbury, and Brompton

[1] Ibid., pp. 36, 45, 56, 77, 78, 83, 160, 178. Milton also refers to Spelman's *Concilia*, p. 143.   [2] *History of Britain*, p. 3.
[3] Ibid., p. 29.   [4] Ibid., p. 173.

in succession, prefacing them with the remark, 'It may seem a wonder that our Historians, if they deserve that name, should in a matter so remarkable, and so neer thir own time, so much differ'. He declines to accept William of Malmesbury's version. In another instance, dealing with Harold's visit to William of Normandy, he sets side by side the statements of five authors, Malmesbury, Ingulf, Eadmer, Simeon of Durham, and Matthew Paris. 'So variously are these things reported' that he finds it impossible to decide.'[1]

Incidentally he criticizes with some acuteness Ingulf's story, for, like seventeenth-century historians in general, he accepted his *Chronicle of Croyland* as a genuine authority. Ingulf had said that Edward the Confessor sent Robert Archbishop of Canterbury to acquaint Duke William with his intention of bequeathing the English crown to him. 'The former part may be true, that King *Edward* upon such considerations had sent one or other; but Archbishop *Robert* was fled the land, and dead many years before.'[2] In the same way Milton rejects a statement of Simeon of Durham's which describes Uthred, son of the Earl of Northumberland, as fighting against Malcolm of Scotland: 'But heer *Simeon* the relater seems to have committed some mistake, having slain *Uthred* by *Canute* two years before, and set *Eric* in his place: *Eric* therfore it must needs be, not *Uthred*, who manag'd this War against the *Scots*.'[3]

Milton's wide reading showed him that some of the statements he found in his authorities were merely conventional imitations of earlier historians. Speaking of the omens which accompanied William's landing on the English shore, he says, 'These are things related of *Alexander* and *Caesar*, and I doubt thence borrow'd by the Monks to inlay thir story'.[4] At other times his good sense prevented him from believing implicitly

[1] *History of Britain*, pp. 265, 278, 297.   [2] Ibid., p. 296.
[3] Ibid., p. 269.   [4] Ibid., p. 303.

what others had been content to accept on authority. Holinshed and Speed, for instance, repeat as a fact Malmesbury's statement that the English in Edgar's time owed their vices to the 'too frequent resort' of strangers to the country, learning rudeness of 'the outlandish *Saxons*', daintiness of the Flemings, and drunkenness of the Danes. 'I doubt', comments Milton, 'these vices are as naturally home-bred heer as in any of those Countries.'[1]

Yet Milton, to use his own phrase, was not 'of too strict an incredulity', and tells us a few lines farther, on the authority of Ingulf, 'This year dy'd *Swarling* a Monk of *Croyland*, the 142. year of his Age, and another soon after him in the 115*th*. in the Fenn and watrish air, the more remarkable.'[2]

To conclude this discussion of Milton's treatment of his authorities and his relation to previous historians.

It seems plain that Professor Masson went too far when he described the *History of Britain* as 'not a work of real research and criticism', but 'a mere popular compilation of such matter as was easily at hand'.[3] Milton aimed higher and achieved more than this verdict admits. There is some attempt both at research and at criticism in the book. Milton frequently shows a very true conception of the value of the evidence at his disposal, as well as the independence of judgement one naturally expects from him.

The style also possesses the individuality which marks all Milton's writings. The earlier books are more carefully finished than the later ones. In books four and six Milton seems somewhat weary of his task; he is less attentive to the arrangement of his matter or the effective statement of what he has to say. In the early part of the *History* he relates a story or describes a scene with a certain deliberate care—not only with touches that reveal the poet, but in the more highly-wrought passages

[1] Ibid., p. 235.   [2] Ibid.   [3] *Life of Milton*, vi. 644.

with a certain sententious brevity entirely unlike the
fervid and unrestrained diction of his first prose pamphlets. The explanation of this change of style is to be
found in Milton's theory of the manner in which history
should be written.

His views on the nature of historical writing in
general are set forth in two passages in the *History*.

Every age, Milton hints, obtained the historians it
deserved, for there was a close relation between the
deeds and the written records of the deeds. In certain
times, what happened was hardly worth recording.
'Oft-times we see that wise men, and of best abilitie
have forborn to write the Acts of thir own daies, while
they beheld with a just loathing and disdain, not only
how unworthy, how pervers, how corrupt, but often
how ignoble, how petty, how below all History the
persons and thir actions were; who either by fortune,
or som rude election had attain'd as a sore judgment,
and ignominie upon the Land, to have cheif sway in
managing the Commonwealth.'[1] Even then there were
historians of a sort. ''Tis true that in obscurest times,
by shallow and unskilfull Writers, the indistinct noise
of many Battels, and devastations, of many Kingdoms
over-run and lost, hath come to our Eares.' But in such
periods of decay true history was hardly possible; and
good historians were discouraged.

'When the esteem of Science, and liberal study waxes low in
the Common-wealth, wee may presume that also there all civil
Vertue, and worthy action is grown as low to a decline: and then
Eloquence, as it were consorted in the same destiny, with the
decrease and fall of vertue corrupts also and fades; at least
resignes her office of relating to illiterat and frivolous Historians; such as the persons themselvs both deserv, and are best
pleas'd with; whilst they want either the understanding to
choose better, or the innocence to dare invite the examining,
and searching stile of an intelligent, and faithfull Writer to the

---

[1] *History of Britain*, p. 2.

survay of thir unsound exploits, better befreinded by obscurity then Fame.'[1]

On the other hand, 'worthy deeds are not often destitute of worthy relaters: as by a certain Fate great Acts and great Eloquence have most commonly gon hand in hand, equalling and honouring each other in the same Ages'. For great men knew that history was necessary to their greatness.

'He whose just and true valour uses the necessity of Warr and Dominion, not to destroy but to prevent destruction, to bring in liberty against Tyrants, Law and Civility among barbarous Nations, knowing that when he Conquers all things else, he cannot Conquer *Time*, or *Detraction*, wisely conscious of this his want, as well as of his worth not to be forgott'n or conceal'd, honours and hath recourse to the aid of Eloquence, his freindliest and best supply; by whose immortal Record his noble deeds, which else were transitory, becoming fixt and durable against the force of Yeares and Generations, he fails not to continue through all Posterity, over *Envy*, *Death*, and *Time*, also victorious.'[2]

As to the manner in which the historian should relate the deeds he undertook to record, Milton set forth his views in two letters to a young foreign scholar, Henry de Brass.[3]

The model for all historical writers was Sallust. The man who appreciated Sallust had made no small progress in the art of history.[4] 'Dicam libere ... *Sallustium* cuivis *Latino* Historico me quidem anteferre; quae etiam constans fere Antiquorum sententia fuit. Habet suas laudes tuus *Tacitus*; sed eas meo quidem judicio maximas, quod *Sallustium* nervis omnibus sit imitatus.'

---

[1] Ibid., p. 32.　　　　　　　　　　　[2] Ibid., pp. 31–3.

[3] *Ioannis Miltoni Angli Epistolarum Familiarum Liber Unus* (1674), pp. 53, 58; and *Works of John Milton*, vii. 401, 405. See Masson, *Life of Milton*, v. 363, 379. The letters are dated July 15 and Dec. 16, 1657.

[4] 'Sciat se haud parum in re Historica profecisse cui placeat *Sallustius*.'

He proceeds then to explain his view of what Sallust meant when he said 'facta dictis exaequanda sunt'.

'Ego vero sic existimo; qui gestas res dignas digne scripserit, eum animo non minus magno rerumque usu præditum scribere oportere, quam is qui eas gesserit: ut vel maximas pari animo comprehendere atque metiri possit, et comprehensas sermone puro atque casto distincte gravitérque narrare: nam ut ornate, non admodum laboro; Historicum enim, non Oratorem requiro. . . . Addiderim et illud Sallustianum, qua in re ipse *Catonem* maxime laudavit, posse multa paucis absolvere; id quod sine acerrimo judicio, atque etiam temperantia quadam neminem posse arbitror. Sunt multi in quibus vel sermonis elegantiam, vel congestarum rerum copiam non desideres; qui brevitatem cum copia conjunxerit, id est, qui multa paucis absolverit, princeps meo judicio *Latinorum* est *Sallustius*. Has ego virtutes Historico inesse putem oportere, qui facta dictis exæquaturum se speret.'[1]

This 'Sallustiana brevitas', as Quintilian terms it, Milton endeavours to imitate, not only in certain highly-wrought passages, but in the pregnant or picturesque phrases interspersed through his narrative. Take, for instance, his summary of the results of the Roman Conquest. 'Of the *Romans* we have cause not to say much worse, then that they beate us into some civilitie.'[2] Or his comment on the attempt of Ethelred to buy off the Danes. 'The King and his Courtiers . . . send now the fourth time to buy a dishonorable peace, every time still dearer, not to be had now under 36 thousand pound (for the *Danes* knew how to milk such easie Kine).' Or his description of the incursions of the Danes 'salying again out of thir Ships as out of Savage Denns', to plunder and then 'like wild Beasts glutted, returning to thir Caves'. To vary the phrase in a second case he says 'or rather Sea-Monsters to thir Water-stables'.[3]

---

[1] *Epistolae*, pp. 54–5.   [2] *History of Britain*, p. 49.
[3] Ibid., pp. 252, 255.

The same quality marks some of Milton's characters of persons. He describes Carausius as usurping the government because he was 'grown at length too great a Delinquent to be less than an Emperor', and Vortigern as a tyrant who was 'yet of the people much belov'd, because his vices sorted so well with theirs'.[1] At times this attempt to put much meaning into few words produces obscurity. At other times it results in something like conceits; as when he describes the Britons 'with a stern compassion' slaying their wives and children to prevent them from falling into the hands of the Romans, or a Dane 'with a pious impiety' killing Archbishop Alfage in order to put an end to his sufferings.[2]

In one passage of his letters to Henry de Brass Milton lays down another principle which should be observed in historical writing. 'Crebras etiam sententias, et judicia de rebus gestis interjecta prolixe nollem, ne, interrupta rerum serie, quod Politici Scriptoris munus est Historicus invadat; qui si in consiliis explicandis, factisque enarrandis, non suum ingenium aut conjecturam, sed veritatem potissimum sequitur, suarum profecto partium satagit.' But he is far from following this counsel himself. It is true he does not insert many general reflections, but there are a few. On the Britons calling the Saxons to help them against the Picts and Scots he observes: 'So much do men through impatience count ever that the heaviest which they bear at present, and to remove the evil which they suffer, care not to pull on a greater: as if variety and change in evil also were acceptable.'[3] When he relates the repentance of Canute and his resolve to make amends to his people, he adds: 'It is a fond conceit in many great ones, and pernicious in the end, to cease from no violence till they have attain'd the utmost of thir ambitions and desires; then to think God appeas'd by thir seeking to bribe

[1] Ibid., pp. 86, 109.   [2] Ibid., pp. 76, 256.
[3] Ibid., p. 110.

him with a share however large of thir ill-gott'n spoils, and then lastly to grow zealous of doing right, when they have no longer need to do wrong.'[1]

But generally Milton's comments are not so much to the point: on the contrary, they are as far away from it as possible. He inserts reflections of every kind. Some are references to contemporary manners. When he describes the ancient Britons as 'painting thir own skins with severall Portratures of Beast, Bird, or Flower', he adds, '*a Vanitie which hath not yet left us, remov'd only from the skin to the skirt behung now with as many colour'd Ribands and gewgawes*'.[2] Others contain references to contemporary politics. Having to mention the expedition sent by a Northumbrian king to Ireland, he introduces an allusion to the Irish massacres in 1641: 'A harmless Nation, saith *Beda*, and ever friendly to the English; in both which they seem to have left a posterity much unlike them at this day.'[3] Milton's comments continually remind us that he held very strong views about the subjection of women. He is as bitter against 'the monstrous regiment of women' as John Knox himself. Cordelia's nephews rebel against her in spite of her virtues, 'not bearing that a Kingdom should be govern'd by a Woman', and Cartismandua is dethroned by the Britons, not because of her crimes, but on account of 'the uncomeliness of thir Subjection to the Monarchie of a Woeman'.[4] When he relates, after Holinshed, the legend of Martia, wife of King Guitheline, who is said 'to have excell'd so much in wisdom, as to venture upon a new Institution of Laws', the story seems so monstrous that he has to rationalize it away. 'In the minority of her Son she had the rule, and then, as may be suppos'd, brought forth these Laws, not her self, for Laws are Masculin Births, but by the advice of her sagest Counselors; and therin she might do vertu-

---

[1] *History of Britain*, p. 272.
[2] Ibid., p. 48.
[3] Ibid., p. 167; cf. p. 82.
[4] Ibid., pp. 20, 60.

ously, since it befell her to supply the nonage of her Son: else nothing more awry from the Law of God and Nature, then that a Woman should give Laws to Men.'[1]

Perhaps the most curious example of Milton's prejudice against women is that afforded by his treatment of Boadicea. Previous historians had regarded the warrior-queen as a national heroine; he represents her merely as a virago, 'a distracted Woeman, with as mad a Crew at her heeles'. Dion Cassius puts a long speech into Boadicea's mouth, which Holinshed and Speed reproduce at length. Milton very properly rejects this oration.

'I affect not set speeches in a Historie, unless known for certain to have bin so spok'n in effect as they are writ'n, nor then, unless worth rehearsal; and to invent such, though eloquently, as some Historians have done, is an abuse of posteritie, raising, in them that read, other conceptions of those times and persons then were true. Much less therefore do I purpose heer or elsewhere to Copie out tedious Orations without decorum, though in thir Authors compos'd ready to my hand.'[2]

The unseemliness of the oration consists in this, that Dion and also Tacitus put into the mouth of Boadicea, besides 'a deal of other fondness', the statement that 'with the *Britans* it was usual for Woemen to be thir Leaders'. Indignantly Milton observes: 'This they do out of a vanity, hoping to embellish and set out thir Historie with the strangness of our manners, not careing in the mean while to brand us with the rankest note of Barbarism, as if in *Britain* Woemen were Men, and Men Woemen.'[3]

Milton's prejudices appear still more strongly and frequently in his references to Church matters. Of set purpose he avoided the ecclesiastical side of British and Saxon history as far as possible, 'not professing to relate of those matters more then what mixes aptly with civil

---

[1] Ibid., p. 25.   [2] Ibid., pp. 65–7.   [3] Ibid., p. 66.

affairs'.[1] The records of political events were often an arid catalogue of names and dates, tragical deaths of princes of whom nothing else was known, and battles without reason or result. 'Such bickerings to recount, met oft'n in these our Writers,' complains Milton, 'what more worth is it then to Chronicle the Wars of Kites, or Crows, flocking and fighting in the Air?'[2]

But he deliberately refused to amplify these meagre annals by drawing upon the fund of information which his authorities supplied about the religious life of the times.

'I am sensible how wearisom it may likely be to read of so many bare and reasonless Actions, so many names of Kings one after another, acting little more then mute persons in a Scene: what would it be to have inserted the long Bead-roll of Archbishops, Bishops, Abbots, Abbesses, and thir doeings, neither to Religion profitable, nor to morality, swelling my Authors each to a voluminous body, by me studiously omitted; and left as their propriety, who have a mind to write the Ecclesiastical matters of those Ages.'[3]

The development of a scientific interest in the monuments and institutions of the past was one of the

[1] *History of Britain*, p. 138.

[2] Ibid., p. 184. Hume quotes this: 'The history of that period abounds in names, but is extremely barren of events; or the events are related so much without circumstances and causes, that the most profound or most eloquent writer must despair of rendering them either instructive or entertaining to the reader. Even the great learning and vigorous imagination of Milton sunk under the weight; and this author scruples not to declare that the skirmishes of kites or crows as much merited a particular narrative as the confused transactions and battles of the Saxon heptarchy.' (*History of England* [1871], i. 16.)

[3] *History of Britain*, pp. 177–8. Hume echoes this passage: 'It is almost impossible, and quite needless, to be more particular in relating the transactions of the East-Angles. What instruction or entertainment can it give the reader to hear a long bead-roll of barbarous names: Egric, Annas, Ethelbert, Ethelwald, Aldulf, Elfwold, Beorne, Ethelred, Ethelbert, who successively murdered, expelled, or inherited from each other, and obscurely filled the throne of that kingdom?' (*History of England*, i. 26.)

characteristics of seventeenth-century England, but so far as it showed itself in researches into ecclesiastical antiquities Milton took no interest in the movement. He scoffed at men like Dodsworth and Dugdale, 'who take pleasure to be all thir life time, rakeing in the Foundations of old Abbies and Cathedrals'.[1] Though he professed to distinguish between antiquaries, 'whose labours are useful and laudable', and 'antiquitarians', that is 'those that over affect antiquity', and consequently oppose necessary changes in the Church, he evidently thought that all antiquaries tended to become antiquitarians. In his pamphlet *Of Reformation in England* he sneers at Camden as 'a fast friend of Episcopacie, . . . who cannot but love Bishops, as well as old coins, and his much lamented Monasteries for antiquities sake'.[2]

Just as Milton failed to appreciate the value of researches into monastic antiquities, so he was insensible to the charm of the monastic legends. He had not hesitated for the sake of the poets to relate Geoffrey of Monmouth's fantastic fictions about the early British kings, but fabulous stories about events which occurred in historic times stood on a different footing. A vision might pass, but no story with a miracle in it should be told in his pages. Legends of martyrs were therefore excluded. Speaking of Alban of Verulam, he says that the story of his martyrdom 'soil'd, and worse martyr'd with the fabling zeal of some idle fancies, more fond of Miracles, than apprehensive of Truth, deserves not longer digression'.[3] The secret murder of Kenelm of Mercia was miraculously revealed, 'but to tell how', says Milton, 'is a long story, told, though out of order, by *Malmsbury*; and under the year 821. by *Mat. West.*, where I leave it to be sought by such as are more credulous then I wish my Readers'.[4]

[1] *History of Britain*, p. 173.
[2] *Of Reformation in England, Works*, iii. 14.
[3] *History of Britain*, p. 88.   [4] Ibid., p. 186.

In Milton's attitude scientific incredulity was reinforced by Puritanical abhorrence of popery, and by contempt for the triviality of ecclesiastical controversy, wherein he anticipates the philosophical historians of the next century. After Augustine had commenced the work of converting the men of Kent, Pope Gregory sent him a supply of fellow labourers. 'What they were', says Milton, 'may be guess't by the stuff which they brought with them, vessels and vestments for the Altar, Coaps, reliques, and for the Archbishop *Austin* a Pall to say Mass in: to such a rank superstition that Age was grown, though some of them yet retaining an emulation of Apostolic zeal.'[1] He is still more contemptuous when, having mentioned the Synod of Whitby, he has to refer to the controversy between the Irish and English clergy about the tonsure. 'Another clerical question was there also much controverted, not so superstitious in my opinion as ridiculous, about the right shaving of crowns.'[2] Of monastic institutions he speaks always with similar contempt, dwelling at length on their worst side and on their decay, never mentioning their services in their prime. 'In the days of *Ina*,' he relates, 'Clerks and Laics, Men and Woemen, hasting to *Rome* in Herds, thought themselves no where sure of Eternal Life, till they were Cloistered there.' Kings imitated their subjects: if one was 'forcibly shav'n a Monk', many others of their own free will got 'into a Monks Hood'. Kelwulf of Northumberland became a monk in Lindisfarne,

'yet none of the severest,' says Milton, 'for he brought those Monks from milk and water, to Wine and Ale; in which doctrin no doubt but they were soon docil, and well might, for *Kelwulf* brought with him good provision, great treasure and revenues of land, recited by *Simeon*, yet all under pretense of following (I use the Authors words) poor *Christ*, by voluntary poverty: no marvel then if such applause were giv'n by Monkish Writers

---

[1] *History of Britain*, p. 141.   [2] Ibid., p. 162.

to Kings turning Monks, and much cunning perhaps us'd to allure them.'[1]

The fruit of this predilection for monkish life was the ruin of Church and State. When at the beginning of the ninth century the Danish storm broke in England, the Saxons were ripe for conquest. They were

'brok'n with luxurie and sloth, either secular or superstitious; for laying aside the exercise of Arms, and the study of all ver-tuous knowledge, some betook them to over-worldly or vitious practice, others to religious Idleness and Solitude, which brought forth nothing but vain and delusive visions; easily perceav'd such, by thir commanding of things, either not be-longing to the Gospel, or utterly forbidden, Ceremonies, Reliques, Monasteries, Masses, Idols, add to these ostentation of Alms, got oft-times by rapine and oppression, or intermixt with violent and lustfull deeds, sometimes prodigally bestow'd as the expiation of cruelty and bloodshed.'

Thus religion itself had grown void of sincerity, and the greatest shows of purity had become impure.[2] There is one omission in Milton's references to ecclesiastical affairs which at first surprises the reader. He does not attack episcopacy. In 1641 he had thought nothing was too bad to say of the bishops.

'Most certaine it is (as all our *Stories* beare witnesse) that ever since their comming to the See of *Canterbury* for neere twelve hundred yeares, to speake of them in generall, they have beene in *England* to our Soules a sad and dolefull succession of illiterate and blind guides: to our purses, and goods a wastfull band of robbers, a perpetuall havock, and rapine: To our state a con-tinuall *Hydra* of mischiefe, and molestation, the forge of dis-cord and Rebellion.'[3]

In the *History*, however, Milton is almost completely silent about the bishops. Incidentally he remarks how

---

[1] Ibid., pp. 172, 173, 176, 180.   [2] Ibid., p. 190.
[3] *Of Reformation, Works*, iii. 60.

quickly Augustine and his successors 'stepp't up into fellowship of pomp with Kings'. On the other hand, he inserts an unexpectedly favourable character of Dunstan: 'a strenuous Bishop, zealous without dread of person, and for ought appeers, the best of many Ages, if he busied not himself too much in secular affairs.'[1]

Perhaps this absence of attacks on bishops is to be explained by the fact that they were suppressed by the licenser. Toland says: 'The Licensers, those sworn Officers to destroy Learning, Liberty, and good Sense, expung'd several passages of it wherin he expos'd the Superstition, Pride, and Cunning of the Popish Monks in the *Saxon* Times, but apply'd by the sagacious Licensers to CHARLES the Second's Bishops.'[2] But the number of attacks upon 'the Popish Monks' which remain seem to refute the story that such indirect thrusts at Milton's old enemies were struck out. Some remarks against the bishops perhaps disappeared owing to the censorship, but there is a better explanation of their absence. . Bishops had been abolished before Milton began to write his *History*. Since 1646 'new presbyter' not 'old priest' had been Milton's mark.[3] In the *History* he used the primitive bishops as a stalking-horse against the Presbyterians. Relating the story that three British bishops who attended the Synod of Rimini in 354 accepted the emperor's offer to pay their expenses rather than the subsidies offered by the brethren, 'esteeming it more honourable to live on the publick, than to be obnoxious to any private Purse', he adds the comment: 'Doubtless an ingenuous mind, and far above the Presbyters of our Age; who like well to sit in Assembly on the publick stipend, but lik'd not the

[1] *History of Britain*, pp. 141, 245.
[2] Toland, *Life of John Milton* (1699), p. 138.
[3] Sonnet 'On the New Forcers of Conscience under the Long Parliament'.

poverty that caus'd these to do so'.[1] Under cover of describing after Gildas the vices of the British clergy in the sixth century, he inserts phrases aimed at modern ministers. 'Pastors in Name, but indeed Wolves', 'seising on the Ministry as a Trade, not as a Spiritual Charge', intent 'not to feed the Flock, but to pamper and well line themselves', who 'keep in aw the superstitious multitude' with 'niceties and trivial points' but 'in true saving knowledge leave them still as gross and stupid as themselves'.[2] Lest there should be any mistake made by his readers, Milton placed at the beginning of Book III a comparison between the state of Britain when the Romans left it and that of England in 1647 and 1648, containing a direct denunciation of the self-seeking of the divines of the Westminster Assembly and their demand for compulsion in matters of conscience.[3]

This great digression shows how impossible it was for Milton to avoid referring to the problems of the present when he was writing about the events of the past. To utter freely what he felt about 'so dear a concernment' as his country's weal was a necessity of his nature. Just as Carlyle was obliged to suspend his study of Cromwell in order to express in *Past and Present* his feelings about the condition of England in 1843, so Milton interrupted his *History of Britain* in order to say what he thought about the condition of England in 1648. As the Civil War drew towards its close, the result of 'all this waste of wealth and loss of blood' became doubtful. In the two years of confusion which followed, no stable settlement was attained, and it seemed as if none was attainable. The king had been practically set aside, but the

---

[1] *History of Britain*, p. 90. He refers to this again in *Considerations touching the Likeliest Means to remove Hirelings out of the Church*, *Works*, v. 376.

[2] *History of Britain*, p. 129.

[3] Ibid., p. 100; *Works*, v. 94–101.

Parliament seemed unable to govern. To Milton, England appeared to be in the position of Britain when the Roman rule ended. When the Romans left the country, the Britons 'thus relinquish't, and by all right the Government relapsing into thir own hands, thenceforth betook themselves to live after thir own Laws'. But they failed to erect a stable government.

'They seem'd a while to bestirr them with a shew of diligence in thir new affairs, som secretly aspiring to rule, others adoring the name of liberty, yet so soon as they felt by proof the weight of what it was to govern well themselves, and what was wanting within them, not stomach or the love of licence, but the wisdom, the virtue, the labour, to use and maintain true libertie, they soon remitted thir heat, and shrunk more wretchedly under the burden of thir own libertie, than before under a foren yoke.'[1]

England now was in a similar condition. Fortune seemed 'to have put Liberty so long desired, like a Bridle into their hands'. The faults of the Britons 'brought *those Antient Natives* to Misery and Ruine, by Liberty, which, rightly used, might have made them happy', as the faults of the English had brought them now, 'after many Labours, much Blood-shed, and vast expence, to Ridiculous Frustration'.[2]

What were the causes of this failure? When the Long Parliament met the people chose to represent them 'such as they thought best affected to the Publick Good'. Some were men of wisdom and integrity, but the greater part merely men of wealth or ambition. These last, when their 'superficial Zeal' was spent,

---

[1] *History of Britain*, p. 100. Milton elsewhere refers to this period to prove that British kings were elected by the people, and could be deposed by them. See p. 107, and *Tenure of Kings and Magistrates*, *Works*, iv. 472.

[2] The ridiculousness of failure to maintain freedom after such efforts to gain it is in 1660 the keynote of Milton's *Ready and Easy Way to Establish a Free Commonwealth*, when the position resembled that in 1648. *Works*, v. 425.

betook themselves every one to follow his own ends. Justice was delayed and denied; spite and favour determined all; everywhere there was wrong and oppression. The members shared offices, gifts, and preferments amongst themselves; instead of enacting good laws they did nothing but impose new taxes; instead of paying the just debts of the State they cheated its creditors.[1] Fearful of being called to account, they fomented fresh troubles and invented new business in order to avoid the necessity of laying down their authority.

Religion was in as bad a plight as the State. The Westminster Assembly had been selected to reform the Church. Its members, after crying down pluralists and non-residents, had become pluralists and non-residents themselves. They called as loudly for compulsion in matters of religion against others as they had complained of it when exercised against themselves, and strove to set up a spiritual tyranny by the aid of the secular power. Seeing the incapacity of their statesmen, the people became disaffected, and seeing the hypocrisy of their ministers, they ceased to believe in religion.

'Thus', continues Milton, 'they who of late were extoll'd as our greatest Deliverers, and had the People wholly at their Devotion, by so discharging their Trust as we see, did not only weaken and unfit themselves to be dispensers of what Liberty they pretended, but unfitted also the People, now grown worse and more disordinate, to receive or to digest any Liberty at all. For Stories teach us, that Liberty sought out of season, in a corrupt and degenerate Age, brought *Rome* itself into a farther Slavery: For Liberty hath a sharp and double edge, fit only to be handled by Just and Vertuous Men; to bad and dissolute, it becomes a mischief unweildy in their own hands: neither is it compleatly given, but by them who have the happy skill to know what is grievance, and unjust to a People, and how to remove it wisely; what good Laws are wanting, and how to frame them substantially, that good Men may enjoy the freedom which they merit, and the bad the Curb which they need. But to do

[1] Compare Milton's Sonnet to Fairfax, written in August 1648.

this, and to know these exquisite proportions, the *Heroick Wisdom* which is required, surmounted far the Principles of these narrow Politicians: what wonder then if they sunk as these unfortunate *Britains* before them, entangled and opprest with things too hard, and generous above their strain and temper?'[1]

Then, having stated the causes of this failure, Milton explained the cure. Englishmen, 'to speak a truth not often spoken', were not born statesmen. England was a land 'fruitful enough of Men stout and courageous in War', but at the same time 'not over-fertile of Men able to govern justly and prudently in Peace'. The national character was in fault: it was rude, intractable, and un-teachable—he almost says unintelligent. Public spirit and similar qualities 'grow not here, but in minds well implanted with solid and elaborate Breeding'. Just as certain products must be imported to our island from sunnier lands, 'so must ripe Understanding, and many civil Vertues, be imported into our mindes from Foreign Writings, and examples of best Ages'. If Eng-land was to succeed in great enterprises she must have men with the education of statesmen to conduct her affairs—not politicians 'trusting only in their Mother-Wit' or tradesmen 'call'd from shops and warehouses . . . to sit in Supreme Councills', but 'men more than vulgar bred up . . . in the knowledge of Antient and Illustrious Deeds'.

Here Milton's tract *Of Education* and his *History of Britain* explain each other. When he wrote in 1644 that the reforming of education was a thing 'for the want whereof this Nation perishes', he did not mean that England was perishing for want of scholars, but for want of statesmen. His imaginary pupils were from the first to be 'stirr'd up with high hopes of living to be brave men, and worthy Patriots, dear to God, and famous to all ages', and in the end to be fit 'to perform justly, skilfully and magnanimously all the offices both

[1] *Mr John Miltons Character of the Long Parliament* (1681), pp. 9-10.

private and publick of Peace and War'. Thus to qualify them one of their studies must be the study of politics. They should be taught to know 'the beginning, end, and reasons of Political Societies; that they may not in a dangerous fit of the Common-wealth be such poor, shaken, uncertain Reeds, of such a tottering Conscience, as many of our great Counsellors have lately shewn themselves, but stedfast pillars of the State'.[1]

'Choise Histories' were also to be put into their hands, and in the *History of Britain* Milton explains what he conceived to be the practical value of his national history to a statesman. It could teach him to understand the character of his countrymen in its strength and weakness. By comparing the past and present, we can 'raise a knowledg of our selves both great and weighty', and judge what we are able to achieve. 'For if it be a high point of wisdom in every private man, much more is it in a Nation to know it self; rather than puft up with vulgar flatteries, and encomiums, for want of self knowledge, to enterprise rashly and come off miserably in great undertakings.'[2]

With the exception of the first paragraph, the whole of this long digression was omitted when Milton published his *History* in 1670. The passage was published in 1681, after his death, under the title of *Mr John Miltons Character of the Long Parliament and Assembly of Divines*. According to the publisher, Mr. Milton had intended the 'Character' to be printed in his *History*, but 'out of tenderness to a Party, (whom neither this nor much more Lenity has had the luck to oblige) it was struck out for some harshness, being only such a Digression, as the History it self would not be discomposed by its omission'.[3]

---

[1] *Works of John Milton*, iv. 384, 385, 388.
[2] *History of Britain*, p. 100. Of the digression there remains in the text thirteen lines on p. 99 and eleven and a half on the next page. The rest was omitted.   [3] Masson, *Life of Milton*, vi. 806–7.

Yet, while the suppressed passage is undoubtedly Milton's, and is correctly placed at the beginning of the third book, the explanation given of its omission is obviously absurd. The publisher recommended it as 'very seasonable for these times', and it would have been equally seasonable in 1670. It was printed now as a controversial weapon against the Presbyterians and the Nonconformists, and it could have been printed eleven years earlier for the same reason. For there was no thought in 1670 of any tenderness towards that party, as the passing of the second Conventicle Act in that year proved. Any licenser would have welcomed the denunciation of the Assembly of Divines as a powerful argument in favour of the policy of the king's government.

The most reasonable explanation is that Milton suppressed the passage himself. All had changed since 1648. The Assembly of Divines was a thing of the past, and its survivors were now persecuted rather than persecutors. The Long Parliament had come to an end: obscurity, or captivity, or the scaffold had been the fate of its leaders, and Milton was more inclined to lament their sufferings than to point out their trespasses or omissions in the day of their power. Englishmen themselves, instead of attempting the high enterprise of erecting a free state, had contentedly relapsed into their old servitude. Milton, therefore, whilst retaining the suggested parallel between the condition of the Britons in the fifth century and that of the English at the close of the first civil war, eliminated the application to the politics of 1648. It had lost all practical utility.

Yet since all history should 'instruct and benefit them that read', the moral of the whole story should be made plain.[1] Poet or historian, Milton was ever a preacher, and used British history for the purpose of edification

[1] *History of Britain*, p. 3.

just as he would have used his British epic. To his eyes
the significance of the revolutions he had related was
clear. Each successive conquest of Britain was a just
judgement on the conquered race. The Britons were
mere barbarians, 'Progenitors not to be glori'd in',
naturally and deservedly subdued by the Romans.
Roman civilization served but to prepare them for
bondage. Freedom made them worse instead of better,
till there was 'scarce the lest footstep, or impression of
goodness left remaining through all ranks and degrees
in the Land; except in some so very few, as to be hardly
visible in a general corruption'.[1] Hence 'the many
miseries and desolations, brought by divine hand on a
perverse Nation; driv'n, when nothing else would reform them, out of a fair Country, into a Mountanous
and Barren Corner, by Strangers and Pagans. So much
more tolerable in the Eye of Heav'n is Infidelity pro-
fess't, then Christian Faith and Religion dishonoured
by unchristian works'.[2] By the ninth century, 'the
Saxons were . . . full as wicked as the *Britans* were at
their arrival'. They fell before the Danes because God
purposed 'to punish our instrumental punishers, though
now Christians, by other Heathen, according to his
Divine retaliation; invasion for invasion, spoil for spoil,
destruction for destruction'. Vain had been the union
of the seven kingdoms under one rule, for 'when God
hath decreed servitude on a sinful Nation, fitted by
thir own vices for no condition but servile, all Estates
of Government are alike unable to avoid it'.[3]

Such, too, were the causes of the Norman Conquest.
By their vices the English had 'fitted themselves for
this servitude'. The clergy had 'lost all good literature
and Religion'; the great men were 'giv'n to gluttony
and dissolute life'; the meaner sort 'spent all they had
in Drunk'ness. . . . Some few of all sorts were much

[1] Ibid., pp. 49, 71, 108, 128.   [2] Ibid., p. 134.
[3] Ibid., p. 190.

better among them; but such was the generality. *And as the long suffering of God permits bad men to enjoy prosperous daies with the good, so his severity oft times exempts not good men from thir share in evil times with the bad.'*

It remained only to apply this moral to the present moment, and to warn the England of Charles II. Milton does this in the last sentence of his *History*, added evidently in 1670: *'If these were the Causes of such misery and thraldom to those our Ancestors, with what better close can be concluded, then here in fit season to remember this Age in the midst of her security, to fear from like Vices without amendment the Revolutions of like Calamities.'*[1]

---

[1] The inseparable connexion between liberty and virtue was the fundamental doctrine of Milton's political pamphlets as well as his *History*, and he emphasized it both in *Paradise Lost* and in *Paradise Regained*. Men, explains the Archangel Michael to Adam, lost their inward freedom when they allowed their passions to 'catch the Government from Reason', and the loss of their outward freedom followed. It was so with nations too.

> '. . . somtimes Nations will decline so low
> From vertue, which is reason, that no wrong,
> But Justice, and some fatal curse annext
> Deprives them of thir outward libertie,
> Thir inward lost.'

Nor is it possible to deliver them. 'Who can of inward slaves make outward free?' replies Christ to the Tempter.

EDWARD HYDE, EARL OF CLARENDON, AS STATESMAN, HISTORIAN, AND CHANCELLOR OF THE UNIVERSITY[1]

TERCENTENARIES and similar celebrations of the births of great men are useful, though becoming somewhat hackneyed. We hear so much about the great men of the moment that we are in danger of ceasing to remember the greater men of the past. I do not mean that we are in danger of forgetting their names, but of forgetting what manner of men they were, and what they did to serve their own generation, and through it ours, and those to come. It is well, therefore, that at set times and seasons we should call to mind the things which are forgotten, and that our University should say to itself, as our colleges do, 'Let us now praise famous men and our fathers that begat us'.

Clarendon filled for many years a great place in English history, and recorded what he did and what he saw in books which fill a great place in our literature. Yet, compared to many men who achieved less, he is to-day but a vague and indistinct personality, and his works are amongst those English classics which educated people put into their shelves, and leave there. When I first undertook to address you on this subject I endeavoured to discover what the popular impression about him was. I thought that to find out what the popular impression was, and then, perhaps, to prove that, erroneous as it might seem, it was in reality fundamentally just, would be sure to please. But I was unfortunate in my researches. I began by asking a learned member of this University—one who was at once a man of culture and a man of affairs—what he

[1] A Lecture delivered at Oxford, Feb. 18, 1909.

thought of Clarendon's *History of the Rebellion*. He replied, 'I have a very beautifully bound copy of the work—I never read it, but I once did some proses out of it'. He had not been tempted to turn over the leaf and try another page. When he had made his verbs and nouns agree his intellectual curiosity was satisfied. And even those who have no love of proses, the gentlemen whom the hard laws of the University compel to read select portions of the History, frequently do not look beyond them, and know little about the life of their writer. For there is no convenient little handbook on Clarendon. He has had bad luck with his immortality. He is not included amongst Lord Morley's *English Statesmen*, or amongst his *English Men of Letters*— probably because he was both. He is not accounted a 'Man of Action' or even worthy to be a 'Worthy'.

Yet any one who reflects for a moment on Clarendon's career must admit that he was a man of no common gifts and no ordinary character. He had no advantages of birth. He did not belong to one of those great families who inherit a claim to govern the state, and sometimes justify it. His father was the younger son of the younger son of a small Cheshire squire, and his mother the descendant of a line of Somersetshire clothiers. He was not rich, though he inherited a competence from his father, and the only relation he had in office was a judge who died too soon to be of much help to a young barrister. Hyde, in short, was one of the first examples in later English history of the man who begins in low estate, and rises by his own abilities to the highest political office:

> Who makes by force his merit known,
> And lives to clutch the golden keys,
> To mould a mighty state's decrees,
> And shape the whisper of the throne.

Let us inquire first how Hyde rose. Unlike some who in our own days have risen to similar heights, Hyde did not greatly distinguish himself at the University. He matriculated at Magdalen Hall in January 1623. He might have matriculated at Magdalen instead, but the President of that Society turned a deaf ear to the letter in which King James I ordered him to give the boy a demyship. He left the University three years later with the degree of B.A. and the reputation, as he tells us, rather 'of a young man of parts and pregnancy of wit, than that he had improved it much by industry'.

Nor was it by his success as a lawyer that Hyde rose to greatness. On leaving Oxford he entered the Middle Temple, and was called to the Bar in 1633. He had not long to wait for employment. Though his name does not appear in the law reports of the period, he was engaged in several causes before the Council, got into good practice in the Court of Requests, and speedily made a good professional income. As a rising young lawyer, he was elected to the two Parliaments which met in 1640. The Long Parliament was full of lawyers of greater knowledge and experience; there were some who had conducted great constitutional cases before he was even called to the Bar, others who had written learned law books that were cited before the judges, and men who held legal offices of various kinds. But he had qualifications for success that most of them lacked. To begin with, it is evident that when he was a young man he had a rare gift of making friends, and his popularity helped him. He prided himself on this power of making friends, and was often heard to say 'that he owed all the little . . . good that was in him to the friendships and conversation he had still been used to, of the most excellent men in their several kinds that lived in that age'. When he was a young law student in London his favourite companions were poets and playwrights—Ben Jonson, Charles Cotton, Thomas May, Thomas Carew, William Davenant, Edmund Waller. But even in that first band of friends there was one man of colossal learning in Hyde's future profession—namely, John Selden—one whose familiar talk must have been full of instruction, for 'in his conversation he was the most clear discourser, and had the best faculty of making hard things easy, and presenting them to the understanding, of any man that hath been known'. A little later Hyde formed a second group of friends; men who were interested in literature too, but interested in the more serious side of it, and were wont to speculate about the highest problems of religion and politics, and to discuss them freely together. Selden was still of the company, but to him were added divines such as Sheldon, Morley, Earle, Hales, and Chillingworth, and, above all, the incomparable Falkland, whose conversation was 'one continued convivium philosophicum, or convivium theologicum, enlivened and refreshed with all the facetiousness of wit, and good humour, and pleasantness of discourse'. Later still, when Hyde began to succeed at the Bar, he became intimate with the leading men in his own profession, but his intimacy was never confined to them. He obtained a footing at the court, too, and became the friend of noblemen such as the earls of Pembroke, Hertford, Holland, and Manchester.

These friendships enhanced Hyde's success at the Bar, and made him a prominent figure amongst the young lawyers of the time. His brethren saw that he was very acceptable to persons of the best quality, observed that 'his condition of living was with more splendour than young lawyers were accustomed to', and regarded him as a man of fashion and a man of influence. From the first he took a good position in the House of Commons. He was not a great orator; he had not the powerful and weighty eloquence of Pym, or the dexterity in debate of Hampden; still less did his speeches stir the emotions of his hearers as the passionate and fiery oratory of Eliot had done. There were a dozen men in the Long Parliament who had a greater reputation as orators. But Mr. Hyde was a speaker whom the House always heard with pleasure. Here was a lawyer who, to use his own phrase, had sacrificed both to the Muses and the Graces. The combination of literary gifts and legal training was rarer then than it is now. Most of the lawyers of the time were pedantic and verbose speakers—unmerciful men to their audiences—and in a word bores of antediluvian vigour and proportions. Hyde could discuss constitutional questions with sufficient knowledge to impress, and in a sufficiently attractive style to please; if he did not rise to the highest flights he was always easy and fluent, and could be dignified or humorous whenever the occasion demanded. Two competent observers have left us descriptions of his manner of speaking five-and-twenty years later, and we can gather from those descriptions what the characteristics of his style must have been in earlier years. 'He spake well', says Burnet, 'his style had no flaw in it, but had a just mixture of wit and sense, only he spoke too copiously; he had a great pleasantness in his spirit, which carried him sometimes too far into raillery, in which he sometimes shewed more wit than discretion.'[1] Mr. Pepys is still more eulogistic. 'I am mad in love with my Lord Chancellor, for he do comprehend and speak out well, and with the greatest easiness and authority that ever I saw man in my life. ... His manner and freedom of doing it, as if he played with it, and was informing only all the rest of the company, was mighty pretty.'[2]

Deduct something from this as the results of long experience and high authority, and we can form a very just conception of what the Lord Chancellor's speaking was like when he was still Mr. Hyde.

Yet it was not Hyde's oratorical, but his literary skill

[1] *A Supplement to Burnet's History of My Own Time*, ed. H. C. Foxcroft (1902), p. 53.   [2] *Diary*, Oct. 13, 1666.

which laid the foundation of his fortune. A moment
came when a skilful writer was of more value to the
King than the most eloquent speaker. In January 1642
Charles I was in extremity. The attempt to arrest the
Five Members had covered him with disgrace, and his
design of introducing foreign forces into England had
been revealed by his tamperings with the governors of
Hull and Portsmouth. The leaders of the Parliament,
full of fears and distrust, were demanding the right to
appoint the King's ministers. Both sides laid their case
before the people, and about eight months of controversial warfare preceded the actual appeal to arms.
During those eight months Hyde was invaluable. There
were no able editors to set forth the case of the two
antagonists in the columns of the newspapers, for
though newspapers were beginning to exist, they were
not yet organs adapted for political controversy. There
were no reports of parliamentary debates to familiarize
everybody with the arguments of party leaders, and,
even if there had been, the secession of the King's party
from Westminster had robbed the debates of their
importance. All at once the capacity to write a state
paper, to set forth a political programme, or to explain
a constitutional theory, in such a way that every
educated man could understand them, became the one
essential gift. That was the gift Hyde possessed, and
at no other time in English history would it have been
so valuable. Whether the King had the better cause
or not, thanks to Hyde he had the best of the controversy. On that point Hallam's verdict is decisive. He
praises 'the temperate and constitutional language of
the royal declarations and answers to the house of
commons . . . known to have proceeded from the pen
of Hyde', and says they are 'as superior to those of the
opposite side in argument as they are in eloquence'.[1]
Modern readers find these declarations dull, contem-

[1] Henry Hallam, *The Constitutional History of England* (1854), ii. 147.

poraries complained that they were too witty and too
elegant for serious political documents. 'Our good pen
will harm us', said one sage nobleman. Another Royalist
complained that Hyde was too constitutional—too
much in love with a thing he called mixed monarchy,
and did not know what real monarchy meant. But the
papers attained the end for which they were written—
they converted and convinced. 'The people were every
day visibly reformed in their understandings.' Hyde
gained the King thousands of partisans, for his main
argument was one which every man could understand;
that it was better to fight for the known laws of the
land than for the 'new Utopia of religion and government' which the Parliament was endeavouring to found
in England.

When the war began the value of Hyde's services
diminished, because the season for arguments was over.
But the King was not ungrateful. Hyde was knighted,
admitted to the Privy Council, and made Chancellor
of the Exchequer—a week or two after his thirty-fourth
birthday. The Chancellorship of the Exchequer was not
in that century the important office it is now—and just
then there was very little in the exchequer—but it was
high promotion for a young man. Hyde calls it 'an
excellent stage for men of parts to tread and expose
themselves upon, and where they have occasion of all
natures to lay out and spread all their faculties and
qualifications most for their advantage'. The post gave
him an acquaintance with official forms, and as much
training in administration as a Royalist could acquire
while the Civil War was in progress. It secured him a
permanent place in the King's councils. Whenever a
negotiation with the Parliament was on foot his skill in
drawing up papers was again in requisition, and sometimes Charles I adopted his advice on a question of
policy. But in the main he played a secondary part
during the Civil War, and I shall not trace his career

through the four years of the war, or the fourteen years of exile which followed.

It was in 1652, after Worcester had put an end to all hopes of a restoration by force of arms, that Charles II called Hyde to his little court, and from that date to the Restoration he was the King's chief adviser.

The policy he persuaded Charles II to adopt was a second edition of the policy which he had persuaded Charles I to adopt in 1642. He had urged Charles I to win back English public opinion by a wise passiveness—to make the law his guide—to concede what the law said he ought to concede, and to refuse what the law empowered him to refuse—holding that the King and the law together would be too strong for any antagonist. He now urged Charles II to adopt a waiting policy, and to seek to conciliate English opinion, with the faith that a time would come when England would recall him to his father's throne. 'All his activity', said Hyde, 'was to consist in carefully avoiding to do anything that might do him hurt.' The King was not to take any step which would alienate the minds of the English people. He was not, for instance, to turn Catholic in order to get the support of Spain and the Pope, nor was he to allow his brothers to become converts to Catholicism. He was not to buy the support of any English party by surrendering the rights of the Crown or the rights of the Church. Monarchy, in short, was to be restored, not by sacrificing constitutional principles, but by sticking to them. When English malcontents made overtures to the exiled King, a clear and consistent line was adopted. The leaders of the party from which the overtures came were promised immunity for past offences and rewards for future service, but there were no concessions of principle. If inconvenient demands were insisted upon, Hyde's plan was to qualify any assent with the saving clause, 'If a free Parliament shall think fit to ask the same of his Majesty'.

In 1660 the long expected revulsion of feeling took place in England, and the King was recalled to his throne. He was recalled unconditionally. Hyde had prevented the King from accepting conditions of his own accord, and Monck prevented Parliament from seeking to impose conditions on the King. All the details of the settlement were left to be determined between the King and Parliament—a Parliament in which the old Royalists were in a majority from the beginning, and became an overwhelming majority a year later. At the moment Hyde seemed indispensable. For years all the threads of the King's policy had been concentrated in his hands. He had more experience in business than any other Royalist possessed; he had the knowledge of the laws and the constitution which the immediate task required; his policy had been crowned with success. Every honour the Crown could confer was conferred upon him. He had been made Lord Chancellor in 1658, was raised to the peerage in 1660, and was created an earl in 1661. The marriage of his daughter to the King's brother gave him the prospect of a throne for his descendants. He had the complete confidence of the King himself. The notes exchanged between Charles and his minister during the sittings of the Council—which you may see in the Bodleian— attest the familiarity of master and servant, and the authority which the servant exercised over the master. Clarendon always disclaimed the name of prime minister —'first minister', he said, 'was a title so newly translated out of French into English that it was not enough understood to be liked.' Nevertheless, he was more in the position of a modern prime minister than any man who had yet held the chief place amongst the coun- cillors of an English king. He was more powerful than Burleigh or Salisbury had been, and more independent than either. For he did not confine himself to carrying out the King's policy, but conceived a policy of his own, and imposed it upon King and country by virtue of the support of Parliament.

It was this in the end which brought about Clarendon's fall. People sometimes talk as if he fell because he reminded Charles of the Decalogue at inconvenient moments, and rashly told him that he had not a prerogative to make vice virtue. As a matter of fact the breach was due to political rather than to personal causes. King and minister held fundamentally different views as to religious policy. Charles desired to make toleration for Catholics and Nonconformists an integral part of the restoration settlement, partly because it seemed essential to the peace of the nation, and partly because he was a Catholic at heart. In the Church as in the State, Clarendon's one aim was to re-establish the state of things which existed before the war began. The Church was to be restored unconditionally as well as the monarchy. This policy the minister successfully carried out. In a few months, almost before the King realized what was happening, the bishops were in possession of their old power, and the Catholics and Nonconformists were under their feet again. All the King's belated efforts to make toleration part of the settlement were frustrated by the steady resistance of Parliament. Clarendon might disclaim responsibility for this result, and plead that public opinion was too powerful to be resisted. He might exhort the clergy to moderation, and blame the Commons for going too far. But the King was convinced that his minister had not supported him as he ought to have done, and felt that he had been outmanœuvred by an old parliamentary hand. Clarendon was saved from overthrow by the fact that he still possessed the confidence of the Commons and by the mistakes of his enemies.

The second cause for the breach was more general in its character. In political as in religious matters Clarendon was more conservative than his master, and this conservatism had been increased by the fourteen years he had passed out of England. Exile, says De Tocqueville, is the most cruel of all punishments, for while it inflicts suffering it teaches nothing. 'It crystallizes, as it were, the minds of its victims, fixes in them the notions acquired in youth or those that were in vogue when they were exiled. For them the facts that occur, or the new customs that are established in their country, do not exist. They stand still, like the hands of a watch at the hour when it stopped.'[1] Without being as blind as a French *émigré* Clarendon had something of this temper. He never realized the new conditions the Rebellion had created, or the new forces which had grown up during the Interregnum. And, above all, he failed to appreciate the change which had taken place in the position of the House of Commons. Charles, on the other hand, had a more open and versatile mind than his minister, and was not hampered by any fixed principles. The King, laments Clarendon, 'had in his nature so little reverence or esteem for antiquity, and did in truth so much condemn old orders, forms, and institutions, that the objection of novelty rather advanced than obstructed any proposition. He was a great lover of new inventions, and thought them the effect of art and spirit, and fit to control the superstitious observation of the dictates of our ancestors'. Hence as new needs arose, and as new expedients had to be devised to meet them, the breach between King and minister continually widened: the one was always eager to adapt his policy to the requirements of the present, the other always firm in his adherence to the traditions of the past. The ill success of the Dutch War brought matters to a climax. Both King and minister had opposed the war, yet both were held responsible for its mismanagement. Parliament, which had gradually lost

---

[1] *Memoirs, Letters and Remains of Alexis de Tocqueville* (translated, 1861), i. 289.

all confidence in Clarendon, demanded certain constitutional changes and certain changes of policy: it wanted
new measures and new men. The minister urged the
King to resist. Parliaments, he told him, were not
formidable unless the King chose to make them so. As
yet it was in the King's power 'to govern them; but if
they found it was in theirs to govern him, nobody knew
what the end would be'. The King thought otherwise.
It seemed to him that an agreement with Parliament
was worth the sacrifice of a few constitutional principles, and even the sacrifice of an unpopular minister.
Personally he was weary of Clarendon. 'The truth is,'
he explained to the Duke of Ormond, 'his behaviour
and humour was grown so unsupportable, to myself,
and to all the world else, that I could not longer endure
it, and it was impossible for me to live with it, and do
those things with the Parliament that must be done, or
the Government will be lost.'

Clarendon's fall was sudden and irreparable. At the
end of August 1667, the Great Seal was taken from him;
in October he was impeached; at the end of November
he fled from England. Vexed at his escape from their
justice, Parliament passed an Act for his banishment,
which made his return high treason, and his pardon
impossible without the consent of both Houses. He
died at Rouen on December 9, 1674. Thus for the last
seven years of his life Clarendon ate once more the
bitter bread of exile, finding what consolation he could
in recounting the vicissitudes of the past, and building
for himself from those memories a monument no vicissitudes could overthrow.

He had commenced his *History of the Rebellion* in one
of the Scilly Islands on March 18, 1646, and continued
it in Jersey during the next two years. By the spring of
1648 he had brought the story down to the opening of
the campaign of 1644, and written seven books of the

History of the Rebellion, and a few sections of the eighth. This narrative was not meant to be published; it was intended solely for the eyes of the King and a few of his counsellors. It was written with a definite practical purpose: he undertook not only to relate the events of the Rebellion and the causes which produced it, but to point out the errors of policy committed on the King's side. The trusty few who read it would learn from it how to avoid like errors in the future; it would teach them not only why the kingdom had been lost, but how it might be regained and kept. In short, the book was to be a private manual for statesmen, and for that reason it was full of political reflections and dissertations on constitutional questions. There was hardly any mention of Hyde himself, but the whole work was an elaborate vindication of the particular section of the Royalist party to which he belonged.

For twenty years Hyde had allowed this narrative to remain unfinished. When he fled to France in December 1667, he left it and all the rest of his other papers in England. As soon as he found a permanent resting-place in France, and leisure for reflection, his thoughts turned once more to the past, and he sat down to write his reminiscences of the great events in which he had taken part. But the work he now began was an auto-biography, not a history. For the information of his children, and in order to vindicate his career in their eyes, he related the story of his own life from his boy-hood to his return to England with Charles II in 1660. Incidentally he told once more the story of the Rebel-lion and its sequel—he could hardly help that—but he naturally dwelt at length on his own part in events and on the personal side of the struggle rather than the constitutional questions it involved.

The interest of the Autobiography lies chiefly in the portraits Hyde draws of himself and his friends. Of himself he speaks with a curious mixture of frankness and complacency. He is very frank about his marriages; we do not gather that there was any frivolous romance about them, and we do gather he wished his children to be equally discreet in the management of their affections. Mr. Hyde's first inclination to marriage, he tells them, had 'no other passion in it than an appetite to a convenient estate'. That match did not come off; when he did marry it was because he found the temptations of literature and society too strong for him, and wished to bind himself down to the study of the law, and 'to call home all straggling and wandering appetites, which naturally produce irresolution and inconstancy in the mind'. The lady died six months after the marriage. Three years passed, during which Mr. Hyde was called to the Bar, and began to practise, but it was somewhat against the grain; he did not feel confident 'that he should not start aside', and he had 'long entertained thoughts of travels'. Accordingly, to 'lay some obligation upon himself, which would suppress and restrain all those appetites', he tried the old remedy, and married again. It proved effectual: 'from the time of his marriage he laid aside all other thoughts but of his profession.' It proved profitable, for he judiciously married the daughter of the judge in whose court he practised. It proved a very happy marriage: with this wife 'he lived very comfortably in the most uncomfortable times, and very joyfully in those times when matter of joy was administered'.

Some critics have complained of this lack of sentiment in Clarendon's character, and of a certain materialism in his nature. He would not have denied the charge, but would have taken it as a tribute to his worldly wisdom, and as one of the causes of his success. He sets forth his own estimate of his character with as much frankness as he relates the incidents of his life. He had great infirmities, he tells us, but providentially they never developed into vices. He had ambition, and 'great designs of raising himself', but not enough ambition to adopt 'crooked and indirect means' of rising. He had some weaknesses too: 'he indulged his palate very much, and took even some delight in eating and drinking well', but he is careful to add that he 'rather discoursed like an epicure than was one'. And though he had 'a fancy sharp and luxuriant' he asserts with confidence that his wit never transgressed the bounds of decorum. It is implied throughout that he was good company, and Evelyn confirms it when he writes many years later of being 'very merry' with my Lord Chancellor, and says that he was 'of a jolly temper after the old English fashion'.

The Lord Chancellor himself, at the close of his career, looking back on what he was at the beginning, sums up decisively in his own favour. Young Mr. Hyde, he tells us,

'was in his nature inclined to pride and passion, and to a humour between wrangling and disputing very troublesome, which good company in a short time so much reformed and mastered, that no man was more affable and courteous to all kind of persons. . . . That which supported and rendered him generally acceptable was his generosity, for he had too much a contempt of money, and the opinion men had of the goodness and justice of his nature, which was transcendent in him, in a wonderful tenderness and delight of obliging. His integrity was ever without blemish, and believed to be above temptation. He was firm and unshaken in his friendships; and, though he had great candour towards others in the differences of religion, he was zealously and deliberately fixed in the principles both of the doctrine and discipline of the church'.

Another judge, Sir Fitzjames Stephen, remarks that 'few men have sung their own praises with such calm assurance', and admires Clarendon's 'solid, deliberate admiration of himself'.[1] A truthful biographer must own that Clarendon did not overcome his passionate

[1] *Horae Sabbaticae* (1892), i. 337.

temper as completely as he alleges. In the days of his power he was often harsh and overbearing, and too easily moved to anger. But we must make allowances for the burden of office, for the contrariety of public affairs, for the gout, and for advancing years. Even the best of us often fail to retain in later life the genial amiability we possessed as undergraduates. Clarendon flattered himself a little—as we should all do if we drew our own portraits—but in the main his portrait of himself is true. He was inflexibly honest. He was 'firm and unshaken in his friendships'. If ever any man had a genius for friendship it was Clarendon. Witness all those portraits of his friends in his History and his Autobiography, in which he brings out with unfailing skill alike the qualities which made them great and the characteristics which made them loveable. Witness above all that incomparable portrait of Falkland; twice over he draws it at length, and each time the long involved periods glow and throb, and one feels behind the words the sense of irreparable loss and undying affection. Statesmen, soldiers, and great noblemen, all the Royalist chiefs move through his pages; each figure has the clear bold outline and the warm colouring of life; each character is a consistent and harmonious conception, and possesses an individuality of its own.

There are some great exceptions. Clarendon frequently failed when he tried to draw the portraits of the leaders of the other party. He could understand men actuated by purely political motives: Parliamentarian nobles such as Pembroke and Salisbury, and antiquarian lawyers such as Selden, were within the range of his sympathies. He could understand a man who was a Puritan because he hated the bishops, but doubts about the doctrine and scruples about ceremonies seemed to him merely the result of 'a working and unquiet fancy', so far as they were not mere factiousness, or downright hypocrisy. His soul could never enter into the secrets of enthusiasts, or, indeed, into any region beyond the range of the Thirty-nine Articles. Just as he fails to understand the nature of the Puritans so he fails to understand Puritanism in general, and his *History of the Rebellion* has the fundamental defect, that it is a history of a religious revolution in which the religious element is omitted.

When Clarendon had completed his Autobiography, or rather brought it down to the date of the Restoration, an event happened which changed his plans. Hitherto he had been prohibited from all communication with England. But in 1671 his son Lawrence was allowed to visit him, and he brought his father the unfinished manuscript of the History written between 1646 and 1648. Clarendon read it through, and a new idea occurred to him. He would complete this History, and make it into something that could be published. Out of the work destined for a few fellow statesmen and the work destined for the eyes of his children alone he would put together something fit, in due season, for the eyes of the world. The vindication of his party and the vindication of himself should be used to complete each other. Accordingly he constructed out of the imperfect History written between 1646 and 1648 and the Autobiography written between 1668 and 1670 the *History of the Rebellion* as we now have it.

The process of construction was very simple.[1] Taking the fragmentary History, which ended at the beginning of 1644, and forms the first seven books of the published *History of the Rebellion*, Clarendon inserted into its framework a great number of passages from the Autobiography he had just completed. Next, to continue this, and to bring the story down to the Restoration, he added the whole of the later part of the Autobiography which forms, roughly, books x to xvi of the

[1] This subject is treated at length in three articles published in the *English Historical Review* during 1904.

published *History*. Finally, to join these two portions of his work, and fill up the gap between the point where the first ended and the point where the second began, he wrote the eighth book and parts of the ninth, and utilized some fragments he had by him. A few amplifications, explanations, and additions tacked the whole together, and the book published in 1702, and republished about twenty times since, had assumed its final shape.

The result is that as an historical authority Clarendon's *History of the Rebellion* is a very difficult and perplexing book for later historians to employ. It is such a patchwork. Parts of it were written with one object, parts with another; parts of it were written at one time, parts at another: some passages were written when he had documents to consult and friends to question about doubtful facts, other passages when he had nothing but his own memory to rely upon. Finally, while some sections were written when his recollections of events were fresh and strong, others were written when the events had been blurred and obscured by the passage of time, and all that was clear was the triumphant or suffering figure of Mr. Hyde in the midst of them.

To estimate the value of any statement made in the *History of the Rebellion*, you have to ask when it was written, why it was written, and whether the writer had any documents at his side when he wrote? The supreme value of Dr. Macray's admirable edition of Clarendon's *Rebellion* lies in the fact that it makes it easy to answer all these questions, for it shows whether a particular passage is taken from the Autobiography, or from the fragmentary History written in 1646, or from the passages added in 1671 to connect them together. And besides this it adds dates, which makes Clarendon's story much clearer, gives occasional references to his correspondence, and corrects in the notes errors caused by Clarendon's defective memory.

Unhappily, there is no equally scholarly edition of Clarendon's Autobiography, or of the continuation of it which contains his account of the first seven years of the reign of Charles II. The *Life of Edward, Earl of Clarendon*, which the University Press published in 1759, is a mere fragment. It includes only the first portion of the life, and not even all of that, with some detached passages from the later portions. This was the result of Clarendon's own act. He mutilated his Autobiography by transplanting three-quarters of it into his *History of the Rebellion*. If we had this life of himself as it stood in 1670, it would, probably, be more read and better known than the *History of the Rebellion* is to-day. For it possessed a unity and homogeneity which the *History of the Rebellion* lacks. Moreover, by some natural instinct, most people prefer autobiography to history; the personal element in the story is what interests them, and they prefer it to the wisest disquisitions about constitutional questions, and even to the most accurate accounts of campaigns and debates. When Clarendon wrote the Autobiography his powers were at their height. It is a more skilful and artistic composition than the History. Most of the scenes and portraits which historians of literature quote as examples of Clarendon's genius are derived from the Autobiography. I sometimes think that he committed a literary crime when he hacked and mangled it to supplement the earlier work.

On the other hand the fragmentary History written between 1646 and 1648, considered merely as an authority, or a piece of documentary evidence, is of far greater value than the Autobiography. It is much more accurate and much more instructive. If it is less picturesque it throws more light on the causes of things. On the whole we need not too much regret the resolution which led Clarendon to combine his two works in order to make the *History of the Rebellion*. By the combination of the two he gave his book variety at the expense of unity. By the blending of the personal and general elements it acquired its unique character, and became something between history and memoirs which partakes of the qualities of both. To the arrangement of the *History of the Rebellion* this combination was certainly detrimental. Clarendon's narrative has not the lucid order of Macaulay's; owing to the process by which it was constructed it is full of digressions, and sometimes confused. But these defects are covered and compensated by his style. It does not hurry his readers along with the rapid and irresistible rush of Macaulay's. It has the ample, easy flow of a great river, that, as Tennyson says, 'moving seems asleep', but carries you to the end of the journey without haste and without noise.

I have spoken of Clarendon as a statesman and as an historian. There is a third character in which he is in still closer relation to us—that of Chancellor of this University. At the beginning of 1660 Richard Cromwell was our Chancellor. He resigned on May 8—the day when Charles II was solemnly proclaimed king. The Marquis of Hertford, who had been Chancellor from 1643 to 1648, was restored to his old position, but died a few months later. Three days after his death, on October 27, 1660, Clarendon was elected Chancellor, and held that office till December 1667. He was not a very active Chancellor. The work of turning out the Heads and Fellows appointed during the Interregnum by the Puritan Visitors had been carried out by a new set of Visitors appointed in June 1660, so that the restoration of the old régime in the University was practically effected before his chancellorship began. But his political and legal position enabled him to further the interests of the University in many ways. Clarendon was not a reforming Chancellor—he preferred old ways in the University as well as in the State, but amongst his miscellaneous writings there is a discourse on Education which proves that he thought the University was not quite perfect.[1] He called it a 'Dialogue' but in reality it is a discussion between half a dozen persons—a courtier, a lawyer, a country gentleman, a colonel, an alderman, and a bishop. They discuss elementary as well as higher education, but limit their aim to the education of 'the Children of Persons of Quality' who can afford to pay for it, and leave the children of common people 'to those common Ways which their Fortunes as well as their Inclinations lead them unto'. After criticizing the public schools they pass to the Universities. There is a general agreement that their discipline is not strict enough. The courtier says that the learning young men get there is 'only a pedantick way of Disputing and Wrangling', which makes them disagreeable to all well-bred persons. Moreover, he adds, the Universities are 'Places of Debauchery, Schools to learn to drink in'. The bishop replies that drinking is a vice too common throughout the kingdom, and that the Universities are, on the whole, soberer than other places. But he thinks their discipline and morals need inquiring into. Quite like a modern bishop, he suggests a Royal Commission composed of 'Persons of the greatest quality, and of known Gravity and Virtue'. Colonel and lawyer both agree that one cause of the decay of discipline is that undergraduates are too old when they come up. No boy should remain in any public school after he is sixteen, says the colonel. The lawyer adds that 'those lubberly Fellows, who come from great Schools after they are Nineteen or Twenty Years of Age, and bring their Debauchery with them' do much to damage the reputation of the University.

[1] *A Collection of Several Tracts of the Right Honourable Edward, Earl of Clarendon* (1727), pp. 313–25.

Another reason for the shortcomings of the under-graduates of the time is also suggested. Our Universities, says the colonel, 'are defective in providing for those Exercises and Recreations which are necessary even to nourish and cherish Their studies'. Clarendon thought that this defect caused too many men of rank to send their sons abroad to the French academies at Paris, where youths were instructed in riding, dancing, and fencing. He held that it would be better to encourage officially the teaching of these arts in the English Universities. The danger of their interfering with the studies of the place might easily be prevented. Regular hours should be set apart for both, and the penalty for the neglect of the studies should be restraint from the exercises. One of his projects was the erection of a handsome riding-school, and the provision of horses and riding-masters for the instruction of young men. It was never realized: but to this idea we owe one of the two buildings associated with Clarendon's name in the Oxford of to-day. In 1751 Henry, Viscount Hyde, Clarendon's great-grandson, left Clarendon's manuscripts to certain trustees for the benefit of the University, with instructions to use the profits derived from their publication as 'the beginning of a fund for supporting a *manège* or academy for riding and other useful exercises in Oxford'.[1] The will was rendered void by his premature death, but his intentions were carried out by his sisters. The fund accumulated till 1868, when it reached the sum of about £12,000, and the trustees then devoted it to the erection of the Clarendon Laboratory. The University, we are told, 'no longer needed a riding-school, and the claims of physical science were urgent', but those who, as they walk down St. Giles's, meet the little bands of future

[1] For a history of this scheme and of others of the same nature see Mr. T. W. Jackson's preface to Dr. Wallis's Letter against Mr. Maidwell, in vol. i of the *Collectanea* of the Oxford Historical Society.

Indian civilians, preparing to witch the world with noble horsemanship rather than actually doing so, will be inclined to hold that our Chancellor's proposed school would not have been entirely useless.

Besides the Laboratory, there is another institution which is a memorial of Clarendon's connexion with us. Mr. Madan has admirably summarized the history of the Oxford University Press in a pamphlet published last year. Its only fault is that it is 40 pages long instead of 400. A detailed history of the development of the Press and its publications is much to be desired, and would be a contribution of great value to the history of learning in England. Mr. Madan points out that there was a printing-press in Oxford as early as 1478, and that as early as 1517 'the aegis of the University was already held over the Press'.[1] The continuous existence of a University Press dates from 1585; but its real importance begins in 1671, when Dr. Fell and his partners took over the management of the Press, after its establishment in the Theatre which Archbishop Sheldon had built to accommodate it. The Theatre proved in many ways unsuitable for the purposes of the printers, so in 1713 a new printing-house was built, in which the Press was housed from 1713 to 1830. This edifice, designed by Hawksmoor, was styled 'The Clarendon Printing House', and is known to us to-day as The Clarendon Building. The question is why Clarendon's name was attached to it? According to the traditional account, given in Ingram's *Memorials of Oxford*, the reason is because it was built out of the profits of the *History of the Rebellion*. According to Hearne, the three printers who leased the press paid £2,000, and the University found the rest of the money. But since the profits of the six editions of the *History of the Rebellion* published before 1713 must have done

[1] Falconer Madan, *A Brief Account of the University Press at Oxford* (1908).

much to fill the purse of the University, there is something to be said for the tradition. Hearne is extremely indignant both at the expensiveness of the new printing-house and the association of Clarendon's name with it. He calls it a magnificent pile, erected 'purely to gratify the Ambition & Desires of some ill, talkative People, who have no manner of regard to ye Credit of Learning or the University'. 'Out of a Whim,' he adds, 'it is to be called Typographéum Clarendonianum, and Archb^p Sheldon is to be forgotten, as a Benefactor to the Oxford Printing, if People will comply with this Whim, purely owing to some vain, ignorant Heads of Houses, such as old Lancaster (commonly called Slyboots . . .).'[1]

Most people will think, however, that Dr. Lancaster, the Provost of Queen's, to whom Hearne refers, was very happily inspired when it occurred to him to connect with the learned press of the University the name of that Chancellor of the University who was most eminent as a man of letters. The application of the name to the institution itself, after its migration in 1830 from the building in Broad Street to its new quarters in Walton Street, is a sign that the University felt the appropriateness of the choice. Archbishop Sheldon himself, far from regarding his own services as slighted, would have rejoiced at this honour done to his old friend, and there is no form of commemoration which would have pleased Clarendon himself more.

Yet of all the memorials of Clarendon's chancellorship in Oxford the most interesting is not either of the buildings called after him, but a manuscript exhibited

[1] *Remarks and Collections of Thomas Hearne* (Oxford Historical Society), iii. 288; iv. 254. In a later passage, dated Sept. 19, 1721, he adds: 'Yesterday was put up, on the South side of the New Printing House . . . a Statue of the Earl of Clarendon y^t writ the History, as if he were Founder, whereas he never thought of it, & 'tis only upon account of the Money they have pretended to lay out upon this House, arising from the Copy of his History.' (Ibid. vii. 280.)

in the Bodleian[1]—the letter which he wrote in December 1667, as he halted at Calais after his flight from England, to resign into the hands of the University the high office it had conferred upon him seven years earlier.

It runs thus:

Good Mr. Vicechancellor,

Having found it necessary to transport my self out of England, and not knowing when it will please God that I shall returne againe, it becomes me to take care that the University be not without the service of a person better able to be of use to them than I am like to be, and I doe therfore hereby surrender the office of chancellour into the hands of the said University to the end that they make choice of some other person better qualified to assist and protect them then I am; I am sure he can never be more affectionate to it. I desire you as the last suit I am like to make to you, to believe that I do not fly my country for guilt, and how passionatly soever I am pursued, that I have not done any thing to make the University ashamed of me, or to repent the good opinion they had once of me; and though I must have no further mention in your public devotions (which I have always exceedingly valued) I hope I shall be always remembred in your private prayers as

Your affectionate servant
CLARENDON.

One word more in conclusion. It has been the happy fate of the University in the past to be closely associated with the fortunes of Clarendon both as a statesman and as an historian. It profited by his influence when he was alive, and by his writings after his death. It still owes him something to-day. If it desires fitly to commemorate the tercentenary of his birth, it should complete the publication of his papers and print a new edition of his life. The last edition of the *Life* and of the *Continuation* of the *Life* was published in 1857. Except

[1] See *The Life and Times of Anthony Wood* (Oxford Historical Society, 1892), ii. 123–4.

as a piece of printing it is utterly unworthy of the University Press. The index is one of the worst in existence. There are no notes. The dates given in the headlines are frequently wrong. As for the text, the reader is given no notice of the fact that large passages of the original have been transferred to the pages of the *History of the Rebellion*, and some passages of the original have not been printed either in the *History* or the *Life*. In every respect the edition is a glaring contrast to Dr. Macray's edition of the companion work.

As to Clarendon's correspondence, a selection from it was published in the eighteenth century. A Calendar of the whole collection was commenced in 1869, but its publication was suspended in 1876, when three volumes had been issued. Volumes iv[1] and v were never published, so that the correspondence for the years 1658 to 1667 remains uncalendared. The completion of this Calendar would be of great service to English historians, and is indeed indispensable to them. Had the papers been in private hands instead of in the Bodleian they would long ago have been calendared by the Historical Manuscripts Commission. And it is not to the credit of the University that it should leave unfinished an enterprise it has once taken in hand. Once more, therefore, I urge the Delegates of the Press to complete the publication of this Calendar.

[1] Volume iv, 1657–60, ed. F. J. Routledge, was published in 1932.

JOHN BUNYAN[1]

THE *Pilgrim's Progress* is so closely related to the life of Bunyan that it is impossible to appreciate the one without some knowledge of the other. How was it, one naturally asks, that a man of little education could produce two centuries ago a masterpiece which is still read wherever the English language is spoken, and has been translated into every European tongue? It is not sufficient to answer that the author of the work was a genius: it is necessary to show what the conditions were which enabled his genius to develop itself, led him to find the form of expression which best suited its character, and secured for what it produced both immediate popularity and lasting fame.

Bunyan belonged to a family of Bedfordshire peasants which can be traced back for many generations in local records, and the theory that he was of gipsy descent has long been disproved. His father, Thomas Bunyan, was a tinker, or, as he calls himself in his will, 'a braseyer'. He is described by one of the biographers of his son as 'an honest, poor labouring man, who, like Adam unparadised, had all the world before him to get his bread in, and was very careful to maintain his family'. John, who was the eldest son of Thomas Bunyan, was baptized in Elstow Church on November 30, 1628. Poor though his parents were, says he, 'it pleased God to put into their hearts to put me to school to learn both to read and write; the which I also attained according to the rate of other poor men's children; though to my shame I confess I did soon lose that little I learnt, even almost utterly'. His school days were over and he was beginning to learn his father's trade when the civil war began.

[1] Reprinted from Introduction to *Pilgrim's Progress*, 1898. By permission of Methuen & Co., Ltd.

He joined the parliamentary army, not as a volunteer, but as one of the young men whom Bedfordshire, like other counties under the Parliament's control, was ordered to impress for military service. His name appears in the muster roll of a regiment forming part of the garrison of Newport Pagnell in November 1644, when he was just sixteen years old, and he served there till the end of May 1645, and perhaps a few months longer.[1]

As he was present with his company at Newport on May 27, 1645, the story that he fought at the siege of Leicester must be definitely abandoned, for the King began the investment of that town on May 28.

In 1647 at the latest Bunyan's military service ended. He had seen something of a soldier's life in a frontier garrison, but can have taken part in no fighting more serious than a trifling skirmish, or possibly the siege of some fortified house. But it must have enlarged the home-bred country boy's knowledge of men and manners, and whatever he saw and learnt remained in his mind, and was put to good use when he came to describe the character of a Puritan soldier in the person of Mr. Great-heart, and the vicissitudes of a besieged town in the history of the City of Mansoul. He returned to his trade, married about the year 1649 a woman of his own rank whose name is unknown, and set up housekeeping at Elstow. 'This woman and I', says he, 'came together as poor as might be (not having so much household stuff as a dish or spoon betwixt us both).' But she brought with her two books: *The Plain Man's Pathway to Heaven*, by Arthur Dent, and Bishop Bayly's *Practice of Piety*. These books they sometimes read together, 'wherein', he tells us, 'I also found some things that were somewhat pleasing to me'. In his

[1] This fact was discovered by Mr. E. G. Atkinson of the Public Record Office, who found there some muster-rolls proving it. See *Notes and Queries*, July 18, 1896.

younger days Bunyan had been, according to his own
account, careless and vicious. 'I had but few equals,
(especially considering my years . . .) both for cursing,
swearing, lying and blaspheming. . . . I was the very
ringleader of all the youth that kept me company, in
all manner of vice and ungodliness.' Yet even then his
imagination was sensitive to supernatural visitings. He
was scared at times by fearful dreams and dreadful
visions, and afflicted with apprehensions of devils. On
his marriage he became a reformed and an outwardly
religious man. He felt 'some desires to religion', he
went to church twice a Sunday, became 'overrun with
the spirit of superstition', and began to reverence both
the church itself and the clergyman who ministered
there with great devotion. 'Our neighbours did take
me to be a very godly man, a new and religious man,
and did marvel much to see such a great and famous
alteration in my life and manners.' But while others
thought him one of the elect his mind was distracted
by doubt and despondency, he doubted the reality of
his conversion, the certainty of his election and salvation. 'I began to sink greatly in my soul, and began to
entertain such discouragement in my heart as laid me
as low as Hell. . . . I fell therefore at the sight of my own
vileness deeply into despair; for I concluded that this
condition I was in could not stand with a state of grace.
Sure, thought I, I am forsaken of God; sure I am given
up to the Devil and to a reprobate mind. And thus I
continued a long while, even for some years together.'
He read the Bible diligently, and at times found comfort in it. More often 'fearful scriptures' would strike
him down as dead, and ring in his ears for days together.
He read religious treatises too; some of the books of the
Ranters which religious friends recommended to him
fell into his hands, but they gave no light, but fresh
doubts. Another book he lighted on was the story of
Francis Spira—an apostate Protestant—which 'was to

my troubled spirit as salt when rubbed into a fresh wound'. Chance at last threw into his hands Martin Luther's commentary on the Galatians, in which, says he, 'I found my condition . . . so largely and profoundly handled as if his book had been written out of my heart'. It seemed to him of all the books he had ever seen, the most fit for a wounded conscience. Much, too, was he helped and comforted by the teaching of John Gifford—the minister of an Independent congregation which had St. John's Church at Bedford for its meeting-place. Bunyan was formally received as a member of this church in 1653. Gifford's doctrine, he says, 'by God's grace was much for my stability'; it was 'as seasonable to my soul as the former and latter rain in their season'. His troubles were not yet ended, but by slow degrees his mind grew less perturbed and he passed from darkness and terror to peace and light.

In Bunyan's *Grace Abounding to the Chief of Sinners*, which he published in 1666, he told the story of his spiritual life with a minuteness that strangely contrasts with his reticence about those outward things on which most modern autobiographies dilate.

He writes as a man to whom the little world within is the only real world, and the great one without something unsubstantial and visionary. *Grace Abounding* is the best preface to the *Pilgrim's Progress*, and the best comment upon it. Bunyan's allegory is the generalization of his own experiences, shadowing the incidents of his own history. The elements of the *Pilgrim's Progress* are in the earlier work, waiting for the moment which is to combine them into an allegorical story. Its style has the same qualities. There is the strong, simple, homely diction, sometimes touched with imagination, and always full of passionate sincerity. There is the same vivid realization of things unseen, which is already becoming a tendency to give concrete form to the promptings of the heart and the abstractions of the brain. Bunyan's struggles with temptation are pictured as struggles with a corporeal tempter, audible and visible. At one time he describes himself as 'much followed by this scripture, "Simon, Simon, behold Satan hath desired to have you"', and 'sometimes it would sound so loud within me, yea . . . call so strongly after me, that once above all the rest I turned my head over my shoulder, thinking that verily some man had behind me called me'. At times as he prayed, 'I have thought I have felt him [Satan] behind me pull my clothes; he would be also continually at me in time of prayer to have done: "Break off, make haste, you have prayed enough, and stay no longer".' Worst of all was the voice that cried in his ear, 'Sell Christ for this, or sell Christ for that'. 'This temptation did put me to such scares . . . that *by the very force of my mind* in labouring to gainsay and resist this wickedness my very body would be put into action, or motion by way of pushing or thrusting with my hands or elbows, still answering as fast as the destroyer said, "Sell Him".' And again, when the temptation is conquered, he says, 'Methought I saw as if the tempter did leer and steal away from me, as being ashamed of what he had done'. Bunyan's hopes took the same distinct and concrete form to his mind's eye. 'Now I had an evidence, as I thought, of my salvation from heaven, with many golden seals thereon all hanging in my sight. . . . My understanding was so enlightened that I was as though I had seen the Lord Jesus look down from heaven through the tiles upon me, and direct these words unto me.' His natural instinct was to express each change of feeling, each vicissitude in his spiritual conflict, in figurative or metaphorical form. In his despair his tumultous thoughts 'like masterless hell hounds roar and bellow' within him, his soul was 'like a broken vessel driven as with the winds'. To describe his despondency, he employs the very image he subsequently uses to depict Christian's experiences in the *Pilgrim's Progress*, and likens himself to a child that has fallen into a pool, or a horse stuck fast in the mire and struggling to reach firm ground.

The instinct which made Bunyan seek to realize his mental conceptions of the spiritual world in the most visible and tangible shape, and to express each vicissitude in his religious experience in a simile or a figure, led him naturally towards allegory. In the verses in which he explains the origin of the *Pilgrim's Progress*, he says:

> . . . thus it was: I writing of the Way
> And Race of Saints, in this our Gospel Day,
> Fell suddenly into an Allegory
> About their Journey, and the way to Glory.

So now in *Grace Abounding* Bunyan, comparing his forlorn condition with the lot of those happy in their certain faith, 'fell suddenly into an allegory'.

'About this time, the state and happiness of these poor people at Bedford was thus, in a kind of Vision, presented to me. I saw as if they were set on the Sunny side of some high Mountain, there refreshing themselves with the pleasant beams of the Sun, while I was shivering and shrinking in the Cold, afflicted with Frost, Snow, and dark Clouds. Methought, also, betwixt me and them, I saw a wall that did compass about this mountain; now, through this wall my soul did greatly desire to pass; concluding, that if I could, I would go even into the very midst of them, and there also comfort myself with the heat of their Sun.

'About this wall I thought myself to go again and again, still prying as I went, to see if I could find some way or passage, by which I might enter therein; but none could I find for some time. At the last, I saw, as it were, a narrow gap, like a little doorway in the Wall, through which I attempted to pass. Now the passage being very strait and narrow, I made many efforts to get in, but all in Vain, even until I was well nigh quite beat out, by striving to get in. At last, with great striving, methought I at first did get in my head, and after that, by a sidling striving, my shoulders and my whole Body. Then was I exceeding glad, and went and sat down in the midst of them, and so was comforted with the light and heat of their Sun.

'Now, this Mountain and Wall, &c., was thus made out to me—the Mountain signified the Church of the living God; the Sun that shone thereon, the comfortable shining of his merciful Face on them that were therein; the wall, I thought, was the Word, that did make separation between the Christians and the World; and the Gap which was in this Wall, I thought, was Jesus Christ, who is the way to God the Father. . . . But forasmuch as the passage was wonderful narrow, even so narrow that I could not, but with great difficulty, enter in thereat, it showed me that none could enter into Life, but those that were in downright earnest, and unless also they left this wicked World behind them; for here was only room for Body and Soul, but not for Body and Soul and Sin.'

'This resemblance abode upon my Spirit many days.'

Many years were yet to pass before Bunyan would make a similar resemblance the groundwork of a story presenting not merely his own experience, but the general experience of all seekers after righteousness. In the meantime the training he went through tended to fit him for the task towards which his natural bent led him. Assiduous reading of the Bible and of the few religious books he possessed had been to him a new education, which replaced the little school learning he had forgotten. Assiduous preaching and controversial writing completed the process. Some two years or so after he joined Mr. Gifford's congregation, brethren who had discovered his gift of utterance, pressed him to exhort the rest in their private meetings, and 'with much weakness and infirmity' he obeyed their desire. Urged by them, he began to exhort more publicly, and at last, about 1656, he tells us, 'being still desired by the church . . . I was more particularly called forth and appointed to a more ordinary and public preaching the Word, not only to and amongst them that believed, but also to offer the Gospel to those who had not yet received the faith thereof'. Besides the desire of the church, he felt in his own mind 'a secret pricking forward thereto'. Conscious that he had a gift, he could not be content unless he exercised it. 'Wherefore,' he says, 'though of all the Saints the most unworthy, yet I, but with great fear and trembling at the sight of my own weakness, did set upon the work, and did according to my gift and the proportion of my faith preach that blessed Gospel that God had showed me.' Soon, from all parts of the country round, men came to hear him in hundreds, and some were touched and greatly affected in their minds. Ministers of the established church warned people against 'the wandering preaching tinker'. Quakers controverted him, he was derided and slandered, but nothing could break the spell which he cast over those who heard him. The secret of his eloquence was its passion and its sincerity. 'I preached what I felt, what I smartingly did feel. . . .' 'I . . . carried that fire in my own conscience that I persuaded them to beware of . . . .' 'I have been in my preaching . . . as if an angel of God had stood by at my back to encourage me. . . .' 'I could not be contented with saying, *I believe and am sure*, methought I was more than sure . . . that those things which then I asserted were true.'

In 1660 the Restoration came, and the forcible suppression of nonconformity began. On November 12, 1660, Bunyan was arrested at a hamlet in Bedfordshire just as he was about to begin to preach. 'At the sessions', he relates, 'I was indicted for an upholder and maintainer of unlawful assemblies and conventicles, and for not conforming to the national worship of the Church of England; and after some conference there with the justices, they taking my plain dealing with them for a confession . . . of the indictment, did sentence me to perpetual banishment because I refused to conform.' He not only refused to conform, but refused to give up preaching. A friend argued with him, that the powers that be were ordained of God, and that therefore it was his duty to obey the law. 'Sir,' said Bunyan, 'the law hath provided two ways of obeying. The one to do that which I in my conscience do believe that I am bound to do actively, and where I cannot obey actively there I am willing to lie down, and to suffer what they shall do unto me.'

For the next twelve years Bunyan was a prisoner in the county jail of Bedford. In 1666 he is said to have been released for a short time, but if so he was speedily rearrested. Towards the close of his imprisonment its rigour was considerably relaxed, for from August 1668 he was able occasionally to attend the meetings of his congregation, and his name is frequently mentioned in its records. On January 21, 1672, while still a prisoner, he was elected to be its minister, having been hitherto merely one of its deacons and an occasional preacher. During his confinement he maintained himself and his family by making laces, and perhaps also by some other handicraft. 'I have been witness', writes a friend, 'that his own hands have ministered to his and his families necessities, making many hundred gross of long tagged laces to fill up the vacancies of his time, which he had learned for that purpose since he had been in prison.' He also wrote much. Four works from Bunyan's pen were published between 1656 and 1660, and eleven others appeared between 1661 and 1672. One was a curious 'map showing the causes of Salvation and Damnation'. Four of them were verse compositions, viz. *Profitable Meditations, Prison Meditations, Ebal and Gerizim,* and *The Four Last Things.* Of the prose works, *Grace Abounding,* published in 1666, was the most important. The friend who visited Bunyan in prison describes him as having with him there 'his library, the least and yet the best that ever I saw, consisting only of two books—a Bible and the *Book of Martyrs*'. The copy of Foxe's *Book of Martyrs,* which Bunyan bought during his imprisonment, is now in the

library of the Literary and Scientific Institute at Bedford. It contains some doggerel verses on the margins
which Southey and other biographers have attributed
to Bunyan himself, but they are in the handwriting of
one of the later owners of the book. Southey is nevertheless right in saying that Bunyan learnt to versify
from Foxe. His earliest verses, and especially his *Prison
Meditations*, closely resemble both in metre and style
'the godly letter of Master Robert Smith in metre',
which Foxe inserts in his account of the sufferings of
the martyrs of Mary's reign. And the farewell speeches
of the martyrs to their friends before they passed
through the fire, probably suggested the similar utterances of Bunyan's pilgrims before they passed through
the river. The influence of Foxe over Bunyan is further
attested by the fact that he is frequently quoted in
Bunyan's religious treatises, and is indeed the only
author so quoted.

In 1672 Charles II, desirous of winning support for
the war against the Dutch, changed his policy towards
the English Nonconformists, and published on March
15, 1672, his Declaration of Indulgence. On May 8,
Bunyan and his fellow prisoners at Bedford petitioned
for their release, and on September 13, 1672, he received
with many others a pardon under the Great Seal. He
had obtained his freedom, however, some months before this formal pardon was granted, and on May 9,
1672, he was given a licence to preach either in the
house of Josias Ruffhead at Bedford, which was the
meeting-place of his little congregation, or in any other
licensed building. Ruffhead's house, or rather his barn,
and the orchard in which it stood, were conveyed to
Bunyan and his congregation in August 1672, and the
present Bunyan Meeting at Bedford now stands upon
its site.

This respite from persecution was only temporary.
Parliament obliged Charles II to annul his Declaration

of Indulgence within a year of its promulgation, and the toleration it had guaranteed came to an end. In 1675, probably towards the end of the year, Bunyan was again imprisoned, and remained a prisoner till the spring of the following year. This time the place of his confinement was the town jail of Bedford, which stood on the bridge over the Ouse, and served the double purpose of a prison and a toll-house. The jail on the bridge was 'the den' to which Bunyan refers, in the opening lines of the *Pilgrim's Progress*, as the place in which he laid himself down to sleep and dreamed his dream. Dr. John Brown—the last and best of Bunyan's biographers—has proved the time and the circumstances under which the composition of the *Pilgrim's Progress* was begun by an ingenious and convincing series of arguments. Bunyan occupied himself during the first part of his imprisonment by writing a catechism entitled, *Instruction for the Ignorant*, which he dedicated to his congregation at Bedford. In the preface to this work, which was published in 1675, he describes himself as 'being driven from you in presence, not affection', obviously alluding in these words to his confinement. He then began a discourse called 'The Strait Gate, or great difficulty of going to heaven, plainly proving by the Scriptures, that not only the rude and profane, but many great professors will come short of that kingdom'. After dwelling on the narrowness of the gate, Bunyan enumerated the different kinds of professing Christians who would seek to enter by it and would be unable, and characterized them one by one. As he wrote a new idea flashed across his mind. He would write not a treatise only but a story, not of the gate only but of the road, with all its difficulties and perils, representing not merely pretended saints, but honest wayfarers on their journey 'from this world to that which is to come'.

Such is the account of the origin of the *Pilgrim's*

Progress given by Bunyan himself in the rough verses prefixed to it, if we interpret them by the light of the contents and history of the *Strait Gate*. When I began to write this, says Bunyan, I did not mean to make a book of it.

> Nay, I had undertook
> To make another, which when almost done
> Before I was aware I this begun.

For I was writing of the way to Heaven, and of the race of Christians who live nowadays, when I 'fell suddenly into an allegory'. Bunyan appears to have intended to make this allegory an episode in his treatise on the *Strait Gate*, but one thought kindled another, and the allegory grew so rapidly that he determined to keep it separate, lest it should quite swallow up and 'eat out' the serious treatise. The various classes of pretenders to religion enumerated at the end of the *Strait Gate* appear in the *Pilgrim's Progress* amongst the persons whom Christian meets upon the road. Those whose religion lieth only in their tongues are represented by Mr. Talkative, the covetous professors who make a gain of religion by Mr. By-ends, and the wilfully ignorant by the 'very brisk lad' whose name was Ignorance. The legalist is heard of as Mr. Legality, and the formalist is one of the two men who 'come tumbling over the wall' because they think it too far round to go to the gate.

Bunyan was released from his imprisonment in 1676, and published the *Strait Gate* before the close of that year. The *Pilgrim's Progress* seems to have been unfinished when he left the jail, and was completed outside its walls. Such at least is the inference which has been drawn from the curious break in the story which occurs on p. 148.[1] After describing the parting of Christian and Hopeful with the shepherds on the Delectable Mountains, Bunyan concludes, 'So I awoke

---

[1] The Hanserd Knollys Society edition, ed. George Offor (1847).

from my dream'. In the next paragraph he continues,
'And I slept and dreamed again, and saw the same two
pilgrims going down the mountains along the highway
towards the City'. Dr. Brown argues with great probability that this breaking of Bunyan's dream alludes
to his release from the den in which he began his dream.
When Bunyan had resumed and completed the first
part of the *Pilgrim's Progress*, he showed it to some of
his friends and asked them whether he should print it
or not. Some had scruples about the treatment of
sacred things in a fictitious narrative, but finding them
divided he determined to publish it, prefixing to it,
however, a preface defending his use of similes and
figures for the purpose of instruction. In December
1677 the book was in the hands of the printer, Nathaniel
Ponder, and was entered by him at Stationers' Hall. It
was licensed on February 18, 1678, and published forth-
with in a little octavo volume of 232 pages at the price
of eighteenpence. A second edition appeared within
the year, a third in 1679, and by 1688 it had reached
an eleventh edition. It was translated into Dutch in
1682, into French in 1685, and into Welsh in 1688.
Additional proof of its popularity was given by unauthorized continuations, some of which were falsely
attributed to Bunyan. The author of another which
appeared in 1683, honestly styled Bunyan's volume
'that necessary and useful Tract, which hath deservedly
obtained such an Universal esteem and commendation',
but complained that certain specified doctrines were
inadequately treated in it, and that some passages occasioned 'lightness and laughter' in 'vain and frothy
minds'.

The second part of the *Pilgrim's Progress* appeared
in 1684. Bunyan's first intention had been to publish
a companion to the *Pilgrim's Progress* rather than a continuation. 'As I was considering with my self', he says,
'what I had written concerning the Progress of the

Pilgrim from this World to Glory; and how it had been acceptable to many in this Nation: It came again into my mind to write, as then, of him that was going to Heaven, so now, of the Life and Death of the Ungodly, and of their travel from this world to Hell.' With this object he wrote the *Life and Death of Mr. Badman,* which appeared in 1680. From this realistic picture of a vicious and swindling tradesman, which recalls both in subject and treatment some of Defoe's novels, Bunyan turned once more to allegory. The *Holy War,* which was published in 1682, is an attempt to treat in prose and for the people the problem which Milton had treated in verse. Its subject is the fall and redemption of mankind, the struggle between God and the devil for the soul of man, narrated under the similitude of the history of a besieged city. The town of Mansoul, as Mr. Froude has pointed out, represents sometimes the soul of a single man, sometimes the collective souls of the Christian world, and it is not always clear which the writer means. The *Holy War* is a much more elaborate allegory than the *Pilgrim's Progress,* and more completely symbolical in all its details, but its subject was less fitted for allegorical treatment. One seeks, like *Paradise Lost* and *Paradise Regained,* to explain the ways of God to man, the other only to represent the way of man to heaven. One embodies the complete system of theology, the other rests not so much on Puritan doctrine as on the Puritan conception of human life. And because our little systems have their day and their place, while the religious instinct is something lasting and universal, the *Pilgrim's Progress* is read and the *Holy War* neglected. Add to this that the personages in the history of Mansoul are for the most part devoid of any human interest. The pilgrims have each their own individuality, while nothing but the label distinguishes Captain Credence from Captain Conviction. The trials of the Diabolonians after the conquest of Mansoul awake more interest than the siege, and the condemned sinners have all the individuality which the saints lack. In the *Holy War* the spontaneity and freedom of the *Pilgrim's Progress* is absent. 'I did it mine own self to gratify,' says Bunyan of his first allegory. His second allegory was too obviously written to instruct others, and the genius of the story-teller is cramped by the theological framework of the story. Possibly Bunyan felt this himself. In the verses at the end of the *Holy War* his mind goes back to the earlier allegory; he turns suddenly to answer the critics who said the *Pilgrim's Progress* was not his own, and asserts his authorship of it in emphatic terms.

It came from mine own heart so to my head.
.   .   .   .
Manner and matter too was all mine own,
Nor was it unto any mortal known
Till I had done it. Nor did any then
By books, by wits, by tongues, or hand, or pen
Add five words to it, or wrote half a line
Thereof; the whole and every whit is mine.

This new allegory, too, he continues, is also 'all my own'; but his claim to have written the *Pilgrim's Progress* is evidently the more important in his eyes.

The best way to refute these critics, and to respond to the general desire which had led to the publication of unauthorized continuations, was to write a second part to the *Pilgrim's Progress*. The story 'of the setting out of Christian's wife and children, their dangerous journey, and safe arrival at the desired country', was completed in 1684. Bunyan's warrant to Ponder, the printer, for its publication is dated January 1, 1684—that is 1685 in our modern reckoning—and the book was published between that date and March 25, when the year 1684 ended. It was nearly as popular as the first part, and reached its sixth edition in 1693.

Charles II died on February 6, 1685, just about the time when the second part of the *Pilgrim's Progress* appeared. The reaction against the Whigs and the accompanying persecution of the Nonconformists which had marked the last years of Charles II's reign continued during the first year of his successor's. In 1684 Bunyan published his *Seasonable Counsel, or Advice to Sufferers*, an exhortation to his persecuted brethren setting forth the duty of suffering cheerfully for the sake of their consciences, and the spiritual uses of adversity. His own freedom was once more in danger, and on December 23, 1685, he conveyed all his property to his wife, in order that his family might have some means of support if he should be again imprisoned. But though threatened and molested he escaped a third imprisonment, and James II's change of policy put an end to the danger.

Each change in the position of English Nonconformity is reflected in Bunyan's allegories. Persecution was at its hottest when he began to write, but even then the number of Nonconformists was increasing. Their sufferings gained them friends. 'The men being patient, and not rendering railing for railing, but contrarywise blessing, and giving good words for bad . . . some men in the Fair that were more observing and less prejudiced than the rest, began to check and blame the baser sort for their continual abuses done by them to the men.' A new candidate for martyrdom filled the place of each who suffered. When Christian left the town of Vanity, says Bunyan, 'I saw in my dream that Christian went not forth alone, for there was one whose name was Hopeful (being made so by the beholding of Christian and Faithful in their words and behaviour in their sufferings at the Fair) who joined himself unto him, and entering into a brotherly covenant, told him that he would be his companion'. As soon as persecution relaxed the number of Nonconformists rapidly increased.

In 1669 it was computed that there were some thirty in Bedford; in 1676, according to Archbishop Sheldon's religious census, their number was one hundred and twenty-one adults. With this increase came a new peril—the peril of false brethren who for the sake of gain made a profession of godliness. How much it occupied Bunyan's thoughts the character of By-ends shows, and above all the manner in which he retouched and further developed the figures of By-ends and his friends in the second and third edition of the first part of the *Pilgrim's Progress*. The grave irony of Mr. Money-love's answer to the case of conscience propounded by his friends is worthy of Swift, and it was not unneeded. Bunyan himself felt no temptation to change a small living for a greater, though greater ones were offered him as his fame spread. 'He was not a man that preached by way of bargain for money,' wrote his first biographer, 'for he hath refused a more plentiful income to keep his station.'

The renewal of persecution which marked the end of Charles II's reign was preceded by an attack on the charters of the corporate towns. All over England Whigs and favourers of Nonconformists were put out of corporations, and Tories and persecutors put in. This process was just beginning when Bunyan wrote the *Holy War*, and it is anticipated in his account of the remodelling of the magistracy of Mansoul by Diabolus. When Mansoul was recaptured by the army of Emmanuel the process was reversed, a new charter given to the town, and godly magistrates appointed. In like fashion James II, when he adopted the policy embodied in the Declaration of Indulgence, remodelled the corporation of Bedford, and filled it with compliant tools of the court and with Nonconformists who were willing to support the king's scheme. Some of Bunyan's congregation were amongst the new councillors, and his influence was eagerly sought by the court candidate for the borough. But Bunyan himself seems to have distrusted the King's aims in granting liberty of conscience. He was glad to lay hold of this liberty as 'an acceptable thing in itself', but he would have nothing to do with the regulators employed to remodel the government of the municipalities. 'When a great man in those days, coming to Bedford upon some such errand, sent for him, as it is supposed, to give him a place of public trust, he would by no means come at him, but sent his excuse.'

Dread of the progress of Catholicism explains Bunyan's reluctance, as it accounts for the lukewarmness of the Nonconformists in general towards the toleration policy of James II. When he wrote the first part of the *Pilgrim's Progress* he had hardly regarded Catholicism as a serious danger. Giant Pope was still alive, but grown so crazy and stiff in his joints that he could only sit at the mouth of his cave 'grinning at pilgrims . . . and biting his nails because he cannot come at them'. The fierce excitement of the Popish Plot produced a change of feeling in Bunyan's party and in Bunyan himself. In the second part of the *Pilgrim's Progress* the Roman Church appears in the shape of the monster living in the woods near the town of Vanity, a monster that was 'very rampant', and 'made great havoc of children'. Like Mr. Great-heart and his 'valiant worthies', Bunyan was eager to check the monster's ravages. One of his last works was a posthumously published treatise against the Roman Church, called *Of Antichrist and his ruine, and the Slaying of the Witnesses*. He did not live to see the fall of King James put an end to his fears, or the Revolution which guaranteed the freedom of conscience he desired. Bunyan died about ten weeks before William of Orange landed in England, on August 31, 1688, and was buried in the cemetery in Bunhill Fields.

To contemporaries outside his own sect the author

of the *Pilgrim's Progress* was nothing but a dissenting preacher with some little reputation among Nonconformists, a preacher, as a news-letter which mentioned his death remarked, 'said to be gifted in that way, though once a cobbler'. The literary fame of the author was a thing of growth as slow as the popularity of his book had been immediate. Addison cited Bunyan as a proof that even despicable writers had their admirers, Young compared his prose to Durfey's poetry, and when Cowper praised him he apologized for his praises:

> I name thee not, lest so despised a name
> Should move a sneer at thy deserved fame.

Yet before the eighteenth century ended the dictators of taste had begun to praise the work of the unlettered preacher. Swift wrote that he had been more entertained and more confirmed by a few pages in the *Pilgrim's Progress* than by a long discussion upon the will and the intellect. Johnson compared passages in it to Spenser and Dante, and told Boswell it was one of the three books which readers wished longer. It had great merit, he declared, 'both for invention, imagination, and the conduct of the story', and when Bishop Percy's little girl confessed that she had not read it, he put her off his knee at once, and said he would not give a farthing for her. In 1830 the publication of Southey's edition of the *Pilgrim's Progress*, followed by Macaulay's essay, showed that the critics had at last accepted the verdict of the people on Bunyan's masterpiece, and in 1880, with the publication of Froude's life of the author, Bunyan was formally included in the roll of 'English Men of Letters'. It was not a dignity which he ever desired, and he would probably have classed most of his associates with Talkative, the son of Saywell, who dwelt in Prating Row, and discoursed glibly of the history and mystery of things.

To explain the immediate popularity of the *Pilgrim's*

Progress with Bunyan's contemporaries is more necessary than to trace the growth of his posthumous fame.
A certain amount of success the very choice of his subject secured. Religious books were almost the only
serious reading of the class for which Bunyan wrote.
Any allegory which appealed to Puritans of the lower
and middle classes, and represented in an imaginative
form feelings they had experienced, struggles they had
gone through, and ideals they cherished, was sure of a
wide circle of readers. The inner meaning of Bunyan's
narrative was plain enough, and a hundred pious commentators have pointed out the significance of every
incident. But considered simply as a story, there was
in what Bunyan terms 'the outside of my dream' much
to explain its immediate popularity.

In the first place it was a great advantage that the
idea on which Bunyan based his allegory was one with
which people had long been familiar. Different commentators have pitched upon different books as containing the germ of the *Pilgrim's Progress*. A long list
of such works is given in the preface to Mr. Offor's
edition, and Guillaume de Guilleville's *Pilgrimage of the
Soule*, of which Caxton printed a translation in 1483,
has been gravely republished as Bunyan's original. If
Bunyan took the hint from any book it was from the
Bible.[1] But the truth is the idea that life was but a
pilgrimage through this world to the next was common property. In the Middle Ages the sight of the
crowds of men who with staff and scrip and pilgrim's
weeds travelled to the shrines of the Holy Land,
had suggested to contemplative minds the obvious
parallel. As late as the middle of the sixteenth century English pilgrims flocked to visit the shrines of
St. Thomas of Canterbury or our Lady of Walsingham. The Middle Ages bequeathed the idea to the
Protestants of the sixteenth and seventeenth centuries,

[1] Hebrews xi. 13.

and long after pilgrimages had ceased, the pilgrim of tradition—

> With his cockle hat and staff,
> And his sandal shoon

was a figure familiar to the minds of the people. To give the traditional equipment of the pilgrim a spiritual significance also was easy and natural. Sir Walter Raleigh, for instance, does so in the poem called the 'Pilgrimage', which he wrote when he was condemned to death.

> Give me my scallop shell of quiet,
>   My staff of faith to walk upon,
> My scrip of joy—immortal diet,
>   My bottle of Salvation,
> My gown of glory, hope's true gage,
> And thus I'll take my pilgrimage.

Emblem writers like Whitney and Quarles had popularized the same idea in their pictures, and George Herbert had embodied it in one of the poems in his *Temple*.

Thus the fundamental conception of the *Pilgrim's Progress* was one with which English readers were perfectly familiar, and when Bunyan made it the basis of an allegory, their minds were prepared to understand his hidden meaning.

Another cause of the book's success was its style. It addressed the unlettered Puritan in a speech which unlettered Puritans could understand. The people for whom Bunyan wrote were illiterate people like his pilgrims themselves. Christian 'was a scholar', and could read a notice board, but Hopeful could not even do that. But they knew their Bible well, and were never at a loss for a text. They could follow Bunyan in his highest flights, and in his most serious theological arguments, because he used the language of the Bible, and adopted its words, its phrases, and its imagery.

Bunyan's English, says Mr. J. R. Green, is the English of the Bible. In no book 'do we see more clearly the new imaginative force which had been given to the common life of Englishmen by their study of the Bible'.

This is true, but it is not the whole truth. In the narrative part of the *Pilgrim's Progress*, and in much of the dialogue, Bunyan used the everyday language of the seventeenth-century workman or shopkeeper, which was a much more homely and less dignified dialect than the language of the Bible.

As Macaulay remarks, the vocabulary of the *Pilgrim's Progress* is the vocabulary of the common people, and with the limitation just pointed out the statement is correct. Hence come the colloquialisms, the obsolete words, and the homely expressions. For instance, when the pilgrims got to the top of the hill called Difficulty 'they were very willing to sit down, for they were all in a pelting heat'. When they reached their inn after a long day's walking, the host says to them, 'You have gone a good stitch, you may well be a-weary'. Their talk is full of proverbs and proverbial expressions. Christian says that the house of Talkative 'is as empty of religion as the white of an egg is of savour'. The common people that know Talkative say that he is 'a saint abroad and a devil at home'. When Hopeful says something Christian disapproves, Christian, in the words of the margin, 'snibbeth his fellow for unadvised speaking', and tells him he talks like a newly hatched chicken. 'Thou talkest like one upon whose head is the shell to this day.'

Sometimes Bunyan drops into the language of his unregenerate days. Old Mr. Honest is described by Great-heart as 'a cock of the right kind'—an obvious reminiscence of a profane sport, which Bunyan had doubtless taken part in in the old times. There was a bad relapse in his account of the escape of the prisoners from Doubting Castle. Even when Christian had discovered the key in his bosom, he found the iron gate difficult to unlock, for 'that lock went damnable hard'. Scrupulous modern editors have often altered the adjective.

The colloquial language of the *Pilgrim's Progress* was not an accident. Bunyan purposely chose the style most likely to appeal to the readers he wished to reach. The fowler, he remarks, sometimes finds his gun and his net insufficient, and must pipe and whistle to catch his birds. The fisherman when hook and line fail him is driven to tickling for trout. In the same way the fisher of men must attract in order to capture.

A similar reason explains the introduction of the symbolical sights and pictures which the pilgrims see in the House Beautiful and elsewhere. The man with the muck-rake, the parlour full of dust, the two little children in their little chairs, the robin with the great spider in its mouth, and the rest—these transparent parables were introduced by Bunyan because he was writing for the young and the unlearned. 'I make bold to talk thus metaphorically', explains Mr. Great-heart, 'for the ripening of the wits of young readers.' So when Mr. Interpreter led Mercy and Christiana into his 'Significant Rooms' to see the hen and chickens and other moral spectacles, he condescendingly told them, 'I chose, my darlings, to lead you into the room where such things are, because you are women, and they are easy for you'.

These symbolical pictures also illustrate the way in which Bunyan made use of the popular literature of his time. For a century before his day emblem-books had enjoyed a wide popularity both in England and in Europe. The little pictures symbolically setting forth moral and religious truths, and accompanied by prose and verse explanations, were familiar to everybody. Hundreds of such works had been published both at home and abroad, both by Catholics and Protestants.

The most popular of English emblem-writers, especially
with the Puritans, was Francis Quarles, whose *Emblems,
Divine and Moral* appeared in 1635. No book was
commoner in Puritan households, and it cannot be
doubted that Bunyan knew a work so easy to meet with,
and so valued by his party. He even tried his hand at
composing emblems himself, and published in 1686
what he called *A Book for Boys and Girls, or Country
Rhymes for Children.* It was republished in the next
century under the title of *Divine Emblems,* and equipped
with curious cuts. The sights which Mr. Interpreter
shows the pilgrims are attempts to express in plain
prose what Bunyan himself afterwards tried to express
in rough verses, and what the emblem-writers had expressed in woodcuts or copper plates. Having taken a
popular idea and made it the basis of his allegory,
Bunyan now took a hint from popular literature, using
it to embellish his story, and to make his moral purpose
clearer.

But whatever suggestions Bunyan derived from literature, he drew more from the world around him than
from books. One of the most remarkable qualities of
his story is the faithfulness with which it pictures the
life of the times. The road on which the pilgrims travel
is as realistically described as the pilgrims themselves.
It is like an old Roman road in some respects, for it goes
up the hill called Difficulty, and across the 'delicate
plain called Ease' as straight as a rule can make it.
Sometimes there is a high wall to tempt the children.
Dogs bark at the travellers as they pass by, and frighten
the women 'with the great voice of their roaring'.
Other travellers overtake them or meet them on the
road; they see men lying asleep by the roadside; they
see criminals hanging in irons a little way from it.
Sometimes 'a fine pleasant green lane' comes down into
the road; on one side of it there is 'a meadow and a
style to go over into it', or a by-path such as that which

leads Christian and Hopeful into the grounds of Giant
Despair. It may be called the road to the Celestial
City, but it is very like a common English seventeenth-
century high-road. The dangers which beset the wayfarers are (in most cases) dangers which every seventeenth-century traveller had to face. Compare for
instance Macaulay's description of an English road in
the time of Charles II. 'It was only in fine weather that
the whole breadth of the road was available for wheeled
vehicles. Often the mud lay deep on the right and the
left; and only a narrow track of firm ground rose above
the quagmire. . . . It happened, almost every day, that
coaches stuck fast, until a team of cattle could be procured from some neighbouring farm, to tug them
out of the slough.' Does not this description at once
recall that 'very miry slough' named Despond, where
Christian and Pliable 'wallowed for a time, being griev-
ously bedaubed with the dirt', just because they missed
'the good and substantial' stepping-stones in the middle?
A more serious danger than the mud was the frequent
floods. Macaulay illustrates this from Ralph Thoresby's
account of his journeys from Leeds to London. 'On
one occasion he learned that the floods were out between Ware and London, that passengers had to swim
for their lives, and that a higgler had perished in the
attempt to cross. In consequence of these tidings he
turned out of the high-road, and was conducted across
some meadows, where it was necessary for him to swim
to the saddle skirts in water. In the course of another
journey he narrowly escaped being swept away by an
inundation of the Trent.' In like manner Christian and
Hopeful were surprised in By-path Meadow by the
sudden rising of the river. 'By this time the waters
were greatly risen, by reason of which the way of going
back was very dangerous. . . . It was so dark, and the
flood was so high, that in their going back they had like
to have been drowned nine or ten times.'

If the traveller escaped the mud and the waters, there was a third danger equally common and more terrible. The latter part of the seventeenth century was the golden age of the British highwayman. Then flourished Claude Duval, John Nevison, the Golden Farmer, Muldsack, and many others whose fame lives in the pages of Johnson's *Lives of Highwaymen and Pirates*. The open heaths and moors round London were their favourite hunting-grounds, or they lay in wait in the woods that bordered the great roads. Cambridge scholars on their way to London, says Macaulay, trembled as they approached Epping Forest. Oxford scholars for equally good reasons thanked God when they had passed Maidenhead Thicket. The mounted highwaymen attacked horsemen and coaches, the poor pedestrian was preyed upon by the footpads—gangs of sturdy rogues armed with cudgels, who assaulted and robbed the foot-traveller as he tramped on his weary way, and it was much if they spared his life. Such were the villains who attacked Valiant-for-truth, and plundered Little-Faith. Alter the names, and the robbery of Little-Faith reads like a page from the *Police News* of the period.

'The thing was this:

'At the entering in at this passage, there comes down from Broadway Gate, a Lane called Dead Man's Lane; so called because of the murders that are commonly done there; and this Little-Faith going on pilgrimage as we do now, chanced to sit down there, and slept. Now there happened at that time, to come down that lane from Broadway Gate, three sturdy rogues, and their names were Faint-heart, Mistrust, and Guilt (three brothers), and they espying Little-Faith, where he was, came galloping up with speed. Now the good man was just awaked from his sleep, and was getting up to go on his journey. So they came all up to him, and with threatening language bid him stand.

'At this Little-Faith looked as white as a clout, and had neither power to fight nor fly. Then said Faint-heart, Deliver thy purse. But he making no haste to do it (for he was loathe to lose his money), Mistrust ran up to him, and thrusting his hand in his pocket, pulled out thence a bag of silver. Then he cried out, Thieves! Thieves! With that, Guilt with a great club that was in his hand, struck Little-Faith on the head, and with that blow felled him flat to the ground: where he lay bleeding as one that would bleed to death. All this while the thieves stood by. But, at last, they hearing that some were upon the road, and fearing lest it should be one Great-grace, that dwells in the city of Good-confidence, they betook themselves to their heels, and left this good man to shift for himself. Now, after a while, Little-Faith came to himself, and getting up, made shift to scrabble on his way. This was the story.'

On the other hand, some of the perils the pilgrims met with are not perils to which seventeenth-century travellers were usually exposed. They did not generally meet a dragon straddling 'quite over the whole breadth of the way', or a giant preparing to pick a passenger's bones, or seven devils carrying a man down a very dark lane. There is a romantic as well as a realistic element in the story, and for this romantic element Bunyan was indebted to the popular literature of the time. Dr. Johnson, discussing the *Pilgrim's Progress* with Boswell, observes, in his confident way, that there is reason to think that Bunyan had read Spenser. A recent editor, Mr. Venables, takes this hint, and works it out, trying to show from certain resemblances between the *Pilgrim's Progress* and the *Faery Queen*, that Bunyan was familiar with Spenser's epic. He compares the House Beautiful to Spenser's House of Holiness, Apollyon to the Dragon vanquished by the Red Cross Knight, and the cave of giants Pope and Pagan with the cave of Despair. Other parallels might be pointed out, but nevertheless it is very unlikely that Bunyan ever read a line of Spenser. The sources of Bunyan's literary inspiration are to be found, not in the books which were read by scholars and gentlemen, but in the litera-

ture of the people. Both Bunyan and Spenser were
indebted to the romances of chivalry for their romantic
machinery, their giants and dragons and enchanters.
Spenser knew the romances in their literary form, and
in the epics of Ariosto and other Italian poets. Bunyan
knew them in their popular form, in the abridgements,
the compilations, and the imitations which ballads and
chap-books had made familiar to Englishmen of the
uneducated classes. They had been his favourite reading when he was unconverted. 'I remember', he says,
speaking of a preacher, 'he alleged many a scripture,
but those I valued not. The Scriptures, thought I,
what are they? A dead letter, a little ink and paper, of
three or four shillings price. . . . Give me a ballad, a
news-book, *George on Horseback*, or *Bevis of Southampton*; give me some book that teaches curious arts, that
tells of old fables; but for the Holy Scriptures I cared not.'

One of the best examples of these story books is
Richard Johnson's *Seven Champions of Christendom*,
originally published in 1607, which went through in-
numerable editions. It begins with the life of St.
George, and is doubtless what Bunyan refers to as
'George'. This book or some other of the same kind
suggested many of the incidents which happen to
Bunyan's pilgrims. The monsters in the *Pilgrim's Progress* are of two kinds. Apollyon was a fiend somewhat
of the nature of a dragon. He had 'scales like a fish',
'wings like a dragon, feet like a bear, and out of his belly
came fire and smoke, and his mouth was as the mouth
of a lion'. He made a 'yelling and hideous roaring' all
the time of the fight, and when he spake he 'spake like
a dragon'. Christian was healed of the wounds he received by applying to them some of the leaves of the
tree of life. In the same way St. George in the *Seven
Champions* was healed of the wounds he got from the
Egyptian dragon, by the virtues of the fruit of a
miraculous tree that grew near the site of the battle.

In the encounters of the pilgrims with the giants the influence of the romances is more plainly perceptible. The giants are of a less complex nature than the monsters. Despair is only an immense man. 'He had a cap of steel upon his head, a breastplate of fire girded to him, and he came out in iron shoes with a great club in his hand.' Slaygood is not only a giant, but a cannibal. 'He was of the nature of flesh eaters,' and is found stripping Feeble-mind 'with a purpose after that to pick his bones.' He resembles the giant thirty feet high, 'who never eats any meat but the raw flesh of mankind', whom St. George vanquishes.

Giant Maul is perhaps the most typical of Bunyan's giants, and his fight with Great-heart is the most minutely described. It begins, as these fights generally begin in the romances, by a defiance and an exchange of taunts between the two champions.

'Then the giant came up, and Mr. Great-heart went to meet him, and as he went he drew his sword, but the giant had a club. So without more ado they fell to it, and at the first blow the giant struck Mr. Great-heart down upon one of his knees; with that the women and children cried out. So Mr. Great-heart recovering himself, laid about him in full lusty manner, and gave the giant a wound in his arm; thus he fought for the space of an hour, to that height of heat that the breath came out of the giant's nostrils as the heat doth out of a boiling caldron.

'Then they sat down to rest them, but Mr. Great-heart betook him to prayer; also the women and children did nothing but sigh and cry all the time that the battle did last.

'When they had rested them and taken breath they both fell to it again, and Mr. Great-heart with a full blow fetched the giant down to the ground. "Nay, hold, and let me recover," quoth he. So Mr. Great-heart fairly let him get up; so to it they went again; and the giant missed but little of all-to-breaking Mr. Great-heart's skull with his club.

'Mr. Great-heart seeing that runs to him in the full heat of his spirit, and pierceth him under the fifth rib: with that the giant began to faint, and could hold up his club no longer. Then

Mr. Great-heart seconded his blow, and smit the head of the giant from his shoulders.'

The incidents of this fight have a general resemblance to the incidents of the battles recorded in the popular romances. Giants in these stories habitually fight with clubs, or even with whole trees. The giant Blanderon in his fight with St. Anthony employed an oak tree, and 'with his great Oke so nimbly bestird him, with soch vehement blowes, that they seemed to shake the earth, . . . and had not the politicke Knight continually skipped from the fury of his blowes, hee had beene bruised as small as flesh unto the pot, for every stroke that the Gyant gave, the roote of his Oke entred at the least two or three inches deepe into the ground'.

Another family characteristic of these giants is that, like Giant Maul, they get extremely hot, while the knight, who is always in good condition, keeps cool. Blanderon, for instance, grows so breathless that he is finally unable to lift his club above his head. 'The sweat of the Gyants browes ran into his eyes, and by the reason that he was so extreame fatte he grew so blinde that hee could not see to endure Combat with him any longer.'

Great-heart is a most chivalrous fighter, and when the giant is knocked down allows him to get up again. St. Anthony is less generous to Blanderon, and refuses him the breathing time for which he petitions, but Guy of Warwick is as obliging as Great-heart. Cole-brand, the giant whom Guy is fighting, becomes very thirsty, and says:

> good Sir, & itt be thy will,
> give me leave to drinke my ffill,
>   ffor sweete St. Charytye;
> and I will doe thee the same deede
> another time, if thou have neede,
>   I tell the certainlye.

On which Guy agrees to wait till he has refreshed himself.
One must not exaggerate these resemblances between

Bunyan's story and the stories in which he had once delighted, but it is plain that he was not uninfluenced by them. They suggested the adventures to which he gave an allegorical meaning, and his recollections of them sometimes supplied him with appropriate details.

There is the same mixture of realism and romance in Bunyan's description of the countries through which the pilgrims travel, and of the scenery through which the road passes. Here and there reminiscences of popular literature colour his pictures, or even suggest his scenes, but for the most part he draws what he had seen with his own eyes. Bunyan's feeling for natural beauty is very keen, but it is the landscape of his native Midlands which pleased him most. From the roof of the House Beautiful Christian sees afar off 'a most pleasant mountainous country, beautified with woods, vineyards, fruits of all sorts; flowers also with springs and fountains very delectable to behold'. But when he gets amongst rocks he is rather afraid of them. In the story they threaten to topple down on the traveller's head, or to give way under his feet. Woods and green fields, rich meadows and softly-sliding waters attract Bunyan's imagination most. In his ideal country, the land of Beulah, the air is 'sweet and pleasant', 'the sun shineth night and day'. 'They heard continually the singing of birds, and saw every day the flowers appear in the earth.' More mundane, because further from the celestial city, is the beauty of the Valley of Humiliation. It is empty and solitary; 'I love to be in such places where there is no rattling with coaches nor rumbling with wheels', exclaims Mercy. It 'consisteth much in meadows,' says Mr. Great-heart, 'and if a man was to come here in the summer time as we do now, if he knew not anything before thereof, and if he also delighted himself in the sight of his eyes, he might see that that would be delightful to him. Behold how green this valley is, also how beautified with lilies'.

The shepherd boy feeding his father's sheep supplies
the one touch necessary to complete the picture. 'The
boy was in very mean clothes but of a very fresh and
well-favoured countenance, and as he sate by himself
he sung. . . . Then said their guide, Do you hear him?
I will dare to say that this boy lives a merrier life, and
wears more of that herb called Heartsease in his bosom,
than he that is clad in silk and velvet.'

The song the shepherd sings is a song of content—a
Puritan echo of a hundred similar songs of the Elizabethan poets—like in temper, if simpler in expression,
to 'Art thou poor, yet hast thou golden slumbers', or,
'My mind to me a kingdom is', or, 'How happy is he
born and taught'. We are back in Arcadia, with
Sidney's shepherds piping as if they would never grow
old, or with the happy melodist of Keats 'forever piping
songs forever new'. These fair lands of Bunyan's fancy
are a kind of homely Arcadia—like the Arcadia of earlier
poets, and yet different, a Puritan instead of a pagan
Arcadia. Marlowe's passionate shepherd promises his
shepherdess 'a thousand fragrant posies'. In the land
of Beulah 'the children of the town would go into the
king's gardens and gather nosegays for the pilgrims, and
bring them to them with much affection'. In Marlowe's Arcadia there are 'shallow rivers to whose falls
melodious birds sing madrigals'. In the grove outside
the House Beautiful the birds sing with a 'most curious
melodious note', but they sing the psalms of Sternhold
and Hopkins.

Amidst these landscapes from Bedfordshire and the
echoes of Arcadia appear once more the reminiscences
of popular romance. One of the chief characteristics of
romances is what Milton terms

> . . . Forests, and inchantments drear,
> Where more is meant then meets the ear.

Of this nature is Bunyan's Enchanted Land. 'By this

time', he says, 'they were got to the enchanted ground, where the air naturally tended to make one drowsy. And that place was all grown over with briars and thorns; excepting here and there, where was an enchanted arbour, upon which if a man sits, or in which if a man sleeps, 'tis a question, some say, whether ever they shall rise or wake again in this world. Over this forest therefore they went.' In one of these arbours Great-heart and his band find Heedless and Too-bold in their unwaking slumbers.

Just so in the *Seven Champions*, when St. David ventured into the Enchanted Garden of the Magician Ormandine, 'all his sences were overtaken with a suddaine and heavie sleepe'. He fell flat on the ground, 'where his eyes were so fast locked up by magicke Art, and his waking sences drowned in such a dead slumber, that it was as much impossible to recover himselfe from sleepe, as to pull the Sunne out of the firmament'. So he lay asleep for seven years. Further on in the same romance occurs an enchanted bed, which is not unlike one of Bunyan's arbours. 'Whosoever but sate upon the sides, or but toucht the furniture of the Bed, were presently cast into as heavy a sleepe, as if they had drunke the juyce of Dwaile or the seed of Poppy.'

Even the conception of the Valley of the Shadow of Death, which Bunyan invests with so much spiritual significance, finds its parallels in these romances. St. George has to journey through an Enchanted Vale, when he hears 'dismal croaking of night ravens, hissing of serpents, bellowing of bulls, and roaring of monsters'. St. Andrew traverses in a land of continual darkness the Vale of Walking Spirits amid like sounds of terror. To say that here and elsewhere Bunyan's incidents were suggested by his recollections of popular romance, does not diminish the originality of the *Pilgrim's Progress*, but helps to explain its popularity. The man who, like Bunyan himself, turned from reading romances to thinking about his soul and its salvation, found in Bunyan's pages something of the charm he had found in the old fables of adventure.

When the pilgrims reach Vanity Fair we are once more amid scenes drawn from the life of the times. 'This Fair,' Bunyan tells us, was 'a thing of ancient standing,' and a very great fair. He describes with the most vivid realism the rows of booths where all kinds of merchandise were sold, the shows where jugglings and plays and games of every kind were to be seen, and the noise of buyers and sellers in its streets. It is possible, as commentators suggest, that he had in his mind the actual fair which had been annually held at Elstow ever since Henry II had granted a charter for it to the nuns of Elstow Abbey. Or he may have re-called the greater fair held at Stourbridge, near Cambridge, which he must have seen in his travels, or perhaps the Bartholomew Fair held at Smithfield in London. In Ben Jonson's play on Bartholomew Fair he depicts the adventures of two Puritans who strayed into that scene. All the sights and sounds of the fair shock them. 'Walk on in the middle way,' cries the leader to his companion, 'turn neither to the right hand nor to the left; let not your eyes be drawn aside with vanity, nor your ears with noises. . . . The wares are the wares of devils, and the whole Fair is the shop of Satan.' Zeal-of-the-land Busy—as Jonson's Puritan is named—becomes as uncontrollable as Mr. Fearing when his blood was up. He is moved in the spirit to protest against the abuses of the fair by throwing over a basket of gingerbread, and is put in the stocks for it.

Gifford, in his edition of Jonson, conjectured that Bunyan in the days of his youth read Jonson's play, and asserted that Jonson's drama was the groundwork of Vanity Fair. But nothing is less likely than that Bunyan had read Jonson's satire against the Puritans; similar incidents must have come to his knowledge, for they were not uncommon. The Quakers in the days of the Commonwealth habitually preached in fairs and markets, and suffered accordingly. On the market day, writes George Fox in his journal, I went to Lancaster, and 'spoake through ye markett in ye dreadefull power of God & declared ye day of ye Lord to them & against all there deceitfull merchandise'. In Vanity Fair and in the incidents which followed the arrival of Christian and Faithful, Bunyan is once more copying life, and not borrowing from literature.

Equally realistic is the trial of Christian and Faithful. It resembles, as Macaulay does not fail to point out, the parody of justice which was administered by hostile judges to accused Nonconformists. When Baxter was tried in 1685 for complaining in print of the persecutions of his brethren, Lord Jeffreys behaved very like Lord Hategood. 'This is an old rogue,' said Jeffreys, 'a schismatical knave, a hypocritical villain. . . . It would be no more than justice to whip such a villain through the whole City.' When Baxter strove to argue in his defence, Jeffreys rudely stopped him.

'Richard, Richard, dost thou think we will let thee poison the court? Richard, thou art an old knave. Thou hast written books enough to load a cart, and every book as full of sedition as an egg is full of meat. By the grace of God, I'll look after thee.'

In the same manner Hategood addressed Faithful, saying, 'Thou Runagate, Heretick and Traitor, hast thou heard what these honest gentlemen have witnessed against thee?'

'May I speak a few words in my own defence.'

'Sirrah, Sirrah, thou deservest to live no longer, but to be slain immediately upon the place; yet that all men may see our gentleness towards thee, let us see what thou . . . hast to say.'

The trial at the town of Vanity should be compared with the trials which took place at the town of Mansoul as related in the *Holy War*. There is a singular resemblance in the deliberations of the two juries, and when the good men have the upper hand they give the bad men just as short a shrift as Faithful received.

A comparison of the trials in these two books also brings out more clearly the influence which another species of popular literature had exercised upon Bunyan. Allegorical trials played a great part in English and foreign polemical literature. There are several anti-Catholic pamphlets of the time of the English Reformation in which the form of a trial is adopted. Such for instance is the Examination of the Mass published in 1547. In the seventeenth century the same device was often employed by controversialists on both sides. When the Presbyterians got the upper hand, and endeavoured to suppress the worship of the Independents, a bold Independent printed the *Trial of Mr. Persecution*. Under the Protectorate, when the Government was engaged in suppressing the old festivals of the Church, there came to its assistance a *Trial of Father Christmas* for corrupting the world by riotous living.

A Puritan divine, Richard Bernard, of Batcombe, employed this device of a trial for much the same purpose as Bunyan used it, that is for moral rather than for controversial purposes. Bernard's book, which was published in 1627, went through nine editions by 1634, and was very popular with Puritans of the class to which Bunyan belonged. The title of the book is the *Isle of Man:. or the Legall Proceeding in Man-shire against Sinne. Wherein, by way of a continued Allegorie, the chiefe Malefactors disturbing both Church and Common-Wealth, are detected and attached, with their Arraignment, and Judiciall triall, according to the Lawes of England.*

Manshire is the name of the county in which the trials take place. The assizes are being held at the county town which is called Soul. 'That worthy judge

Conscience' presides, and before him the criminals
appear one after another. The names of these offenders
are Old Man, who represents what in theological language is called 'the old Adam', his wife, Mistress Heart,
his servant, Wilful Will, Covetousness, and others. A
few extracts from the trial of Old Man will supply a
specimen of Bernard's method of handling his allegory.
The indictment is set forth in the usual legal form.

'Old-man, thou art indited here by the name of Old-
man of the Towne of Evahs Temptation, in the Countie
of Adams consent, that upon the day of Mans fall in
Paradise, when he was driven out, thou diddest corrupt
the whole nature of man.'

David and St. Paul bear witness against the Criminal,
who argues in his own defence much as the Pelagians
do vainly talk. He is condemned to death and prays
for mercy. 'Good my Lord, I beseech you, be good
unto me, and cast not away so poore an Old man: (good
my Lord) for I am at this day 5556 yeeres old.'

But his plea for mercy and his request to be allowed
benefit of clergy are all in vain. He is sentenced to be
hung, or rather, as the judge says, to be 'cast off, with
all thy deeds'.

Bernard's handling of his allegory is awkward and
cumbrous; he can neither tell a story, nor draw a
character, and he has very little humour, though he
apologizes for showing too much. But there are, nevertheless, certain resemblances between the *Isle of Man*
and the *Holy War* which seem to show that Bunyan
had read the work of the earlier allegorist. The town
of Soul in the county of Manshire naturally suggests
Bunyan's town of Mansoul. Bernard's Wilful Will is
the prototype of Bunyan's Lord Will be Will. There
are touches in the trials described by Bernard which
remind the reader of incidents in those related by
Bunyan. Lord Covetousness in Bunyan's book changes
his name to Prudent-thrifty, and in the same way

Bernard's Covetousness finds a flaw in his indictment,
pleading that his real name is Thrift. And Judge Conscience addresses Covetousness much in the manner
that Judge Hategood addresses Faithful.

'Sirrha, Sirrha, thou that hast so impudently denied
thy name, here before the face of thy country: being
so clerely prooved against thee every way, what canst
thou yet alleadge for thy selfe that now the sentence of
death should not be pronounced against thee?'

All I wish to show is that in introducing these trials
in his two allegories Bunyan was adopting a literary
device with which English readers were already familiar,
and one which was specially popular with the readers
for whom he wrote. In his hands the old idea received
a new life, and the tedious abstractions of the allegorical
courts became living persons. It is in this power of
giving life to his characters that the supreme excellence
of Bunyan as an allegorist lies. Whatever adventures
his pilgrims pass through they are always flesh and
blood Englishmen of the seventeenth century, speaking and acting as English Puritans of their class would
have acted under the conditions which Bunyan's imagination created. The serious discourse with which
Christian and Faithful while away their march is as
true to life as the road or the fair through which they
pass. Ellwood the Quaker tells us in his autobiography
how he and his friend Ovy set forth to learn from Isaac
Pennington the true principles of Quakerism.

'We met by appointment at Stoken Church,' he says,
'with our staves in our hands, like a couple of pilgrims,
intending to walk on foot; and having taken some
refreshment and rest at Wiccomb, went on cheerfully in
the afternoon, entertaining each other with grave and
religious discourse, which made the walk the easier.'

It has often been said that the pilgrims in Bunyan's
story are as individual as Chaucer's pilgrims. Coleridge
goes so far as to complain that the allegory is so strongly

individualized that it ceases to be allegory, the characters become real persons with nicknames. Bunyan's characters themselves seem to feel that they are not abstractions, but men. Mr. By-ends protests when he is addressed by his name, 'That is not my name, but indeed it is a nickname given me by some that cannot abide me'. Another character modestly explains that his name is too good for him.

' "Your name is old Honesty, is it not," asks Greatheart. . . . So the old gentleman blushed and said, "Not Honesty in the abstract, but Honest is my name, and I wish that my nature shall agree to what I am called." '

Bunyan conceives his characters so clearly that he gives them not merely the utterances, but the features and the gestures appropriate to their parts. Mr. Honest recognizes Mr. Feeble-mind by his likeness to Mr. Fearing. 'He was mine uncle,' answers Fearing, 'he and I have been much of a temper; he was a little shorter than I, but yet we were much of a complexion.' At which old Honest observes with awkward candour, 'I am apt to believe you were related to one another: for you have his whitely look, a cast like his with your eye, and your speech is much alike.' Old Honest indeed is a keen observer of the little tricks of manner and bearing in which character reveals itself. 'Madam Bubble', he reflectively remarks to Mr. Stand-fast when he hears her name mentioned, 'Madam Bubble, is she not a tall comely dame, something of a swarthy complexion?' 'Right, you hit it,' says Stand-fast, 'she is just such a one.'

'Doth she not speak very smoothly, and give you a smile at the end of the sentence?'

'You fall right upon it again, these are her very actions.'

'Doth she not wear a great purse at her side, and is not her hand often in it fingering her money as if that was her heart's delight.'

' 'Tis just so—Had she stood by all this while, you could not more amply have set her forth before me.'

It is curious that Bunyan's power of individualizing his personages seems for a moment to leave him when he gives them proper names. Christiana and Mercy are clearly drawn, but Matthew, Joseph, Samuel, and James are little better than lay-figures. Beyond the fact that one was fond of his catechism and another too fond of green plums, there is little to distinguish them. And this is stranger because in the second part—inferior as it is on the whole to the first part—Bunyan handles his allegorical characters with more freedom and ease than in the first. The most vivid and impressive figure in it is Great-heart, the servant of Mr. Interpreter. He is a combination of two persons mentioned in the first part—of Mr. Great-grace, who is 'excellent good at his weapons' and bears in his face the scars of former battles, and of the nameless 'man of a very stout countenance' who fights his way through the armed men into the palace, 'cutting and hacking most fiercely'. But Great-heart is not merely the strong man armed; he beguiles the journey of the pilgrims he protects by the charms of his conversation. He begins, it is true, by a lengthy discourse on justification by faith, but he soon becomes humanized, and tells humorous stories of the pilgrims he has known, such as Mr. Fearing, 'one of the most troublesome pilgrims that ever I met with in all my days'.

To the children he is always kind and affable. He takes the little boy by the hand up the Hill Difficulty, and cheers the others on, 'Come, my pretty boys; how do you like going on a pilgrimage?'

He jokes with them because they run and get behind him when they meet the lions.

But when there is more real danger—when they go through the valley—he is first behind and then in front, saying to them: 'Be of good cheer—we shall be out by

and by,' or 'Let them that are most afraid keep close
to me.'

A very pleasing and natural touch is his delight in
pilgrims of his own temper. When they meet old
Honest asleep he at first takes them for thieves.

'What would, or could you a done, to a helped your-
self, if indeed we had been of that company,' asks
Great-heart.

'Done,' answers Honest, 'why I would a fought as
long as breath had been in me.'

'Well said, Father Honest,' quoth the guide, 'for by
this I know thou art a cock of the right kind.'

So, too, when they meet the man with his sword
drawn and his face all bloody from a three hours' fight
with three thieves, all the old soldierly instincts break
out in Great-heart at his story. 'Then said Great-heart
to Mr. Valiant-for-truth, "Thou hast worthily behaved
thyself; let me see thy sword." So he showed it him.

'When he had taken it in his hand and looked thereon
a while, he said, "Ha, it is a right Jerusalem Blade."

'Mr. Great-heart was delighted in him (for he loved
one greatly that he found to be a man of his hands).'

So vivid is the portrait, so characteristic the touches,
that one thinks Bunyan must have had in his mind's
eye when he drew it some real soldier, some one whom
he had served under at Newport, or some scarred
veteran of Naseby and Worcester, who had come back
to live in Bedford and turned his sword into a reaping-
hook.

In the second part of the *Pilgrim's Progress*, which
was published in 1684, six years after the first part,
Bunyan handles his allegorical characters with more
freedom. Sometimes he seems to forget the allegory for
a moment, and to let the sense of humour, or the story-
telling instinct, run away with him. Look, for instance,
at two episodes in the second part.

Matthew's illness after his over-indulgence in plums

is a little crudely described, but it is humorous as well
as realistic. 'Pray Sir,' says the afflicted mother to the
'antient and well-approved physician', 'try the utmost
of your skill with him, whatever it costs'; to which he
replies with professional dignity, 'Nay, I hope I shall
be reasonable'.

Matthew's reluctance to take his physic, and his
mother's moving entreaties to him, are copied from the
life. 'With that she touched one of the pills with the
tip of her tongue, "Oh, Matthew," said she, "this
potion is sweeter than honey." ' As to the pills themselves, 'he was to take them three at a time fasting, in
half a quarter of a pint of the tears of repentance'.

In the end, after the cure is wrought, the ancient
physician praises his pills. 'It is an universal pill, 'tis
good against all the diseases that pilgrims are incident
to.' 'Pray Sir,' replies the provident parent, 'make me
up twelve boxes of them'; and he does.

All this is, of course, allegorical, but the reader for-
gets all about its spiritual significance, and takes no
notice of the texts in the margin. He may be edified
by it in the end, but for the moment he is simply 'merry
and jocund', as the pilgrims are when they dance in
the road.

A page or two earlier comes the episode of Mercy's
love affair. At the House Beautiful Mercy

'had a visitor that pretended some goodwill unto her and his
name was Mr. Brisk, a man of some breeding, and that pretended
to religion; but a man that stuck very close to the world. So he
came once or twice or more to Mercy, and offered love unto her.
Now Mercy was of a fair countenance, and therefore the more
alluring.

'Her mind also was, to be always busying of herself in doing;
for when she had nothing to do for herself she would be making
of hose and garments for others, and would bestow them upon
them that had need. And Mr. Brisk, not knowing where or
how she disposed of what she made, seemed to be greatly taken,

for he found her never idle. "I will warrant her a good house-wife," quoth he to himself. Mercy then revealed the business to the maidens that were of the house, and enquired of them concerning him, for they did know him better than she. So they told her, that he was a very busy young man, and one that pretended to religion; but was, as they feared, a stranger to the power of that which was good.

' "Nay, then," said Mercy, "I will look no more on him; for I purpose never to have a clog to my soul."

'Prudence then replied that there needed no great matter of discouragement to be given to him, her continuing so as she had begun to do for the poor would quickly cool his courage. So the next time he comes, he finds her at her old work a-making of things for the poor. Then said he, "What! always at it?" "Yes," said she, "either for myself or for others." "And what canst thee earn a day?" quoth he. "I do these things", said she, "that I may be rich in good works, laying up in store a good founda-tion against the time to come, that I may lay hold on eternal life." "Why, prithee, what dost thou do with them?" said he. "Clothe the naked," said she. With that his countenance fell. So he forebore to come at her again; and when he was asked the reason why, he said, "Mercy was a pretty lass, but troubled with ill-conditions." '

Mercy's comment puts the finishing touch to the whole picture. 'Mercy and he', observes Prudence, 'are of tempers so different, that I believe they will never come together.' Then says Mercy, with an air of modest pride, and doubtless with her usual blush, 'I might a had husbands afore now, tho' I spake not of it to any; but they were such as did not like my conditions, though never did any of them find fault with my person.'

Here the allegory disappears altogether. We have simply an incident in the life of a fair Puritan described with absolute fidelity to nature; the actors are ordinary men and women of the time, and the fact that their names have a moral significance makes no difference to the story. We are passing, in fact, from allegory to the novel with an improving tendency. Bunyan is here the forerunner of Hannah More and a whole generation of novelists who sought to combine realistic fiction and moral teaching, while Mr. Brisk is the not very remote ancestor of Coelebs in search of a wife. In the days when the English novel did not exist, an allegory which was so like a story of everyday life had a charm which it is not easy for us to appreciate now. Bunyan was not merely the first of English allegorists; he is one of the founders of the English novel and the forerunner of Defoe.

It is time to sum up this analysis of the causes of the popularity of the *Pilgrim's Progress*. Bunyan took a familiar idea as the basis of his story, and told it in a language that was simple or elevated just as the subject required. He put the essence of his own life into the story; put into it reproductions of the life he saw round him, and recollections of the books he had read; made his actors real men and women, and made his narrative by turns satirical and enthusiastic, humorous and pathetic, realistic and romantic. It was no wonder that 'the outside of his dream' attracted his readers, but what united and harmonized all these different elements was the inner spirit of his dream. That which gives the book a lasting power is the ideal of life which underlies it all—of life as the Puritan conceived it then and conceives it still. The *Pilgrim's Progress* is the prose epic of English Puritanism; it contains much that is only temporary and local in its application, but unlike Milton's epic it can be understood everywhere, and has been translated into most tongues. Its real foundation is not a doctrinal system but a moral conception. Omit a few theological discussions, and it appeals to the Puritan of all creeds and all races. Everywhere the seeker after personal holiness or ideal perfection turns his face from his own home, and sets forth on the same journey: let others stay by their farm or their merchandise, he must follow the light which he sees, or thinks he sees; happy if at last he beholds the shining spires of the city he travels to, glad if he catches by the way only a glimpse of the glory of it. Some may laugh at him as a fool, others may tell him there is no such city; like Bunyan he heeds them not, but dreams his dream and holds it true.

BURNET AS AN HISTORIAN[1]

BURNET has a place to himself in English historical literature, midway between the historians proper and the writers of memoirs. He belongs to both groups, for he attempted first to tell the story of a portion of the past from written records and afterwards to tell the story of the age in which he lived from his own reminiscences and the recollections of others. Posterity sets most value on Burnet as the narrator of contemporary history, but that should not make us forget that he began as a professional historian and that his own age rated him highest in that capacity. It is partly to Burnet's experience in writing the history of the past that the value of his memoirs of his own time is due. He had learnt to appreciate the relative importance of events by writing history as he had learned to appreciate and describe character by writing biography. His early writings possess an intrinsic value of their own, and an examination of their characteristics throws light on the character of his most lasting achievement, the *History of My Own Time*. For both reasons they deserve study.

Burnet's first historical work was the *Memoirs of the Lives and Actions of James and William Dukes of Hamilton*.[2] The book was rather a history of the times of the two dukes than their biographies. In the catalogue of books printed and published in Easter Term, 1678, it stands on the next page to an announcement of the fourth edition of Spottiswoode's *History of the Church and State of Scotland*. Originally it was designed

[1] Reprinted from Introduction to *A Life of Gilbert Burnet*, by T. E. S. Clarke and H. C. Foxcroft, 1907. By permission of the Cambridge University Press.

[2] See T. E. S. Clarke and H. C. Foxcroft, *A Life of Gilbert Burnet* (1907), pp. 98, 115, 150.

to be a continuation of Spottiswoode's work, and it is said that the title-page of some copies of the first edition actually described it as the second volume of Spottiswoode. In the introduction prefixed to the *Lives*, Burnet set forth at length his views on the function of the historian and the qualities which he should possess. Some histories, he said, were nothing but romances; full of great and palpable errors because their authors 'lived out of business', and took too many things upon trust. Others were full of slanders and lies. There was 'such foul dealing in the histories of our own time' that people had learnt to suspect histories of past times, and to regard all other writings of that nature as equally untrustworthy. In reality only two classes of historians deserved credit. First, those who had helped to make history. 'Of all men those who have been themselves engaged in affairs are the fittest to write history, as knowing best how matters were designed and carried on.' Secondly, those who write with authentic documents at their disposal. 'Those that have had the perusal of the cabinets of great ministers, and of public records, are the best qualified for giving the world a true information of affairs.'

Burnet himself belonged to the second class. He had been given free access to the abundant and important correspondence of the first Duke of Hamilton—a correspondence which no previous English historian had seen, and one full of revelations about the policy of the late King and the origin of the civil troubles in England and Scotland. At first he intended merely to extract the information the letters contained and to summarize the results. Afterwards Sir Robert Moray persuaded him to adopt a different method. He 'gave me', says Burnet, 'such reasons to change the whole work, and to insert most of the papers at their full length, that prevailed on me to do it'. The reason Burnet gives is that 'the common failings of historians have in this last age made

people desire to see papers, records, and letters published at their full length'. The public in short wanted
authentic documents instead of narrative of very dubious
value, and the reception accorded to the first volume
of Rushworth's *Collections*, published in 1659, had
shown how thirsty people were to learn the truth about
the late revolution. Dull though that book may seem to
us now it was full of interest then, and to study it
became an indisputable part of every gentleman's political education. Pepys, who bought a copy of the
volume in November 1663, read it with avidity. 'So
to my office writing letters,' says his *Diary* under
December 26, 1663, 'and then to read and make an end
of Rushworth, which I did, and do say that it is a book
the most worth reading for a man of my condition or
any man that hopes to come to any publique condition
in the world that I do know.'

Burnet's book was welcomed for the same reason, but
it was a great deal more than a mere collection of documents like Rushworth's: it was the first political biography of the modern type, combining a narrative of a
man's life with a selection from his letters, so the novelty
of the form added to the attractions of the matter.

Though the materials on which Burnet based his
work made it infinitely superior to the productions of
the 'scribbling historians' he condemns in his preface,
he did not exclusively rely on the Hamilton Papers.
Where they failed him he sought and obtained information from Hamilton's officers, as for instance Sir James
Turner, who contributed an account of the Preston
campaign, and from other 'persons of great honour and
worth'. Burnet also says that he owed some of his
knowledge of the time to his father, whose conversations had given him 'a great deal more of the truth of
these affairs than is generally known'.

Accordingly the *Lives* of the Hamiltons at once
became an authority, as indeed it deserved. Sir Robert

Moray, charmed with the result of his advice, declared that he 'did not think there was a truer history writ since the apostles' days'.[1] As it was originally written it was too true, or at least too frank. The long delay in the publication of the book was due to this. The dedication is dated October 21, 1673, the warrant for a license November 3, 1673, and the title-page 1677, but the book is not advertised in the *Term Catalogue* as published until Easter Term, 1678.[2] Political reasons, such as the quarrel between the third Duke of Hamilton and Lauderdale, no doubt contributed to hinder publication, for from November 1673 Lauderdale became Burnet's enemy.[3] But there was much in the book which it must have seemed doubtful policy to print when the questions touched were so closely connected with existing political controversies.

Charles II was willing to admit a certain amount of freedom of speech. When Burnet represented that he would be obliged to show the faults of some of his father's ministers, the King said that 'such things were unavoidable in a history; and therefore he allowed me to tell the truth freely'.[4] Charles read parts of the *Lives* himself, 'particularly', says Burnet, 'the account I give of the ill-conduct of the bishops, that occasioned the beginning of the wars: and told me that he was well pleased with it'.[5] The King's ministers seem to have been less easy to satisfy, and the manuscript of the *Lives* (now in the British Museum) shows signs of many insertions and many omissions.[6] Burnet had,

---

[1] *Burnet's History of My Own Time*, ed. Osmund Airy (1900), i. 27.

[2] Arber, *Term Catalogues*, i. 312; *Cal. State Papers, Dom. 1673-75*, p. 4.　　　　[3] Clarke and Foxcroft, *Life*, p. 118.

[4] Preface, p. xv.　　　　[5] *Own Time*, i. 356.

[6] Add. MS. 33259. See an article by Mr. Robert Dewar, entitled 'Burnet on the Scottish Troubles', in the *Scottish Historical Review* for July 1907, pp. 384-98. The preface is different to the printed one, and the manuscript is imperfect, ending in July 1647, i.e. on p. 404 of the edition of 1852, which contains 555 pp.

according to his own account, exercised considerable discretion and reticence. 'Neither shall I tell', says a passage in the original preface, 'how soon it was finished, nor with what caution it was considered, what things concerning those times were fit to be published, or what were to be suppressed.'[1] He confesses that he 'did conceal several things that related to the king', and 'left out some passages that were in his letters', because 'in some of them there was too much craft and anger'.[2] Some of the passages in the manuscript were obviously omitted because they revealed the King's insincerity in his negotiations with the Covenanters in 1639. Other passages deleted referred to Lauderdale or Lauderdale's father. Some things Burnet had left out as injurious to the reputation of various noble houses, and when he came to relate the delivery of Charles I to the English in January 1647, he again confessed that 'in invidious passages I have spared the memories and families of the unhappy actors'.[3] It was also desirable not to go into the precise nature of the treaty which Charles I made with the Scottish commissioners at Carisbrooke in December 1647, but it is doubtful whether Burnet knew the whole truth about that subject, since the details of the agreement were not revealed until the publication of the second volume of Clarendon's *History of the Rebellion* in 1703. For political reasons it was still more necessary to slur over the pledges which Charles II had made to the Scots in 1650 and 1651. No one would gather from the *Lives of the Hamiltons* that Charles II took the Covenant, and the brevity of the account of the events of those two years given in the life of the second Duke is no doubt due to considerations of this nature quite as much as to the scantiness of the papers relating to the period.[4] Finally, there was the great difficulty that

---

[1] *Scottish Historical Review*, iv. 398.
[2] Clarke and Foxcroft, *Life*, p. 99.   [3] *Lives*, p. 397.
[4] Cf. *Lives*, pp. 529, 537, and *Own Time*, i. 53, 110.

Burnet had undertaken to eulogize both Charles I and the first Duke of Hamilton, which made it necessary to handle very delicately the causes of the breach between the two, the Duke's imprisonment in 1643, and the King's distrust of the Duke even after their reconciliation in 1646.[1]

Yet though Burnet suppressed some passages in the letters he published, and omitted some material facts, it is not just to charge him with dishonesty. For some of the suppressions and omissions the censorship to which his book was subjected is responsible; the reticence obligatory upon a man writing about such recent political events accounts for others. That he was biased in favour of the royalist cause is evident, but he is much fairer than most writers of the period, and on the whole it must be said that he told as much of the truth as it was possible to publish at the time when he wrote.

Having learnt the difficulties which beset the writer of contemporary history Burnet had next to struggle with a new problem. In judging the *History of the Reformation* it is necessary to take into account the difficulties under which a seventeenth-century historian laboured. He wrote before the British Museum existed, before the historical manuscripts in the Bodleian were catalogued, when the State Papers and the Public Records were in two separate repositories and both collections in a state of chaos. An historian who attempted to base his book on unprinted authorities met with obstacles of every kind. Fuller, who undertook a similar task to Burnet, describes his own experience thus.

'A greater volume of general Church-Historie might be made

[1] The third Duke of Hamilton was evidently dissatisfied with the original draft of the *Lives*. He complained that it contained 'great errors' and that Burnet was too precipitate in trying to publish it. Probably, however, he referred to the account of the Preston campaign. (Sir James Turner's *Memoirs*, 1829, p. 254.)

with less time, pains, and cost: for in the making thereof, I had *Straw* provided me to burn my *Brick*; I mean, could find what I needed, in printed Books. Whereas in this Brittish Church-History, I must (as well as I could) provide my own Straw, and my pains have been scattered all over the Land, by riding, writing, going, sending, chiding, begging, praying, and some times paying too, to procure manuscript materials.'[1]

Burnet met with difficulties of a similar nature. He was allowed, he tells us, free access to the State Paper Office, by a warrant which the Earl of Sunderland procured for him.

'That office', he adds, 'was first set up by the care of the earl of Salisbury, when he was secretary of state in king James' time: which though it is a copious and certain repertory for those that are to write our history ever since the papers of state were laid up there, yet for the former times it contains only such papers as that great minister could then gather together; so that it is not so complete in the transactions that fall within the time of which I write.'[2] Burnet procured some papers from that source, but the privilege of access was of little value so long as the documents it contained were unarranged. When he was preparing his third volume he visited the office again and found it 'in much better order and method than it was above thirty years ago, when I saw it last.'[3]

Much more serviceable to Burnet was the great collection of manuscripts in the Cotton Library, but there his difficulty was to get at them. The modern researcher, guaranteed by two respectable householders, obtains access to them at the British Museum without any trouble. But Sir John Cotton refused Burnet admission to his library unless he could obtain recommendations from the Archbishop of Canterbury and one of the Secretaries of State, and Archbishop Sancroft declined to interfere on Burnet's behalf. Burnet obtained admission through one of Cotton's relations,

---

[1] *The Appeal of Iniured Innocence* (1659), pt. i, 23–4.
[2] *History of the Reformation*, ed. N. Pocock (1865), ii. 217–18.
[3] Ibid. iii. 41.

and copied hard for ten days till Cotton's return to town again shut him out of the library. This was when the first volume was in preparation; after it was published and had met with universal applause no more difficulties were put in his way.[1] There were other manuscripts in other collections of which Burnet procured copies, all duly enumerated and traced in Pocock's admirable edition of his book.[2] In his own words, 'I laid out for manuscripts and searched into all the offices'. He even went so far as to publish an advertisement in the *London Gazette* asking people to lend him papers.

'All persons that have any Papers concerning the Reformation of the Church of *England*, or of any Ministers of State or Clergymen, during the Reigns of King *Edward the Sixth*, Queen *Mary*, or Queen *Elizabeth*, are most earnestly desired to give notice of them to Mr. *Richard Chiswell* Bookseller at the *Rose and Crown* in *St. Pauls* Churchyard, that they may be perused by the Author of the first part of that History, already extant, in order to the compleating of that necessary Work.'[3]

These documents were not simply employed to serve as a basis for Burnet's narrative. Imitating the method he had already followed in his *Lives* of the Hamiltons he appended to each volume of his text a collection of 'records', intended not only to justify his statements but to inform public opinion and to serve future historians. Hallam praises Burnet's book for this particular feature.

It 'has the signal merit of having been the first in English, as far as I remember, which is fortified by a large appendix of documents. This, though frequent in Latin, had not been so usual in the modern languages.'[4]

Unluckily Burnet's energy and zeal in searching for truth was not accompanied by equal care in stating it.

[1] *Reformation*, iii. 19.   [2] Ibid. vii. 65–122.
[3] *London Gazette*, no. 1473, Jan. 1, 1679/80.
[4] Henry Hallam, *Introduction to the Literature of Europe* (1872), iv. 369.

He wrote in a hurry and his work swarms with inaccuracies of detail. On that point the testimony of his editor is emphatic and conclusive. 'It is scarcely', writes Mr. Pocock, 'an exaggeration of the state of the case to say that the author's dates are nearly as often wrong as right.' In his quotation or summaries of other writers: 'It is not hastily to be taken for granted that he represents the sense of the author from whom he copies, for such were his inaccurate habits of thought, that where there is but a slight alteration in the words, there will often be some change in the sense. His strong prejudices again seem in some cases to have led him unconsciously to alter the sense of a passage to which he is referring.' The papers he printed had been copied in haste, and by unskilled transcribers, and they were also carelessly printed. In the three volumes of documents selected for publication 'after making allowance for all the alterations in the spelling both of common words and proper names, there remained about ten thousand downright mistakes'. Yet none of these shortcomings seem to this austere critic to justify the acrimony with which Burnet's enemies assaulted his honesty. Quoting a crucial instance Mr. Pocock remarks:

'There is no reason whatever to accuse Burnet of wilfully misrepresenting this document, yet in point of fact it was copied with so many mistakes, and so large an omission, that it afforded a good handle for the accusation brought against him, of having purposely falsified documents to suit his purpose. . . . Yet in truth nothing more is shewn by it, than to how great an extent an inaccurate and prejudiced mind can be deceived into the belief that certain facts make for its own view of a given case.'[1]

One proof of Burnet's honesty was his willingness to own and correct his blunders. When he was printing his second volume a clergyman sent him a number of corrections to the first. These he published at the end of the second volume, 'being neither ashamed to confess

[1] *Reformation*, vii. 54, 55, 174–5.

my faults, nor unwilling to acknowledge from what hand I received better information. My design in writing is to discover truth, and to deliver it down impartially to the next age; so I should think it both a mean and criminal piece of vanity to suppress this discovery of my errors'.[1] What Burnet did in this case with Fulman's corrections he did later with those sent him by Baker and Strype.

The candour which this procedure shows is not common amongst historians, and is very much to Burnet's credit. He endeavoured to be equally candid in his general treatment of the subject, not to conceal the faults of the Reformers themselves and to state fairly the views of the different leaders and the conflicting parties. In this he was but partially successful, for he was neither impartial nor unprejudiced, and he wrote at a moment when popular feeling in England was vehemently excited against the Catholics, and shared himself the fears and passions of the time. Nevertheless, the author of the latest history of the Reformation finds it possible to praise his honesty in spite of the reservations he is forced to make about his accuracy.

'No book', wrote Canon Dixon, 'has been more severely criticised. . . . For myself, I am far from joining in the unmeasured condemnation of this work which has been pronounced by some writers of authority. It should be remembered that it was the first work of the nature of a general history, founded on authentic records, that appeared in this country. The author was very laborious, and he studied to be exact. It is true that he has strong prejudices; but who is free from prejudice? The question is, whether his prejudices make him dishonest. I do not think they do. He now and then makes a downright blunder; but it is usually one of pure prejudice, being often an unwarrantable inference from authorities fairly given; and he usually furnishes the means of confuting himself. But he is never found giving to all appearance the whole of a

[1] Ibid. ii. 2.

story, and suppressing everything that makes against his own view. He is never found passing entirely over events that do not favour him.'[1]

In judging an historical book on a great subject the design as well as the execution has to be taken into consideration. It is not merely accuracy in details and honesty we require, but some conception of the general significance of the events narrated and of their place in the world's history. Judged in this respect, Burnet's book was as much superior to the books of his predecessors, Fuller and Heylyn, as it was in knowledge and research. A recent writer does not hesitate to say that it marks the beginning of a new epoch in historical science and that Burnet's *History* raised the controversy it handled to a higher plane of thought.

'It was the first attempt to write a judicial account of the English Reformation from authentic sources. The point of view is frankly Protestant; but Burnet has sufficient breadth of mind and sufficient confidence in his own case to be above the vulgar artifices of concealment and misrepresentation. He approaches his subject in a philosophic spirit. The Reformation was to his mind a work of providence accomplished through human and imperfect agents. There were deadly errors to be rooted out and priceless truths to be recovered from oblivion. But the errors were only recognized by slow degrees; the truth was long in dawning on the minds of Protestants. Hence the fluctuations of opinion which delayed the progress of reform. Hence too the disagreements of reformed communions on matters of speculation: there must be differences when finite intellects are independently engaged in the exploration of the infinite. But on essentials all the Reformers were agreed: and this is sufficient to confirm our faith in human reason. There is a spiritual unity among the Protestants which has more value because it is more spontaneous and sincere than the formal unity of Rome. Results, then, justify the Reformation. We need not shrink from owning that its course was marked by crimes and influenced by personal ambitions. The work of Protestantism can neither

[1] R. W. Dixon, *History of the Church of England* (1895), ii. 359.

be proved by vindicating nor refuted by aspersing the characters of those who smoothed the way for it. The highest ends of Providence are always brought about through natural causes, often by the hands of most unworthy agents. Good is educed from evil, and many selfish wills are yoked together to fulfil a purpose of which they are at best but half conscious.

'Burnet in fact is the exponent of a new historical method. He is less concerned with persons than with the genesis of new ideas in the turmoil of events. His vindication of reformed religion rests upon a contrast between the system into which the earliest reformers were born, and that which was established as the consequence of their revolt.'[1]

Possessing all these great merits—research, honesty, and breadth of view—it is not surprising that the minor defects of Burnet's book were overlooked, and that the *History of the Reformation* became at once a popular success. The House of Commons publicly thanked him for the service he had rendered to the Protestant religion. The book was read not only by scholars and politicians, but by men of the world. The most brilliant courtier and wit of the period, John Wilmot, Earl of Rochester, solaced his illness by reading the book of the hour. 'He was also then entertaining himself', says Burnet, describing the origin of their acquaintance, 'in that low state of his health, with the first part of the *History of the Reformation* then newly come out, with which he seemed not ill pleased.'

About November 1680, in the interval between the publication of the first and second volumes of the *History of the Reformation*, Burnet published *Some Passages of the Life and Death of the right honourable John Earl of Rochester*.[2] The little book deserves the praise which Johnson bestowed upon it.[3] Judged simply as literature, it is the finest thing Burnet ever wrote,

[1] 'Gilbert Burnet,' a lecture by H. W. C. Davis, in *Typical English Churchmen*, S.P.C.K., 1902, pp. 173-4.
[2] *Term Catalogues*, i. 417.
[3] *Lives of the English Poets*, ed. G. B. Hill (1905), i. 222.

and represents his style at its best. Historically, its value lies in the picture it gives us of the character and the ideas of a man who was at once a nobleman and a wit, and in the light it throws upon the life and thought of the time. As Miss Foxcroft points out, the dialogues between Burnet and Rochester are rendered with singular felicity, and they appear to be reproduced with singular fidelity, too.

'As far as I can remember', writes Burnet, 'I have faithfully repeated the substance of our Arguments: I have not concealed the strongest things he said to me, but though I have not enlarged on all the Excursions of his Wit in setting them off, Yet I have given them their full strength, as he expressed them; and as far as I could recollect, have used his own words.'

And, again:

'I do not pretend to have given the formal words that he said, though I have done that where I could remember them. . . . I did not take Notes of our Discourses last Winter after we parted; so I may have perhaps in the setting out of my Answers to him, have enlarged on several things both more fully and more regularly, than I could say them in such free Discourses as we had. I am not so sure of all I set down as said by me, as I am of all said by him to me. But yet the substance of the greatest part, even of that, is the same.'[1]

This account which Burnet gives us of his way of reporting Rochester's conversations is of particular interest. We see him learning the art and developing the method which he practised later to so much purpose in the *History of My Own Time*.

A year later, in November 1681, Burnet's *Life and Death of Sir Matthew Hale* appeared.[2] To it he prefixed a short disquisition on the principles of biographical writing. No part of history, said he, was more instructive and delighting than the lives of great and worthy

---

[1] *Some Passages*, pp. 124, 162-3.
[2] *Term Catalogues*, i. 461.

men, but to the general reader biographies of heroes and princes were on the whole more entertaining than useful. Not only were their authors often too biased by interest or resentment to write the truth, but even when such biographies were truthfully written they were lacking in instructiveness. The lives of private men were more profitable. They set before the eyes of the average man 'things that are more imitable'; they showed him wisdom and virtue 'in such plain and familiar Instances, as do both direct him better, and perswade him more'. Burnet's design in writing was, he tells us, 'to propose a pattern of heroic virtue' to the world in general, and to lawyers in particular, a life which they might take as a model, as Hale himself was said to have taken the life of Pomponius Atticus by Cornelius Nepos.

One great disadvantage Burnet laboured under. He had not known Hale personally, though he had often observed him amongst the congregation in the Rolls chapel. 'In my life I never saw so much Gravity tempered with that sweetness, and set off with so much vivacity, as appeared in his looks and behaviour, which disposed me to a veneration for him, which I never had for any, with whom I was not acquainted.'

He had, however, help from men whose acquaintance with Hale was intimate and of long standing. Robert Gibbon, of the Middle Temple, one of Hale's executors, and apparently for a long time one of his clerks, supplied Burnet with memorials and reminiscences. 'One of the greatest men of the Law,' perhaps Heneage Finch, furnished an abstract of the character of Hale, based upon long observation and much converse with him. This information Burnet employed with much skill and tact, producing a life-like portrait of the great lawyer. The book was plainly and simply written, for its object was to set Hale out 'in the same simplicity in which he lived'. Dates are few, and some important biographical facts are not very exactly stated. Yet compared with

Sprat's account of Cowley, which passed then as a model biography, Burnet's life is a model, for Sprat gives as few facts as possible and drowns them all in a flood of elegant verbiage. Burnet's object was not so much to relate a career as to describe a man, and he succeeds in bringing out the salient points of Hale's character with great distinctness. Little traits, such as the carelessness of Hale about his dress, his care for old horses and dogs, his scrupulousness about bad money and similar characteristics, give life and reality to the portrait, and are just the things which most contemporary biographers would have omitted as too trivial to mention. Contemporaries generally accepted it as a good portrait. Roger North criticizes it, alleging that Hale was timid and too fond of popularity, vain and too open to flattery, and rather scoffs at the scientific and theological attainments of the judge, though admitting that he was 'an incomparable magistrate' and 'a most excellent person'. For the book and its author he had nothing but condemnation.

'Gilbert Burnet', he said, 'has pretended to write his life, but wanted both information and understanding for such an undertaking. Nay that which he intended chiefly, to touch the people with a panegyric, he was not fit for, because he knew not the virtues he had fit to be praised, and I should recommend to him the lives of Jack Cade, Wat Tyler, or Cromwell, as characters fitter for his learning and pen to work upon than him.'[1]

Roger North little knew when he wrote this that Burnet had devoted his pen to Cromwell. He began writing his memoirs about August 1683, a few months after the publication of the life of Hale, and it was about 1687 that he wrote the sketch of Cromwell which, in an enlarged form, occupies so many pages of his greatest work.[2]

[1] *Lives of the Norths*, ed. A. Jessopp (1890), iii. 102.

[2] *A Supplement to Burnet's History of My Own Time*, ed. H. C. Foxcroft (1902), pp. 229–42; *Own Time*, i. 65–83.

Burnet's *History of My Own Time* was the work of many years. Both volumes appeared posthumously, one in 1724, the other in 1734, but the original narrative had been revised throughout and to a great extent rewritten. 'I begun to write in the year 1683. I continued in the year 84, and ended it in the year 1686, and have now writ it all over again and ended it in August 1703, and revised it in March 1711.'[1] This is Burnet's account of the composition of the section narrating the reign of Charles II, and other parts of his work went through a similar process. We have therefore in the *History of My Own Time* something different from most autobiographical memoirs. Such memoirs are generally written at the end of a man's career, looking back over a long period of years when memory is apt to confuse the outline of the landscape, and fancy to alter somewhat its colours. But in the case of Burnet the *History* is based upon a series of impressions written down soon after the events recorded, and sometimes almost at the moment when they happened. For instance, although the portion of the *History* dealing with the reign of James II did not take its present form till much later, it is throughout founded on a strictly contemporaneous narrative, and is therefore of higher authority than the portion relating to the reign of Charles II, which is only in part based on such evidence.

In estimating the value of Burnet's statements we have the further advantage that much of the original narrative is still in existence. Thanks to Miss Foxcroft the portions which survive have been printed and admirably edited in a *Supplement to Burnet's History of My Own Time* (Clarendon Press, 1902), so that a comparison of the two versions is easy. For Charles II's reign we have only a long fragment covering the period 1660 to 1664, and some smaller fragments relating to the years 1679–83. For the fifteen years from 1664 to

[1] *Own Time*, i. 615.

1679 there is a great gap in the manuscript. We have the whole of the first version of the reign of James II and about half of the reign of William III, that is, from October 1684, just before the death of Charles II, to January 1696, just before the Treaty of Ryswick. From January 1696 to August 1708 the original version is again missing, but for the period from 1708 to 1713 it has been preserved.

It is possible, therefore, to compare Burnet's earlier impressions with his later ones, to trace the development of his political views as they were affected by alterations in his own position and changes in English politics, and to see how the *History of My Own Time* gradually assumed its present shape.

Ranke, who was the first to attempt to compare the two versions, thinks the earlier one more vigorous and more clear, the characters fresher and truer to life; 'persons and events', he says, 'appear more as they are', and he concludes by speaking of Burnet as 'ruining his own work'. Politically he describes the later version as intentionally more Whiggish in tone, more hostile to the Tories and to the clergy. Nottingham being a Tory is treated more harshly in the second version than the first, Marlborough being a Whig leader, more indulgently.[1] It was natural, however, that Burnet should revise his earlier estimates of public men by the light of their subsequent careers, and that time should alter his opinions on measures as well as men. Though it is always necessary to compare Burnet's earlier with his later view, there is nothing discreditable to him in the fact that he made such changes, and it does not diminish the value of his *History*.

The nature of the changes which Burnet made is pointed out by Miss Foxcroft in *A Life of Gilbert Burnet*,[2] and they are set forth at length and in detail

[1] Ranke, *History of England*, vi. 73-7.
[2] Pp. 403-4.

in the introduction to her *Supplement* to Burnet.[1] Some alterations were made in self-defence. Burnet suppressed for instance some indications of his early intimacy with Lauderdale, and concealed the radical nature of the difference between his earlier and later views on the question of passive obedience.[2] Many other alterations were merely the natural consequence of the complete change in the scheme of the work which Burnet made in 1703 when he began to recast the whole work. In the original sketch the life of the author formed the thread by which the various episodes were connected, but he finally resolved to convert his autobiographical memoirs into a formal history. Clarendon in exactly the same way turned his life of himself into the *History of the Rebellion,* and in each case the result was the omission of a number of passages relating to the author himself. Burnet's abandonment of his original design 'destroyed to a great extent the unity of the work', and made his narrative less coherent and less orderly. Clarendon's change of plan, for various reasons, was not so detrimental in its literary results as Burnet's, but it also led to much disorder and many repetitions.[3]

From the moment when he began to write Burnet had in view the ultimate publication of his memoirs. 'I must begin', he wrote in 1683, 'with a character of the King and Duke, but I must give them at present very imperfect, otherwise what I write may happen to be seized upon, and I know not what may be made of that; but I will venture a good deal now, and if ever I outlive them I will say the rest when it will be more safe.' In 1687 Burnet told the Earl of Middleton that if the prosecution against him in Scotland was not dropped he would be driven to print 'an *Apology* for myself; in which I will be forced to make a recital of all

---

[1] *Supplement*, pp. xvi–xxi.   [2] Ibid., p. 515.
[3] See articles on Clarendon's *History of the Rebellion*, in the *English Historical Review,* xix. 26, 246, 464.

that share that I have had in Affairs these twenty years past: and in which I must mention a vast number of particulars, *that I am affraid will be displeasing to His Majesty*'. Again, in October 1688, when he was on the point of embarking for England with William of Orange, Burnet left instructions, in case of his death, for the printing of what he then termed 'my secret *History*'.[1]

The phrase is suggestive. In the preface to his *Life* of Hale, Burnet regretted that most biographers who wrote about heroes and princes did not or could not tell the whole truth. 'Few have been able to imitate the Patterns Suetonius set the world, in Writing the Lives of the *Roman* Emperors, with the same freedom that they had led them.' Apparently Burnet wished to write the life of Charles II with similar frankness, and the famous comparison of that sovereign to Tiberius[2] seems to show that he had been reading Suetonius when he wrote it.

In the final version, however, Burnet had a different model before him. He was familiar with the best modern historians. In his *History of the Reformation* he had taken Paolo Sarpi as an example for imitation. Sarpi's *History of the Council of Trent* he described as 'writ with as much life, and beauty, and authority, as had been ever seen in any human writing', and he styled it 'that noble pattern, which the famous Venetian friar has given to all the writers of ecclesiastical history'.[3]

Now Burnet copied De Thou.[4]

'I have made him', he writes at the beginning of his auto-biography, 'my pattern in writing, and as I read most of him manny years ago, and formed my designe in writting from that

---

[1] *Supplement*, pp. 47, 526; Burnet, *A Collection of Eighteen Papers* (1689), p. 149.

[2] *Own Time*, i. 613–14. [3] *Reformation*, i. 581; ii. 355; iii. 10.

[4] Historiarum sui Temporis Libri cxxxviii ab anno 1543 usque ad annum 1607; accedunt ejusdem de vita sua commentariorum Libri sex.

great Originall; so after I had ended my History, I read him all over again, to see how farre I had risen up in my imitation of him, and was not a little pleased to find that if I did not flatter my selfe too much, I had in some degree answered my designe in resembling him.'[1]

It was also the example of De Thou which suggested to Burnet the idea of supplementing the *History* by adding to it as an appendix a short life of himself. In the *History of My Own Time*, however, Burnet diverged in several points from his original. 'I have avoided', says he, 'a particular recital of warlike actions both in battles and sieges.' Marshal Schomberg had advised him 'never to meddle in the relation of military matters', on the ground that civilian writers usually committed great blunders when they did so.[2] Laying this advice to heart he declined to enter into the particulars either of the battle of Sedgemoor or that of the Boyne, and contented himself with stating the results.

In the same way Burnet informs us that he did not endeavour to be as copious as De Thou in the relation of foreign affairs. Although in dealing with the wars of William III's and Anne's reigns he felt obliged to give a tolerably full account of European events during each year, it is evident that his knowledge of them was slight and mainly derived from newspapers. Ranke justly observes that 'of a comprehension of the state of affairs in the world at large, such as Thuanus attempted, there is, however, in Burnet scarcely the faintest trace. He keeps to the province of Scottish and English affairs, with which he unites those of Holland and France, but only so far as these affect the former, and as they came to his knowledge by staying in those countries.'[3]

Burnet again diverged from his model in saying very little about 'the lives and writing of learned men'. The literature of the fifty years of English history with

[1] *Supplement*, p. 451. [2] *Own Time*, i. 49; cf. *Supplement*, p. 165.
[3] Ranke, *History of England*, vi. 46.

which he deals is passed over, and his references to the few great writers of the period he does mention are of the briefest character. Hobbes is mentioned as the author of 'a very wicked book with a very strange title', and there are a few sentences setting forth the evil principles it inculcated, and their effect in corrupting his contemporaries. Locke is never mentioned at all, and though Hoadly is praised for his confutation of Filmer's *Patriarcha*, there is no reference to the more effective answer contained in Locke's *Two Treatises of Government*. Of the poets Dryden is named as a dramatist only, as the man who above all others debased the stage and demoralized the public. He is stigmatized as 'the great master at dramatic poesy' who was 'a monster of immodesty and of impurity of all sorts'. Marvell's name could hardly be omitted on account of his controversy with Parker; he is styled 'the liveliest droll of the age, who writ in a burlesque strain, but with so peculiar and so entertaining a conduct, that from the king down to the tradesman his book was read with great pleasure'.[1]

Nobody would gather from these allusions that Dryden wrote anything besides plays, or Marvell anything but prose. The only sign of any appreciation of poetry on the part of Burnet is his praise of *Paradise Lost*. After relating Milton's escape at the Restoration the Bishop says that Milton lived many years afterwards, 'much visited by all strangers, and much admired by all at home for the poems he writ, though he was then blind; chiefly that of Paradise Lost, in which there is a nobleness both of contrivance and execution, that, though he affected to write in blank verse without rithm, and made many new and rough words, yet it was esteemed the beautifulest and perfectest poem that ever was writ, at least in our language'.[2]

On the other hand, though Burnet was indifferent to the literature of the time in which he lived, or rather

[1] *Own Time*, i. 187, 260, 269.   [2] Ibid. i. 163.

to *belles lettres* in general, he devotes a considerable space to the Royal Society and incidentally to the scientific movement of the age. At one time he dabbled in science himself: 'I run thro some courses of Chimistry which helped me in my Philosophicall notions.'[1] At another he began to study mathematics, and found the subject enthralling. 'I was much taken with them and I had such a memory that I could carry on a progresse of equations long without pen ink or paper, so that I was pursued with them day and night.'[1] These things, however, were but diversions. The fullness with which theological and ecclesiastical controversies are treated in his pages and the space devoted to the different schools of religious thought and the characters of the great churchmen show plainly what Burnet's real interests were. For him the great event of the time in the intellectual sphere was the rise of that 'new set of men' in the church of the Restoration upon whom 'men of narrower thoughts and fiercer tempers' afterwards fastened the 'name of Latitudinarians'. He explained their position; he set forth their aims and their hopes; he traced their influence on church and state; that is his contribution to the history of English thought in the seventeenth century.[2]

The aim with which Burnet wrote his *History*, or rather recast his autobiographical memoirs as a history, is several times explained in his pages. 'My chief design in writing was to give a true view of men and of counsels, leaving public transactions to gazettes and the public historians of the times.'[3] In another passage he insists still more strongly on the moral purpose which inspired him.

'My intention in writing was not so much to tell a fine tale to the world, and to amuse them with a discovery of many secrets, and of intrigues of state, to blast the memory of some,

---

[1] *Supplement*, pp. 469, 489.
[2] *Own Time*, i. 186–91. [3] Ibid., Preface.

and to exalt others, to disgrace one party and to recommend another: my chief design was better formed, and deeper laid: it was to give such a discovery of errors in government, and of the excesses and follies of parties, as may make the next age wiser, by what I may tell them of the last.'[1]

He seems to have thought that it would serve to guide the governing classes. It would undeceive, he suggests, the 'good and well meaning' section of the clergy, and 'deliver them from common prejudices and mistaken notions' about public affairs.[2] It would help to educate the English gentry, who were worse instructed in England than in any other country with which Burnet was acquainted. He held that the study of history should be a necessary part of their training in order to make them better qualified to take part in the government of their country and more attached to its constitution. They should study it, not in abridgements, 'but in the fullest and most copious collectors of it, that they may see to the bottom what is our constitution, and what are our laws, what are the methods bad princes have taken to enslave us, and by what conduct we have been preserved'.[3]

In the last lines Burnet seems to be referring to his own *History*. But the drawback was that when the *History* appeared its veracity and its value were at once disputed. Many people denied that it was history. On November 15, 1723, Dr. Stratford wrote to the Earl of Oxford that he had just been reading 'Gibby Burnet's history'.[4] It was 'a strange rhapsody of chit-chat and lies, ill tacked together'. In many things it was plain that the author was very ignorant, and much that he could have given an account of he had purposely omitted. About the same time John Potenger, in his advice to his grandson on going to the University, warned him against reading Burnet.

'Be careful of what history you read of late reigns, for it is

[1] *Own Time*, ii. 633.   [2] Ibid., Preface.   [3] Ibid. ii. 649.
[4] Hist. MSS. Comm., *MSS. of the Duke of Portland*, vii. 367–8.

full of legend and false secret tradition, especially Burnet's, which is no more to be credited than *The Seven Champions of Christendom*, and if you will believe me, you will never be imposed on by that fallacious historian, who

Peccare docentes
Fallax historia monet:—

for generally what he says comes short of truth, or tells it with a bad design. His characters for the most part are not according to the merits of the persons, but as they pleased or displeased him. This Scotch prelate, a mere father-in-law to our church, was in his nature so fiery a *boute-feu*, that he was not contented to disturb the peace of the church or state in all king's reigns whilst he lived, but has left a posthumous piece of history to seduce posterity, and to disquiet the nation when he is in his grave.'[1]

Bolingbroke classed Burnet with party pamphleteers.

'Even pamphlets, written on different sides and on different occasions in our party disputes, and histories of no more authority than pamphlets, will help you to come at truth. Read them with suspicion, for they deserve to be suspected; pay no regard to the epithets given nor to the judgments passed; neglect all declamation, weigh the reasoning, and advert to fact. With such precautions, even Burnet's history may be of some use.'[2]

Other critics complained that Burnet misrepresented events in order to exaggerate his own importance. Lord Hervey prefaces his own memoirs with a disclaimer directed against his predecessors.

'I leave these ecclesiastical heroes of their own romances— De Retz and Burnet—to aim at that useless imaginary glory of being thought to influence every considerable event they relate; and I very freely declare that my part in this drama was only that of the Chorus's in the ancient plays, who, by constantly being on the stage, saw everything that was done, and made

[1] *Private Memoirs of John Potenger*, ed. C. W. Bingham (1841), p. 5.
[2] Bolingbroke's *Letters on the Study and Use of History* (1870), p. 136.

their own comments upon the scene, without mixing in the action or making any considerable figure in the performance.'[1]

Nevertheless, even Burnet's contemporary opponents could not deny that in spite of prejudice and exaggeration there was much of value in the volumes they denounced. 'D—— him,' Atterbury is reported to have said, 'he has told a great deal of truth; but where the Devil did he learn it?'[2] What discredited Burnet was his lack of discrimination: truth and legend were mixed together, and the better metal was alloyed with too much dross. He had 'a prodigious memory, and a very indifferent judgment', explained Lord Dartmouth. 'He was extremely partial, and readily took every thing for granted that he heard to the prejudice of those he did not like: which made him pass for a man of less truth than he really was. I do not think he designedly published any thing he believed to be false.' Afterwards Dartmouth retracted this last sentence, and declared that the Bishop published many things he must have known to be untrue, but his earlier verdict was the correct one.[3] It exactly agrees with the later verdict of Dr. Johnson. 'I do not believe', said that sagacious critic, 'that Burnet intentionally lyed; but he was so much prejudiced, that he took no pains to find out the truth. He was like a man who resolves to regulate his time by a certain watch; but will not enquire whether the watch is right or not.'[4]

The capital instance of this prejudice is Burnet's treatment of the question of the birth of the Prince of Wales. Convinced by the rumours from England that James II and his Queen intended to palm off a supposititious child on the nation, he became so firmly imbued with the theory of fraud that he was incapable of judg-

---

[1] John, Lord Hervey, *Memoirs*, ed. J. W. Croker (1884), i. 3.
[2] Cole's MS. quoted in Bohn's *Lowndes*, i. 320.
[3] *Own Time*, i. 3; cf. iv. 1 (1833 ed.).
[4] Boswell's *Johnson*, ed. G. B. Hill (1887), ii. 213.

ing the evidence when it was submitted to him.[1] Other legends, too, especially if they told against political opponents, he adopted with similar credulousness.

This uncritical habit of mind much diminishes the value of the *History of My Own Time*, since a very large portion of it rests on hearsay evidence. Usually he gives an authority for each of his stories. This fact he learnt from Lauderdale, that from Primrose, or Leighton, or Essex, or Schomberg, or Titus. Something he was told by Lord Holles, much he had heard from old Sir Harbottle Grimstone, and a good deal from Lord Montagu and Colonel Stouppe. But he did not sufficiently sift the information he gathered from these various resources and allowed mere gossip not only too large a place in his narrative but too great an influence on his judgements of men and events.

Nevertheless, he had the inestimable advantage of personal acquaintance with the chief men of his times. 'For above thirty years', he asserted, 'I have lived in such intimacy with all who have had the chief conduct of affairs, and have been so much trusted and on so many important occasions employed by them, that I have been able to penetrate far into the true secrets of counsels and designs.'[2]

The ambition of playing a part in 'intrigues of state, and the conduct of affairs' had for many years attracted him, and it was only in the latter years of his life that it had ceased to do so. 'I was for some years deeply immersed in these, but still with hopes of reforming the world, and of making mankind wiser and better: but I have found, *that which is crooked cannot be made straight.*'[3]

Burnet's career had really enabled him to know a great deal about the political history of his time, and his character had led him always to seek for such

[1] See Clarke and Foxcroft, *Life*, pp. 238, 240, 253.
[2] *Own Time*, Preface.   [3] Ibid. ii. 669.

knowledge with singular pertinacity. Atterbury's surprise that he knew so much was unreasonable. No doubt Burnet, as Hervey implies, exaggerated his own influence and importance, but what he writes about affairs in which he was personally employed and matters which came directly under his observation is always trustworthy. His account of affairs in Scotland between the Restoration and the year 1673 has been subjected to minute examination in Dr. Osmund Airy's edition of the *History*, and bears the test of comparison with contemporary documents extremely well. Equally valuable in a different way are Burnet's accounts of English politics immediately after the Revolution, and of his earlier intercourse with William and Mary when he was an exile at The Hague.

Bearing in mind the distinction between the parts which rest on personal knowledge and those which depend on secondary evidence, it is not difficult to determine the value of particular statements contained in the *History*, especially since for a large portion of it we have the advantage of being able to compare the earlier and later versions. After all necessary deductions have been made, it remains an authority of mixed quality it is true, but of primary importance. Put the whole mass into the crucible, and eliminate the inferior elements; the amount of true and valuable information left represents a high percentage. Burnet bears the test of comparison with the writers of memoirs very well.

A comparison between Burnet and Clarendon naturally suggests itself. The *History of the Rebellion* appeared in 1702-4. It very probably suggested to Burnet, as Miss Foxcroft thinks, the idea of converting his autobiographical narrative into a formal history. There was some resemblance in the position of the two authors. Each wrote of men he had known and of events in which he had taken part. Each was prejudiced and partial, honest in intention but holding a brief for a particular party. But Clarendon played a far greater part on the political stage than Burnet, and wrote from a larger knowledge of affairs and a more intimate acquaintance with the problems of government. He was throughout nearer to the centre of things than Burnet. Part of his *History* is of first-rate value, part of very slight value. Some portions of it, and those the most trustworthy, are based on documentary evidence: some on recent, others on distant recollections. When Clarendon depends on memory alone he is much less trustworthy than Burnet, whose memory was at once more exact and more retentive.

But the difference between the character of the two historians is more striking than the resemblance which exists between the substance of their works. It reveals itself in every word they write. Clarendon is always dignified; he has a large vocabulary and a great choice of words. Burnet is vulgar and familiar as well as occasionally elevated; he has no great choice of words, and repeats some of his phrases far too often. Clarendon's constructions are sometimes involved, but Burnet's relatives and antecedents are frequently so mixed that it is difficult to determine what person is meant by some particular 'he' or 'who'. Swift is never tired of commenting on the inelegancy of Burnet's expressions or the awkward construction of his sentences. 'I never read so ill a style' is his verdict. He condemns it as 'rough, full of improprieties, in expressions often Scotch, and often such as are used by the meanest people'. When Burnet observes that *Paradise Lost* is the perfectest poem ever written, 'at least in our language', Swift comments, 'a mistake, for it is *in English*'.[1]

There is a great difference also between the long, sonorous, rolling periods of Clarendon, which seem a last echo of the Elizabethans in our literature, and the short disconnected sentences of Burnet. As we read

[1] Swift's *Prose Works*, ed. Temple Scott, x (1902), 327, 331, 336.

what Swift calls his 'jumping periods' we seem embarked on a rough choppy sea, as it might be the Channel passage.

On the other hand, when we get beyond the style and come to the matter there is a realism in Burnet which one misses in Clarendon. Clarendon is a little overpowered by literary conventions: the dignity of history is always with him: a long row of great historians, Roman or Italian, are before his eyes: we feel that he is consciously seeking to rival them, to reproduce their effects and to follow their rules. Certain facts must only be mentioned in the most roundabout fashion. When Clarendon has to speak of Lady Castlemaine he introduces her thus: 'There was a lady of youth and beauty, with whom the King had lived in great and notorious familiarity from the time of his coming into England,' and he never refers to her by name, but always calls her vaguely 'the Lady'.[1] Burnet, on the other hand, bluntly describes her as 'the King's first and longest mistress', and mentions not only her name but those of many other ladies of the same kind. It was not merely that the literary taste of Burnet's generation differed from that of Clarendon's; Burnet preferred a straightforward phrase and had none of Clarendon's reticence. If one of his *dramatis personae* had used a broad jest or an indecent proverb to point an argument he did not hesitate to insert it in relating the incident.

Clarendon and Burnet have a totally different way of telling the anecdotes with which they illustrate the character of the times or of the men they describe. Clarendon tells a story in a large, leisurely, oratorical manner, making almost a small epic or a little drama out of it. See, for instance, the stories of the ghost of Sir George Villiers and of the King's attempt to borrow

[1] *The Continuation of the Life of Edward Earl of Clarendon* (1857), § 359.

money from Lords Deincourt and Kingston.[1] Burnet's stories are little bits of gossip that drop naturally from his pen, with a sort of artless garrulity, as they used to do from his tongue; he seems to tell them not so much to produce an effect, but because having heard or seen something of interest he cannot keep it to himself. His writing has all the qualities of his conversation which, if report can be trusted, was as full of historic scandal as his book. 'He hath told me many passages not mentioned in this history', says Swift.[2]

For though Burnet had liberal ideas as to what might be published there were a few things which he thought it desirable not to print. White Kennet records a story which Burnet told in order to prove the principle that it was not expedient to publish everything that was true. 'Is this story now fit to be told?' he asked his hearers, after he had related it. 'All the company stood amazed and held up their hands,' thus agreeing that it was not.[3] A still more amazing story recorded in Spence's *Anecdotes* on the authority of the Dean of Winchester, is omitted here in deference to the principle just laid down.[4]

As a narrator on a large scale Clarendon is much superior to Burnet; his account of the progress of a movement or the development of a situation is more coherent and more clear. But in telling an anecdote, or describing a scene or an interview Burnet frequently excels him. When Clarendon reports a conversation the personages all speak in much the same style, in the Clarendonian dialect in short. As Goldsmith said of Johnson, his little fishes talk like whales. Burnet, on the other hand, tries to give the *ipsissima verba* of the persons with whom he conversed. Even in an abridged

---

[1] *Rebellion*, i. 89–94; 59–60.   [2] Swift, *Prose Works*, x. 329.
[3] Thomas Birch, *Enquiry in the share which King Charles I had in the Transactions of the Earl of Glamorgan*, 2nd ed. (1756), p. 372.
[4] Joseph Spence, *Anecdotes*, ed. S. W. Singer (1820), p. 329.

form they talk naturally and in their proper character. There is more individuality and more life in Burnet's conversations. His pages give a much truer idea of what Charles II's talk was like than those which Clarendon in his account of his administration devotes to the same subject, and yet Clarendon knew Charles much better than Burnet and had spent many years in close association with the King.

Burnet's characters, on the other hand, are admittedly inferior to Clarendon's. Swift says, 'His characters are miserably wrought, in many things mistaken, and are all of them detracting, except of those who were friends to the Presbyterians'.[1] To a certain extent the criticism is true: they are rough and unfinished; often they are merely a bundle of characteristics and comments bound together anyhow. In Dryden's phrase, 'he faggoted his notions as they fell'. Hence he often provides materials for a portrait-painter rather than a picture. He had more observation than insight. When he notes a trait which he observed or records the impression which some person produced upon him his evidence is of the greatest value. Hence the superiority of the first characters of Charles II and his ministers contained in Burnet's original manuscript to those embodied in the published *History*. As Ranke remarks they 'have internal truth and give proof of his power of comprehending human nature'.[2] They are more vivid and vigorous, too, for they represent his first impressions, unalloyed by late accretions of prejudice or legend, and unsophisticated by attempts to polish his style.

One distinction between Burnet's characters and Clarendon's is that the former notices a number of minor particulars of every kind which Clarendon neglects or disdains. Clarendon's description of the exterior of the personages he mentions is usually vague. He tells you that Sir Harry Vane 'had an unusual

[1] *Prose Works*, x. 328.   [2] Ranke, *History of England*, vi. 77.

aspect' which 'made men think there was somewhat in
him of extraordinary', but does not explain what the
peculiarity in Vane's look was. He mentions that Oliver
St. John 'had naturally a great cloud in his face' simply
in order to explain the significance of his smile at a
particular political crisis, and that Lauderdale's tongue
was too big for his mouth in order to heighten a description of the effectiveness of one of his speeches.[1] Burnet
piles details on details. Take his description of Lauderdale. 'It may be expected that I should be a little copious
in setting out his character; for I knew him very particularly. He made a very ill appearance: he was very big:
his hair was red, hanging oddly about him: his tongue
was too big for his mouth, which made him bedew all
that he talked to: and his whole manner was rough and
boisterous, and very unfit for a court.'[2] Burnet enumerates moral features in the same fashion as physical,
pouring forth, with hardly any attempt at selection
or arrangement, a number of traits and reminiscences,
and leaving his readers to construct a character from
a catalogue of characteristics.

Clarendon's characters on the other hand are works
of art. He selects and arranges the particular traits he
thinks most significant as indications or illustrations of
character. Instead of individualizing his personages by
noting the little peculiarities which differentiated them
from other men he seems to endeavour to generalize,
and to reduce them all to certain universal types.

In reading the *History of the Rebellion* one is continually reminded of the fact that the description of
imaginary types of character was a popular literary
exercise in Clarendon's day. Burnet's rough sketches,
inferior though they may be as artistic compositions,
have an individuality which Clarendon's finished
portraits sometimes lack. But as a rule he is more

[1] Clarendon, *Rebellion*, ii. 78; iii. 34; *Continuation of the Life*, § 105.
[2] *Own Time*, i. 101.

convincing when he gives a glimpse of a character rather than a full-length picture, and sometimes hits in a sentence what he misses in a paragraph. He rises highest when he writes from his heart, as in his account of Archbishop Leighton. 'I bear still', he says, 'the greatest admiration for the memory of that man than I do to any person', and the sincerity of this feeling inspires and elevates the pages he devotes to the representation of his friend.

In the latter half of the *History of My Own Time* William and Mary are the central figures. Burnet's narrative makes a fresh start when they come upon the stage, and flags after they leave it. We owe much to the chance which brought his wandering steps to The Hague in 1686, and so associated him with the Prince in his expedition to England. Anecdotes, impressions, and records of conversation acquire a double value when they reveal to us one of the greatest men of the age at the crisis of his career, and light up one of the turning-points in English history. Burnet draws both William and Mary with convincing truthfulness. Of the two he understood Mary better. For her he cherished a feeling which was a mixture of affection, loyalty, and admiration. 'I never admired any as I admired her,' he declared in the *History*, and the fervid *Essay on the Memory of the Late Queen* should be read side by side with the briefer and better known commemoration in his account of the reign of William and Mary. For William, Burnet's attachment was political rather than personal; changes in the situation of English politics, in the policy of the King, and in the relations of the bishop and his master influenced Burnet's judgement as an historian. The character of William which Burnet wrote in 1686 is far more favourable than that written in 1702, but the main features are the same, and the final estimate if less enthusiastic is just and acute. For however they differed William remained throughout in Burnet's eyes 'a glorious instrument raised up by God' to redeem the civil and religious liberties of Englishmen, though he became more sensible of the imperfections of the instrument, and more critical.

This question of characterization is more important than it seems. The great difference between historical writers of the seventeenth century and those of our own day lies in their varying conceptions of the relative importance of personal and general causes. Clarendon, for instance, has hardly any conception of the working of general causes in history. He mentions indeed the 'immediate finger and wrath of God' as one of the causes of the revolutions he undertakes to relate, and vaguely alludes to the 'natural causes and means which have usually attended kingdoms swoln with long plenty, pride, and excess'. These, however, are but formal and perfunctory prefaces; as soon as he gets to work on the story of events he attributes everything to the action of particular persons. For him to know the chief actors is to know the causes of things, and he seeks to make them known in order that his readers may see 'the pride of this man, and the popularity of that; the levity of one, and the morosity of another; . . . the spirit of craft and subtlety in some, and the rude and unpolished integrity of others . . . like so many atoms contributing jointly to this mass of confusion'.[1] Motives which influenced masses of men escape his appreciation, and the *History of the Rebellion* is accordingly an account of the Puritan Revolution which is unintelligible because the part played by Puritanism is misunderstood or omitted altogether.

Burnet's task, like Clarendon's, was to write the history of a political revolution which was mainly due to religious causes, and he was better qualified for it than Clarendon because he understood better the significance

[1] *History of the Rebellion*, i. 2, 4.

of the questions at issue. Wider theological sympathies, a natural breadth of view, and the character
of his historical studies enabled him to appreciate the
standpoint of different sections of Protestants, to realize
the difficulties with which English statesmen had to
deal, and to perceive their solution. He succeeds in
making the Revolution of 1688 intelligible while
Clarendon leaves that of 1649 unexplained.

At the same time Burnet's conception of general
causes is consistently theological. It was very clear
to him that the course of events was providentially
ordered, and that it was part of the business of an
historian to vindicate the ways of God to man. In the
events of 1688 he saw plain evidence of divine intervention. One proof was the little damage which William's
fleet suffered when it was driven back at first setting
out. This was 'a mark of God's great care of us, who,
though he had not changed the course of the winds and
seas in our favour, yet had preserved us while we were
in such apparent danger, beyond what could have been
imagined'. So, too, when 'a Protestant wind' facilitated
the prosperous passage of William's fleet, kept that of
James in harbour, and then shifting to the west frustrated pursuit, Burnet says 'I never found a disposition
to superstition in my temper: I was rather inclined to
be philosophical upon all occasions. Yet I must confess,
that this strange ordering of the winds and seasons, just
to change as our affairs required it, could not but make
deep impressions on me, as well as on all that observed
it.' Later still, in the wars which followed the Revolution, Burnet commented on the recurrence of similar
phenomena. A sudden fog preserved a fleet of British
merchantmen from French cruisers, an unusually dry
autumn facilitated Marlborough's sieges, and so on. 'I
know', he comments, 'it is not possible to determine,
when such accidents rise from a chain of second causes
in the course of nature, and when they are directed by

a special providence: but my mind has always carried me so strongly to acknowledge the latter, that I love to set these reflections in the way of others, that they may consider them with the same serious attention that I feel in myself.'[1]

A larger survey of the past seemed to furnish ground for Burnet's faith. What struck him when he looked back on the history of Europe since the Reformation was the progress of the Protestant religion and the vicissitudes through which it had passed. Five times in the course of the last two centuries European Protestantism had been in great peril, almost, it seemed to him, in danger of extinction; yet at each crisis Providence had raised up some one to deliver it—Maurice of Saxony, Queen Elizabeth, Gustavus Adolphus, and last of all William of Orange.[2] The fifth crisis, of which William was the hero, was 'of the longest continuance'. It had begun in 1672, or at the latest in 1685, and it was not over yet. 'We are yet in the agitations of it', nor did it end till the accession of George I secured a Protestant line of kings for England. Burnet's *History of My Own Time* is an account of England during this fifth crisis, and this conception of the meaning of events and of their cause links his later book to his *History of the Reformation* and gives unity to his historical writings.

---

[1] *Own Time*, i. 783, 789; ii. 388, 512.

[2] For the five crises, which Burnet computes somewhat differently in the different recensions of his *History*, see *Supplement*, pp. 172–7, and *Own Time*, i. 310–21, 655.

THE POLITICAL SIGNIFICANCE OF 'GULLIVER'S TRAVELS'[1]

A CRITIC who seeks to explain the political significance of *Gulliver's Travels* may be guilty of too
much ingenuity, but he cannot fairly be charged with
exaggerated curiosity. He is searching for a secret
which Swift tells us is hidden there, and endeavouring
to solve riddles which were intended to exercise his wits.
Swift loved to mystify the public; he often preferred
to speak in parables when there was no reason for doing
so. In this case there was good reason for his preference.
At that time, and for many years later, it was dangerous
to write plainly about public affairs, or to criticize
public men with any freedom.

When Swift wrote his *History of the Last Four Years
of the Queen* he proposed to prefix to it characters of the
party leaders of that period in order to make it more
intelligible. In 1738 he contemplated the publication
of this *History*. Though it was about five-and-twenty
years after the events described, he was warned by his
friend Erasmus Lewis, that if the characters he had
drawn were published as they stood, 'nothing could
save the author's printer and publishers from some
grievous punishment'.[2] Accordingly it was not published till 1758, thirteen years after Swift's death.

Authors who wrote about public affairs immediately
after they had happened and about ministers of state
while they were actually in office were obliged to use
literary artifices of various kinds in order to express
their opinions with impunity. But it was not without
some compensating advantage, for to be allusive and

[1] Reprinted from *Proceedings of the British Academy*, vol. ix. By
permission.

[2] *Correspondence*, ed. F. Elrington Ball, vi. 78.

indirect, while it protected the author, stimulated the curiosity of the reader.

In *Gulliver's Travels* many figures which seem to be imaginary are meant to depict real personages, or at all events are drawn from them. Swift says in one of his earlier writings: 'In describing the virtues and vices of mankind, it is convenient upon every article, to have some eminent person in our eye, from whence we copy our description.' Again he says: 'I have . . . thought of another expedient, frequently practised with great safety and success by satirical writers: which is, that of looking into history for some character bearing a resemblance to the person we would describe; and with the absolute power of altering, adding or suppressing what circumstances we please, I conceived we must have very bad luck, or very little skill to fail.' He admitted that this method of writing had one serious drawback. 'Though the present age may understand well enough the little hints we give, the parallels we draw, and the characters we describe, yet this will all be lost to the next. However, if these papers . . . should happen to live till our grandchildren are men, I hope they may have curiosity enough to consult annals, and compare dates, in order to find out.'[1]

Gulliver's Travels was published on October 28, 1726, but some portions of the book were written much earlier. They were intended to be a contribution to the *Memoirs of Martinus Scriblerus*. 'It was from a part of these memoirs', Pope told Spence, 'that Dr. Swift took his first hints for Gulliver. There were pigmies in Schreibler's travels; and the projects of Laputa.'[2]

As Pope's statement is confirmed by internal evidence, and is inherently probable, it may be accepted in an inquiry into the composition of the *Travels*, and

[1] *The Prose Works of Jonathan Swift*, ed. Temple Scott, ix. 81, 101, 110; cf. also 271 and v. 297.

[2] Spence, *Anecdotes*, ed. Singer, p. 10.

parts of the First and Third Voyages may be assigned to the year 1714. At that date, as Swift's correspondence shows, Swift and a circle of his friends were engaged upon the *Memoirs*.[1] Swift's return to Ireland and the political revolution which followed Queen Anne's death (August 1, 1714) broke up the circle, and it was not till 1741 that the *Memoirs of Scriblerus* were printed. In the meantime Swift's intended contribution to the joint work had been transformed into the Travels of Captain Lemuel Gulliver.

The development was a slow process. After the revolution of 1714 Swift had no heart to continue his story. 'I must be a little easy in my mind before I think of Scriblerus,' he wrote on June 28, 1715. 'You know how well I loved both Lord Oxford and Bolingbroke, and how dear the Duke of Ormond is to me. Do you imagine I can be easy while their enemies are endeavouring to take off their heads. . . . Truly I must be a little easy in my mind before I can think of Scriblerus.'[2]

About six years later he had regained his ease of mind, and he began to write again. He took up his pen in defence of Ireland, writing about May 1720 his *Proposal for the Universal Use of Irish Manufacture*. He took out of his desk his half-finished contribution to the *Memoirs of Scriblerus*, and converted it into the *Voyages of Captain Gulliver*. In a letter written to Charles Ford and dated April 15, 1721, he says, 'I am now writing a History of my Travells, which will be a large Volume, and gives Account of Countryes hitherto unknown; but they go on slowly for want of Health and Humor'.[3] Three years later the *Travels* were nearly completed.

---

[1] *Correspondence*, ii. 144, 155, 158, 162, 186, 288, 416.

[2] Ibid. ii. 286, 288.

[3] For these extracts from Swift's letters to Ford I am indebted to the kindness of Mr. D. Nichol Smith, who is now editing them for the Clarendon Press. (This work was published in 1935 as *The Letters of Jonathan Swift to Charles Ford*.)

'I have left the Country of Horses', he told Ford on
January 19, 1724, 'and am in the flying Island, where
I shall not stay long, and my two last Journyes will be
soon over.' He was able to tell his friend on August 14,
1725: 'I have finished my Travells, and I am now
transcribing them; they are admirable Things, and will
wonderfully mend the World.' On September 29 in the
same year he told Pope: 'I have employed my time . . .
in finishing, correcting, amending, and transcribing my
Travels, in four parts complete, newly augmented, and
intended for the press, when the world shall deserve
them, or rather when a printer shall be found brave
enough to venture his ears.'[1] This reference to the
printer's ears is an acknowledgement that the book
contained political allusions which might bring the
publisher to the pillory, and draw upon him the fate
which befell Defoe.

Political allusions abound in the *Travels*. Some are
to the events of the end of Queen Anne's reign, others
to events in the reign of George I. Naturally those
events which happened during the five years in which
the *Travels* were completed left most traces on the
work. In England at the beginning of the period there
was the South Sea Bubble (1720), which was followed
by the return of Walpole to office (1721) and by the
return of Bolingbroke from exile (1723), by the ejection
of Carteret from the English cabinet (1724), and by the
supremacy of Walpole in it (1725). In Ireland during
the same period the struggle over Wood's patent began
and ended (1722–5).

These references to public events and public personages are most frequent in the First and Third Voyages.
Each of these Voyages consists of a part which was
written about 1714, as Pope's statement proves, and
internal evidence confirms. Each of these Voyages also
contains other parts written later, as Swift's letters

[1] *Correspondence*, iii. 276.

indicate, and the contents of the additions show. Moreover, there are signs in the text itself, such as repetitions, explanations, and alterations, which show where the matter was added.

Let us begin by examining the Voyage to Lilliput. The first part of it, which contains the story of Gulliver's shipwreck, and of his early adventures among the pigmies, has no political significance. It is simply what Shakespeare terms 'very gracious fooling'. This no doubt represents the part written in 1714. On the other hand, the account of the laws and customs of Lilliput contained in Chapter VI was probably written later. It seems to be an afterthought, because in Chapter IV Gulliver had announced that he proposed to reserve 'for a greater work' the very subjects treated of in Chapter VI.[1] There is also a distinct change of tone; a serious didactic purpose becomes apparent. The institutions of Lilliput are described for the instruction of Swift's fellow countrymen, just as Sir Thomas More described the institutions of Utopia. 'There are some laws and customs in this empire very peculiar,' says Gulliver; 'and if they were not so directly contrary to those of my own dear country, I should be tempted to say a little in their justification.'[2] Thus he directs the attention of his readers to the impunity of certain crimes in England and the shortcomings of English education.

By a curious contradiction, as soon as Swift turns to describe the politics of Lilliput it ceases to be Utopia and becomes England itself, instead of being an example to England. 'We labour', says Gulliver's informant, 'under two mighty evils; a violent faction at home, and the danger of an invasion by a most potent enemy from abroad.'

---

[1] *Gulliver's Travels*, pp. 48, 59. The edition referred to throughout this paper is that edited by Mr. G. R. Dennis in 1899, forming vol. viii of the *Prose Works*, edited by Temple Scott. [2] Ibid., p. 59.

In Lilliput there are two struggling parties called *'Tramecksan* and *Slamecksan,* from the high and low heels on their shoes, by which they distinguish themselves'.[1] These typify the High Church and Low Church parties, or the Tories and Whigs. The potent enemy abroad is the island of Blefuscu, which typifies France, engaged in an obstinate struggle with its neighbour for a whole generation. The conversion of Lilliput into England marks the change of plan made by Swift when he took up the half-finished story of the First Voyage again, about 1720, and turned his story into a political allegory. This change involved other changes. The majestic Emperor of Lilliput of the second chapter, with his 'Austrian lip and arched nose',[2] was a purely conventional monarch, not representing George I or any other real king. It was now necessary to convert this personage into George I, which was effected by making him a Whig 'determined to make use of only low heels in the administration of the government', and wearing himself heels lower than any of his court. The parallel was emphasized by making the heir to the throne show an inclination to the High Heels, as the Prince of Wales did to the Tories.[3] Finally, Swift inserted an ironical passage on the lenity and mercy of the King, intended to call to the minds of his readers the executions which had taken place after the rebellion in 1715, and the encomiums on the King's mercy which the Government had published at the time.[4]

The King was not the only personage who underwent a sort of transformation when Swift took his half-told story in hand again. Gulliver is changed too. At first Gulliver to a certain extent represented Swift himself —that is, certain incidents in Gulliver's adventures were an allegorical representation of certain incidents

[1] Ibid., p. 48. [2] Ibid., p. 29.
[3] Ibid., pp. 48–9. [4] Ibid., p. 74.

in Swift's life. Editors of *Gulliver's Travels* rightly agree in their interpretation of the story of Gulliver's extinction of the fire in the palace at Lilliput, and of the resentment of the Empress in consequence. Sir Walter Scott says: 'It is perhaps a strained interpretation of this incident, to suppose, that our author recollected the prejudices of Queen Anne against the indecency and immorality of his own satirical vein, though it was so serviceable to the cause of her ministry.'[1] Mr. Dennis says: 'Queen Anne was so much disgusted with the "Tale of a Tub" that, in spite of Swift's political services, she could never be induced to give him preferment in the Church.'[2] J. F. Waller and W. C. Taylor, in their editions of *Gulliver*, interpret the incident in a similar fashion. It is not an unreasonable interpretation, for it is clear that Swift's satirical writings stood in the way of his promotion. He failed to obtain the Irish bishopric which he hoped to get in 1708,[3] and it was with great difficulty that he obtained a deanery in 1713.[4]

The tradition is that the first failure was due to the influence of Dr. Sharp, the Archbishop of York, who showed the Queen the *Tale of a Tub*.[5] The second, it is alleged, was due to the influence of the Duchess of Somerset, incensed by Swift's *Windsor Prophecy*, written in December 1711.[6] Swift believed that this was the case, and in the lines entitled 'The Author on Himself', written in 1714, he mentioned both causes, and spoke of Queen Anne as 'a royal prude', whose opposition to his preferment was due to the efforts of his enemies. In

---

[1] Swift's *Works* (1824), xi. 74.   [2] *Gulliver's Travels*, p. 57.

[3] Sir Henry Craik, *Life of Jonathan Swift* (1882), pp. 145, 183.

[4] Craik, p. 259; *Correspondence*, ii. 22.

[5] Craik, p. 114; *Correspondence*, i. 73, 152; ii. 212; Johnson, *Lives of the Poets*, ed. G. B. Hill (1905), iii. 10, 68.

[6] *Poems*, ed. W. E. Browning (1910), ii. 150; The Earl of Cork and Orrery, *Remarks on the Life and Writings of . . . Swift*, p. 48; *Correspondence*, ii. 212; *Prose Works*, v. 463.

that poem he names firstly the Duchess of Somerset and the Archbishop of York, and secondly the Earl of Nottingham and Robert Walpole as the enemies in question.

In *Gulliver's Travels* the captain's chief enemy is a certain lord named Bolgolam, who was pleased, says Gulliver, 'without any provocation, to be my mortal enemy.... That minister was *Galbet*, or Admiral of the Realm, very much in his master's confidence, and a person well versed in affairs, but of a morose and sour complexion'. He is referred to later as Gulliver's 'mortal enemy', and his 'malice' is mentioned and insisted upon.[1]

This person is clearly intended to represent the Earl of Nottingham. The 'morose and sour complexion' attributed to Bolgolam at once suggests the identification. In one of his pamphlets Swift says that Nottingham's 'adust complexion disposeth him to rigour and severity', and time after time he refers to him by his nickname of 'Dismal'. 'Dismal, so men call him from his looks,' explains Swift to Stella.[2] The earl had long been Swift's personal enemy. In 1711, when Nottingham joined the Whigs in their attack on the foreign policy of the Government, Swift wrote two ballads against him, 'An orator *dismal* of *Nottinghamshire*' and 'Toland's Invitation to Dismal'.[3] Nottingham retaliated by using whatever private influence he possessed at court to stop Swift's preferment, and finally by an open and bitter attack upon him in Parliament. On June 1, 1714, when the Schism Act was debated in the House of Lords, Nottingham opposed the Bill, saying that it was dangerous because it gave too much power to the bishops, 'though now they had the happiness of having so worthy bishops, yet it possibly might

[1] *Gulliver's Travels*, pp. 43, 69, 72, 73.
[2] *Prose Works*, ii. 294; x. 29.
[3] *Poems*, ii. 148, 156.

happen that a person who wrote lewdly, nay, even atheistically, might by having a false undeserved character given him be promoted to a bishopric by her Majesty'.[1] Another version makes Nottingham say: 'I own I tremble when I think that a certain Divine, who is hardly suspected of being a Christian, is in a fair way of being a Bishop.'[2] More than any other statesman of the period, he might be described with justice as Swift's 'mortal enemy'. On the other hand, it is more difficult to explain why Nottingham should be designated 'High Admiral'. There was no Lord High Admiral in England after 1709, and the different noblemen who held the post of First Lord of the Admiralty between 1709 and 1726 were none of them enemies of Swift. One reason for the designation can be suggested. Nottingham had been First Lord from February 1680 to May 1684, and ever afterwards 'peeked himself upon understanding sea affairs'. In William III's reign, when he was Secretary of State, he was continually interfering in the management of the fleet. 'All men', says Lord Dartmouth, 'that had been bred to that profession unanimously agreed, that he was totally ignorant in their science, and were highly provoked, when he pretended to contradict, or give them directions.'[3] To term Nottingham 'High Admiral' may be an ironical reference to this notorious foible.

Nottingham was President of the Council in the first Ministry of George I, and held that post till February 29, 1716, when he was dismissed because he pressed for the pardon of the leaders of the late rebellion.[4] This attack upon him under the character of Bolgolam must have been written in the summer of 1714, when

---

[1] *Wentworth Papers* (1883), p. 385.

[2] Mahon, *History of England* (1872), i. 82.

[3] Gilbert Burnet, *History of My Own Time* (1833), v. 95.

[4] W. M. Torrens, *History of Cabinets* (1894), i. 116–18; Nicholas Tindal, *History of England*, iv. 487.

his offences against Swift were fresh and Swift's anger against him was hot. The prose character is the counterpart of the verses entitled 'The Author on Himself', which belong to the same summer. It is not likely that it was written after 1716, when Nottingham's clemency had led to his fall from office.

When Swift, in 1720 or 1721, took up his unfinished story again, and converted it into a political allegory, he changed his plan, developed, as we have seen, the character of the Emperor, and shadowed forth under the misfortunes of Gulliver the fate of Bolingbroke. That statesman must have been much in Swift's mind about that time. He had resumed his correspondence with his exiled friend in February 1719, at which time there was some prospect of Bolingbroke's pardon and his return to England, though the hope was not realized till 1723. During that period several long letters passed between them. It was towards the end of 1721 that Bolingbroke came to know of *Gulliver's Travels*. 'I long to see your Travels', he wrote, answering on January 1, 1722, a letter from Swift dated September 29, 1721.[1]

The parallel between the fate of Bolingbroke and that of Gulliver was very close. Like Gulliver, Bolingbroke had brought a great war to an end and concluded a peace 'upon conditions very advantageous' to his country, but was denounced by his political opponents for not prosecuting the war to the complete subjugation of the enemy. He was accused of treasonable intercourse with the ambassadors of France, as Gulliver was with those of Blefuscu. Gulliver fled from Lilliput because he felt that he could not obtain a fair trial, 'having in my life', says he, 'perused many state-trials, which I ever observed to terminate as the judges thought fit to direct', and because he knew that powerful enemies sought his life. Bolingbroke declared that he fled from England because 'I had certain and

[1] *Correspondence*, iii. 24–32, 40, 88, 109, 113, 170.

repeated information from some who are in the secret of affairs, that a resolution was taken by those who have power to execute it to pursue me to the scaffold. My blood was to have been the cement of a new alliance; nor could my innocence be any security, after it had once been demanded from abroad and resolved on at home that it was necessary to cut me off.'

Bolingbroke was pardoned in May 1723, and returned from exile in July 1723. In April 1725 he was restored to his ancestral estates, but remained excluded from the House of Lords because Walpole refused to agree to his complete restoration. The enmity between the two, which was concealed between 1723 and 1725, when Bolingbroke was hoping to obtain full restitution, and endeavouring to earn it by services to the Government, broke out once more about 1725, when he found his hopes were vain.

One result of the transformation of Gulliver into Bolingbroke was the development of the character of Flimnap, who was obviously designed to represent Walpole, as all commentators agree. Flimnap, as originally sketched, was a somewhat colourless character, secretly hostile to Gulliver because the prodigious appetite of the monster made him a burden to the treasury, but not his mortal enemy as Bolgolam was. At the end of Queen Anne's reign Walpole was not a personage of the first rank in English politics; in 1721 he became one of the most powerful members of the Government, and by 1726 he was practically Prime Minister. Hence three or four additional touches were added to give Flimnap additional importance, and to bring out the resemblance to Walpole.

Candidates for great employments in Lilliput competed for them by dancing on a rope for the entertainment of the Emperor. 'Flimnap, the Treasurer,' says Gulliver, 'is allowed to cut a caper on the straight rope, at least an inch higher than any other lord in the whole empire.' This symbolizes Walpole's dexterity in parliamentary tactics and political intrigues. 'The King's cushion,' which broke Flimnap's fall when he leaped too high, and saved him from breaking his neck, is agreed to symbolize the Duchess of Kendal, one of the King's mistresses, by whose influence Walpole, after his fall from power in 1717, was again restored to favour.[1]

Another passage in the text must have been added just before the publication of the *Travels*. It is the account of the silken threads, green, red, and blue, given to the courtiers who showed most agility in leaping over or creeping under a stick.[2] The green thread typifies the Order of the Thistle, revived by Queen Anne in 1703. The red typifies the Order of the Bath, revived by George I in May 1725. Its revival, according to Horace Walpole, was due to Sir Robert 'and was an artful bank of thirty-six ribands to supply a fund of favours in lieu of places'. The blue thread typifies the Order of the Garter, which was bestowed on Sir Robert himself in May 1726, after which he was known to satirists by the title of Sir Blue-String. Swift's verses on the revival of the Order of the Bath explain the meaning of his prose.[3]

A third passage is more difficult to explain. It is the account of Flimnap's jealousy of his wife, who was reported to have conceived a violent affection for Gulliver, and the story is introduced to explain the Treasurer's enmity to Gulliver. This may be an ironical hit at Walpole, whose first wife, Catherine Shorter, was not above suspicion, while Walpole's indifference to her levities was notorious. Pope hints at it when he calls Walpole 'a tyrant to his wife'.[4]

Another explanation is that the episode is a reference

---

[1] *Gulliver's Travels*, p. 39.   [2] Ibid., p. 40.
[3] *Poems*, ii. 203; H. Walpole, *Letters* (1877), i. cxiv.
[4] *Gulliver's Travels*, p. 66; Pope, *Works*, ed. Elwin and Courthope, iii. 481.

to Bolingbroke's attempt to win the favour of the Duchess of Kendal, hitherto Walpole's firmest ally, in order to utilize her influence with George I to Walpole's detriment. Sir Robert, who was aware of the intrigue, 'bestowed some fitting language on her Grace, and said she would at any time have sold her influence with the King for a shilling advance to the best bidder'. Bolingbroke, according to Walpole, had paid her £11,000 for her support, and she was entirely in his interest.[1]

Besides Flimnap, another minister of the Lilliputian court is mentioned. Gulliver says: 'My friend Reldresal, principal Secretary for private Affairs, is, in my opinion, if I am not partial, the second after the Treasurer.' Reldresal was the lord who explained to Gulliver the intricacies of Lilliputian politics and proved himself throughout his true friend.[2] Commentators have not identified him, but it is clear that the person meant is Lord Carteret. He was Secretary of State from March 5, 1721 to April 1724, and stood so high in the King's favour that he might fairly be described as the second man in the Government at that time. 'Principal Secretary of State' or one of our 'Principal Secretaries of State' was Carteret's official title. As the two Secretaries of State who then existed divided the conduct of foreign affairs between them, and the care of home affairs was the common function of both of them, there was strictly no 'principal Secretary for private Affairs' at the time. The choice lies between Carteret and his colleague Townshend; as Carteret was Swift's friend he must be the person meant. In April 1724 Walpole got rid of Carteret by making him Lord-Lieutenant of Ireland. In that capacity Carteret was obliged to issue a proclamation (October 27, 1724) offering a reward of £300 for the discovery of the author of the *Drapier's Letter to the People of Ireland*, just as

[1] Torrens, i. 348, 358; Sichel, ii. 190, 208, 266.
[2] *Gulliver's Travels*, pp. 39, 71.

Reldresal was obliged to suggest a method of punishing his friend Gulliver.[1]

The Second Voyage, the Voyage to Brobdingnag, requires less commentary. It was written at one time and is all of a piece. There are no references to persons which require explaining, and the allusions to contemporary politics are only general. Some of the institutions and customs of Brobdingnag are briefly described and praised; for instance, the brevity of the laws, the cultivation of useful knowledge rather than speculative philosophy or abstract sciences, and the simplicity of the literary style in fashion. The method adopted throughout is not to hold up ideal institutions for imitation as in the case of Lilliput, but to describe existing institutions so as to show their defects. In five interviews Gulliver explains to the King the constitution and government of England, and then the King, by astute 'doubts, queries, and objections', forces him to reveal the difference between the practice and the theory of the institutions described. Gulliver has to admit that the working of the parliamentary government is vitiated by the method of selecting peers, bishops, and members of the House of Commons, so that, as the King points out, the original idea of the institution is 'blurred and blotted by corruptions'.[2]

The comments of the King of Brobdingnag express on many questions the political views of Swift's party. He was amazed, says Gulliver, 'to hear me talk of a mercenary standing army in the midst of peace, and among a free people'. Every year, over the Mutiny Act or the Estimates, the House of Commons resounded with denunciations of standing armies, and Chesterfield recommended the question to his son as the best subject for a young member's maiden speech. In the same way the King of Brobdingnag echoed the criticisms of the

---

[1] *Prose Works*, vi. 109, 235.
[2] *Gulliver's Travels*, pp. 135-6.

Tories on the financial system, and their alarm at the existence of the National Debt.[1]

On most questions, however, the King is the mouth-piece of Swift, not merely that of the Tory party, and the opinions he expresses are those Swift had already set forth in his pamphlets. Swift's condemnation of gaming, Swift's complaint of the neglected education of the upper classes, Swift's theory of the best way of treating Dissenters and his rooted animosity to lawyers, lose nothing in vigour in issuing from the King's lips. 'I shall never forget', says Swift at the close of the *Drapier's Letters*, 'what I once ventured to say to a great man in England; "That few politicians, with all their schemes, are half so useful members of a common-wealth, as an honest farmer; who, by skilful draining, fencing, manuring, and planting, hath increased the intrinsic value of a piece of land; and thereby done a perpetual service to his country"; which it is a great controversy, whether any of the former ever did, since the creation of the world.'[2] The King of Brobdingnag puts this in a more epigrammatic form. 'He gave it for his opinion, that whoever could make two ears of corn, or two blades of grass to grow upon a spot of ground where only one grew before, would deserve better of mankind, and do more essential service to his country than the whole race of politicians put together.'[3]

In this way the specific reference to Ireland in the *Drapier's Letters* is made a general maxim in *Gulliver's Travels*, but at the back of Swift's mind there is always the thought of Ireland. In a letter written in 1732 he makes his meaning still clearer. 'There is not an acre of land in Ireland turned to half its advantage, yet it is better improved than the people; and all these evils

---

[1] *Gulliver's Travels*, p. 134. The views expressed by the King refute Sir Walter Scott's opinion (Swift, xi. 8), that the monarch was perhaps drawn from William III.

[2] *Prose Works*, vi. 202.   [3] *Gulliver's Travels*, p. 140.

are effects of English tyranny, so your sons and grand-children will find it to their sorrow.'[1]

There is another passage in the Second Voyage suggested by Irish conditions, and that is an incident in Gulliver's visit to the capital of Brobdingnag. As the carriage in which he and his nurse were conveyed stopped at a shop 'the beggars, watching their opportunity, crowded to the sides of the coach, and gave me the most horrible spectacles that ever an European eye beheld'.[2] He describes with horrid minuteness the exhibition of their sores, and there can be no doubt that the description was inspired by the beggars of Dublin, on whom he has much to say in his pamphlets and sermons.

These passages show that while Swift was entirely wrapt up in English politics when he wrote the First Voyage, Irish social conditions were beginning to occupy his thoughts when the Second was written.

The Fourth Voyage—the Voyage to the island of the horses—seems from Swift's letter of January 19, 1724, to have been written immediately after the second. In it Swift adopts once more the method employed in the Voyage to Brobdingnag.

The traveller describes the institutions and manners of his native country for the information of his temporary master, and his master judges them with all the freedom of a superior being. Once more Swift's views on the education of noblemen, and the education of women and on the iniquities of lawyers, are restated. Once more militarism is denounced. A soldier is defined as 'a *Yahoo* hired to kill in cold blood as many of his own species, who have never offended him, as possibly he can'.[3] But the attack on standing armies of the Second Voyage becomes now an attack on war in general, somewhat resembling a passage in the *Tale of a Tub*, written five-and-twenty years earlier. This

[1] *Correspondence*, iv. 312.   [2] *Gulliver's Travels*, p. 115.
[3] Ibid., p. 255.

tendency to generalize and to deal with abstract principles, rather than particular manifestations of them,
is noticeable in the Fourth Voyage. In the Voyage to
Lilliput, Swift had personally satirized Walpole as chief
minister of state, describing not simply Walpole but a
typical minister compounded out of many examples
living and dead. Swift is no longer content with condemning the faults of English society: he assails the
foundations of the social system, capital, trade, and
private property, exalting the natural life at the expense
of civilization, and horses at the expense of men.

Even the most devoted admirers of Swift are shocked.
Scott calls the Fourth Voyage 'the basest and most
unworthy part of the work'.[1] 'The satire', declares
Mr. Dennis, 'is here turned against human nature itself,
and in his morbid effort to degrade mankind below
the level of the brutes, Swift has violated every law of
probability and outraged every canon of propriety.'[2]
It is 'painful and repulsive', complains Stephen. 'Swift
tears aside the veil of decency to show the bestial element in human nature. . . . The Yahoo is the embodi-
ment of the bestial element in man; and Swift in his
wrath takes the bestial for the predominating element.'[3]

But was it simply blind wrath against the human
race which inspired Swift? Isolated expressions lend
some colour to the theory. 'Expect no more from man
than such an animal is capable of,' wrote Swift to
Sheridan, 'and you will every day find my description
of Yahoos more resembling';[4] and again: 'I hate and
detest that animal called man, although I heartily love
John, Peter, Thomas, and so forth.'[5] 'I tell you after
all, that I do not hate mankind: it is *vous autres* who
hate them, because you would have them reasonable

---

[1] Swift's *Works* (1824), xi. 11.
[2] Preface to *Gulliver's Travels*, p. xxiv.
[3] Leslie Stephen, *Swift* (1882), p. 181.
[4] *Correspondence*, iii. 267.   [5] Ibid. iii. 277.

animals, and are angry for being disappointed. I have always rejected that definition, and made another of my own.' His definition of man was not *animal rationale* but *animal rationis capax*.[1]

Even among the Yahoos Gulliver distinguishes two kinds. There are Yahoos of his native land and the Yahoos indigenous to the island in which he finds himself. The English Yahoos, like himself, are a superior breed: it is admitted that they have appearances of glimmerings of reason; perhaps it is not real reason but only some quality like it; it may be they have some small pittance of reason. These are the conclusions of Gulliver's master.

On the other hand, the Yahoos indigenous to the island are a brutal and degenerate race. But they are, as Gulliver has to admit, of the same race as the English Yahoos. With horror and astonishment not to be described, he observed in this abominable animal a perfect human figure: 'the face of it indeed was flat and broad, the nose depressed, the lips large, and the mouth wide. But these differences are common to all savage nations.'[2] The 'degenerate and brutal nature' of the Yahoos was in part explained by their past history. Once they were free, but when they were free they were harmful, and infested the whole country. So after 'a general hunting' the old ones were destroyed, and the young ones 'brought to such a degree of tameness, as an animal so savage by nature can be capable of acquiring; using them for draught and carriage'. Nothing more could be done with them, because they were 'the most unteachable of all animals, their capacities never reaching higher than to draw or carry burdens'. Their untractableness came from perversity of nature. They were 'cunning, malicious, treacherous, and revengeful', mischievous and destructive to cattle and crops; ravenous and averse to labour, lived chiefly

---

[1] Ibid. iii. 277, 293.   [2] *Gulliver's Travels*, p. 238.

on roots, and had a 'strange disposition to nastiness and dirt'.

Gulliver's description of the Yahoos recalls the description given by Swift, in prose pamphlets written about the same time, of the people whom he terms 'the savage old Irish'.[1] By several conquests and long subjection, the old Irish had been reduced to be 'hewers of wood, and drawers of water'.[2] They are 'poor wretches,' says Swift, 'who think themselves blessed, if they can obtain a hut worse than the squire's dog-kennel, and an acre of ground for a potato-plantation, on condition of being as very slaves as any in America'.[3] Wretches 'forced to pay for a filthy cabin, and two ridges of potatoes, treble the worth; brought up to steal or beg, for want of work; to whom death would be the best thing to be wished for on account both of themselves and the public'.[4] They were vicious as well as wretched. 'The poorer sort of our natives', says Swift, 'in all these parts of this kingdom where the Irish abound . . . live in the utmost ignorance, barbarity, and poverty, giving themselves wholly up to idleness, nastiness, and thievery.'[5] Can nothing be done, he asks, 'to reduce this uncultivated people from that idle, savage, beastly, thievish manner of life, in which they continue sunk to a degree, that it is almost impossible for a country gentleman to find a servant of human capacity, or the least tincture of natural honesty; or who does not live among his own tenants in continual fear of having his plantations destroyed, his cattle stolen, and his goods pilfered.'[6]

In short, the 'savage old Irish' who made up 'the poorer sort of our natives', were not only in a position similar to that of the Yahoos, but there was also a certain similarity in their natures. If nothing was done to stop the process of degeneration, they would become

[1] *Correspondence*, vi. 32.   [2] *Prose Works*, iv. 17, 41.
[3] Ibid. vii. 164.   [4] Ibid. vii. 71; cf. vii. 212.
[5] Ibid. vi. 199.   [6] Ibid. vii. 133; cf. iv. 216.

complete brutes, as the Yahoos were already. They were, so to speak, Yahoos in the making.

The Yahoos, on the other hand, were not capable of any amelioration or improvement; they had sunk so far that they could not be raised again in the scale of being. To put an end to the whole species as humanely as possible, and to replace them as beasts of burden by asses, which were 'in all respects more valuable brutes' would be the wisest course.[1] This idea was no doubt suggested by the fact that the ass, recently introduced into Ireland, was beginning to become common in the country when Swift wrote.[2]

Swift's *Modest Proposal for preventing the Children of Poor People from being a burthen to their Parents or Country, and for making them beneficial to the Public*, published in 1729, three years after *Gulliver's Travels*, is a parallel to the proposal for the painless extinction of the Yahoos. The wisest thing, he practically says, would be to treat the 'savage old Irish' and the 'natives of the poorer sort' like beasts, unless you are prepared to do something to relieve their misery and remove its causes. The difference between them and the Yahoos was that their lot could be ameliorated; however low they had sunk they could be raised in the scale. 'Those people may be brought to a less savage manner of life,' says Swift; by proper measures it would be possible to 'civilize the most barbarous among them, reconcile them to our customs and manner of living, and reduce great numbers to the national religion'.[3] Begin, he urged, by educating the young, and teaching them English: the Irish are not unteachable. 'Supposing the size of a native's understanding just equal to that of a

---

[1] *Gulliver's Travels*, pp. 283–4.
[2] See Dr. Mahaffy's paper, 'On the Introduction of the Ass as a Beast of Burden into Ireland', *Proceedings of the Royal Irish Academy*, March 1917. Other evidence might be added.
[3] *Prose Works*, vii. 133.

dog or horse, I have often seen those two animals to be civilized by rewards, at least as much as by punishment.'[1] In a letter written some years later he declared that the English ought to be 'ashamed of the reproaches they cast on the ignorance, the dulness, and the want of courage, in the Irish natives; those defects, wherever they happen, arising only from the poverty and slavery they suffer from their inhuman neighbours, and the base corrupt spirits of too many of the chief gentry, etc. . . . I do assert that from several experiments I have made in travelling over both kingdoms, I have found the poor cottagers here, who could speak our language, to have a much better natural taste for good sense, humour, and raillery, than ever I observed among people of the like sort in England. But the millions of oppressions they lie under, the tyranny of their landlords, the ridiculous zeal of their priests, and the general misery of the whole nation, have been enough to damp the best spirits under the sun.'[2]

In this passage, Swift's pity for the old Irish seems to be developing into sympathy. But in reality he reserved his sympathy for the new Irish—that is, the English colony in Ireland. The inhabitants of that country were two distinct races, and he was anxious not for their union but for the maintenance of the distinction between them. 'Our neighbours', he complains in the *Drapier's Letters*, 'look upon us as a sort of savage Irish, whom our ancestors conquered several hundred years ago.'[3] The first grievance of Ireland, he told Walpole, was 'that all persons born in Ireland are called and treated as Irishmen, although their fathers and grandfathers were born in England.'[4] He rebuked Pope as late as 1737 for making this mistake. 'Some of those who highly esteem you, and a few who know you personally,

---

[1] *Prose Works*, iv. 214; vi. 199; vii. 133.
[2] To Col. Wogan, Aug. 2, 1732. *Correspondence*, iv. 328.
[3] *Prose Works*, vi. 116.   [4] *Correspondence*, iii. 309.

are grieved to find you make no distinction between the English gentry of this kingdom, and the savage old Irish, who are only the vulgar, and some gentlemen who live in the Irish parts of the kingdom; but the English colonies, who are three parts in four, are much more civilized than many counties in England, and speak better English, and are much better bred.'[1] Swift confessed the place of his birth with regret. 'I happened indeed by a perfect accident, to be born here . . . and thus I am a Teague, or an Irishman, or what people please.' But whatever other people said, he regarded himself as an English gentleman born in Ireland—the phrase by which he described Molyneux[2]—and wrote the *Drapier's Letters* in defence of the rights of those he called 'the true English people of Ireland'.[3] The Third Part of *Gulliver* is full of allusions to that famous controversy.

The Third Voyage is admittedly the part of *Gulliver's Travels* 'in which the world took the least pleasure'. Contemporary critics and later critics agreed in this verdict. 'Dr. Arbuthnot likes the projectors least; others, you tell me, the flying island,' wrote Swift to Pope. Swift's friend Erasmus Lewis grumbled, and said he wanted a key to it.[4] One reason why the Third Voyage was less popular with readers was that it was more complicated and more difficult to understand than the rest. Its plot was less simple. It was not a voyage to a single island, but to a group of islands. Captain Gulliver sails from island to island as Lucian's heroes do in his *True History*, or as Pantagruel and his companions do in Rabelais. It consists of four different stories loosely held together by a framework of personal narrative. One part is the story of the Flying Island; another that of the Academy of Projectors, a satire against science and philosophy; a third part is a satire against literary critics and historians; a fourth a satire against too

---

[1] Ibid. vi. 32. [2] *Prose Works*, vi. 115.
[3] Ibid. vi. 119. [4] *Correspondence*, iii. 357, 368.

much love of living. These different sections were written at different times and patched together later. We know from Pope's statement to Spence, that the story of 'the projects of Laputa' was to be inserted in the *Memoirs of Scriblerus*, and must therefore have been written about 1714. Internal evidence confirms Pope's statement; for instance, there is a direct reference to a celebrated divorce case which occurred in 1713.[1]

We know that the story of the Flying Island was written later. 'I am in the Flying Island where I shall not stay long,' wrote Swift to Ford in January 1724, but judging once more from the references to contemporary events which it contains, the final touches were not added till 1725. Swift's own words show that the Third Voyage possessed some political meaning, and that the world had not perceived it. In the lines on his own death, written in November 1731, he refers to himself as the author of

> . . . Libels yet conceal'd from sight,
> Against the court to show his spite;
> Perhaps his travels, part the third;
> A lie at every second word—
> Offensive to a loyal ear.[2]

The libel was an allegory about the relations between Ireland and England concealed in the story of the islands of Laputa and Balnibarbi. The Flying or Floating Island represented England. The application of that title to England was suggested by Sir William Temple. In his *Memoirs*, speaking of England's foreign policy during Charles II's reign, Temple says: 'Our counsels and conduct were like those of a floating island, driven one way or 'tother, according to the winds or tides.' Again, in one of his *Essays*, speaking of the fatal effects of faction, Temple terms England 'this floating island'.[3]

---

[1] *Gulliver's Travels*, p. 170.
[2] *Poems*, ed. W. E. Browning, i. 262.
[3] Temple's *Works* (1754), i. 374; ii. 375.

This Floating or Flying Island hovers over the subject land or continent of Balnibarbi, and 'from the great advantage of such a superior situation' easily keeps it in a state of subjection. If any part of the subject land rebels, the King has two methods of reducing it to obedience. 'The first and mildest course is by keeping the island hovering over such a town, and the lands about it, whereby he can deprive them of the benefit of the sun and the rain, and consequently afflict the inhabitants with dearth and diseases.'[1]

This was the result produced by the laws in restraint of trade which England had enacted to keep Ireland in subjection. 'We are so strangely limited', complains Swift in the *Drapier's Letters*, 'in every branch of trade, that can be of advantage to us; and utterly deprived of those, which are of the greatest importance. . . . For we are denied the benefits that God and nature intended to us; as manifestly appears by our happy situation for commerce, and the great number of our excellent ports.' In one of his pamphlets he contrasts the unhappy lot of Ireland with that of England, 'which is left at liberty to enjoy the benefits of nature, and to make the best of those advantages which God hath given it, in soil, climate, and situation'.[2] These 'benefits of nature' in general are typified by the 'benefit of the sun and rain' in the passage in the *Travels*.

Other pamphlets of Swift dwell on the decay of Dublin and the decadence of Irish agriculture. In that 'beggarly city', wrote Swift in 1724, fifteen hundred of the houses, being a seventh part of the whole city, were left uninhabited and falling to ruin. In Ireland at large land was going out of cultivation, owing to the transformation of tillage into pasture: landlords were prohibiting their tenants from ploughing, 'one effect of which is already seen in the prodigious dearness of corn, and the importation of it from London, as the cheaper

---

[1] *Gulliver's Travels*, p. 176.   [2] *Prose Works*, vi. 201; vii. 115.

market'.[1] Both these features of the economic condition of the country are reproduced in Gulliver's account of the state of Balnibari and its capital Lagado. In Lagado most of the houses are out of repair and the people in the streets generally in rags. In the country outside its labourers were working on the ground, but there was no sign either of corn or grass, though the soil appeared to be excellent. 'I never knew', sums up Gulliver, 'a soil so unhappily cultivated, houses so ill contrived and so ruinous, or a people whose countenances and habit expressed so much misery and want.'[2]

All the economic evils of Ireland were increased by the fact that owing to absentee landlords, English place-holders, and the forced consumption of English manufactured goods, half the rents and profits of the whole kingdom were spent in England. Poor to begin with, Ireland was drained by England of what little wealth it possessed. It is for that reason that Swift baptized England by the significant name of Laputa. He solemnly describes the etymology and meaning of the word at the beginning of his account of the island, and offers a derivation which was no doubt intended to ridicule the philologists of the period.[3] But the name is simply two Spanish words meaning 'the harlot', a comparison suggested by Swift because, as a proverb in his Spanish Dictionary says, a lady of that kind 'leaves the purse empty'.[4] In one of his poems he calls England 'yon ravenous isle'.[5]

Some lighter touches he also added to suggest the identification of Laputa with England. One of the distinguishing characteristics of its people was the 'strong disposition' Gulliver observed in them 'towards news and politics, perpetually enquiring into public affairs,

[1] *Prose Works*, vii. 17, 69.   [2] *Gulliver's Travels*, p. 182.
[3] Ibid., p. 166.
[4] Captain John Stevens, *Spanish and English Dictionary* (1706).
[5] *Verses on the sudden Drying up of St. Patrick's Well* (1726).

giving their judgments in matters of state, and passionately disputing every inch of a party opinion'.[1] This was one of the characteristics Swift had remarked in the English. 'The rabble here', he wrote from London in 1710, 'are much more inquisitive in politics than in Ireland. . . . I never saw so great a ferment among all sorts of people.' In one of his essays he observes that there was in England 'a pragmatical disposition to politics, in the very nature and genius of the people'.[2]

In Laputa Gulliver also observed a remarkable fondness for music. On the second morning after his arrival, about eleven o'clock, 'the King himself in person, attended by his nobility, courtiers, and officers, having prepared all their musical instruments, played on them for three hours without intermission, so that I was quite stunned with the noise; neither could I possibly guess the meaning, till my tutor informed me. He said that the people of their island had their ears adapted to hear the music of the spheres, which always played at certain periods, and the court was now prepared to bear their part in whatever instrument they most excelled.'[3] Now, at the moment when Swift was writing, operas were all the rage at the English court. The King had pensioned Handel, and a great scheme for producing operas, called the Royal Academy of Music, had been set on foot under his patronage. Rivalries between one singer and another, and disputes about the comparative merits of one composer and another, split society into contending factions. 'The reigning amusement of the town', wrote Gay to Swift on February 3, 1723, 'is entirely music. . . . Everybody is grown now as great a judge of music, as they were in your time of poetry, and folks, that could not distinguish one tune from another, now daily dispute about the different styles of Handel, Bononcini, and Attilio.'[4]

---

[1] *Gulliver's Travels*, p. 168.   [2] *Prose Works*, ii. 8; xi. 179.
[3] *Gulliver's Travels*, p. 167.   [4] *Correspondence*, iii. 154.

The Court of Laputa was too much taken up with its amusements to regard what passed below in Balnibarbi. One of the misfortunes from which that country suffered was the promotion of all kinds of schemes by an Academy of Projectors established in it. None of these projects were brought to perfection, and in the meantime the whole country lay miserably waste, the houses in ruins, and the people without food or clothes. Swift uses the words 'projects' and 'projectors' to cover speculative schemes of every kind, not merely mechanical inventions of a pseudo-scientific character. It includes political reforms such as the projected scheme of the Whigs for the repeal of the Test Act in order to benefit the Nonconformists of Ulster. It covers the proposal for the establishment of a National Bank in Ireland, agitated in 1720–1. 'That destructive project', he calls it in the *Drapier's Letters*.[1] It also refers to financial jobs such as Wood's patent for providing Ireland with copper coinage. A 'wicked project,' Swift calls it; 'an open attempt . . . to destroy all arts and sciences, all trades and manufactures, and the very tillage of the ground, only to enrich one obscure ill-designing projector, and his followers'.[2]

The years during which Swift completed *Gulliver's Travels* coincided with the period when Wood's attempt was made and defeated. Wood's patent was sealed on July 12, 1722, and cancelled on August 25, 1725. The votes of the Irish Parliament against the patent were passed in September 1723, and the *Drapier's Letters* appeared in 1724, between March and December. A story in the Voyage to Laputa celebrates Wood's defeat. Chapter III begins with a scientific account of the nature of the flying island, how it was moved, and made to rise and fall, of the substance of which it was composed, and of the thick layer of adamant which formed the under-surface of the island. The last remedy of the

[1] *Prose Works*, vi. 145. [2] Ibid. iv. 185, 189.

King of Laputa against a rebellious district of the continent below, supposing the plan of depriving that district of the benefit of the sun and rain was not effective, was to crush the rebels 'by letting the island drop directly upon their heads, which makes a universal destruction both of houses and men'. It was a dangerous remedy, because if the adamantine bottom were to crack or break the whole mass would fall to the ground. Just before Gulliver arrived in Balnibarbi there had been such a rebellion in one part of it, and the inhabitants, 'who had often complained of great oppressions', had 'provided a vast quantity of the most combustible fuel, hoping to burst therewith the adamantine bottom of the island', if the attempt was made to crush them. In the face of this and other dangers the King of Laputa was obliged to give way, and yielded to the conditions demanded by the rebels.[1]

It appears to me that this story is an allegorical representation of the successful opposition of Ireland to Wood's halfpence.

The 'combustible fuel' represents the resolutions of the Irish Parliament, and Swift's incendiary pamphlets and ballads. In the *Drapier's Letters* he denied that Ireland was what was termed 'a depending kingdom' and told his countrymen that 'by the laws of God, of nature, of nations, and of your own country, you are and ought to be as free a people as your brethren in England'.[2] The 'adamantine bottom' typifies what was called 'the English interest in Ireland', that is, the colony of English descent who formed the foundation on which the rule of England there rested. The governing class in Ireland was divided: some officials and lawyers and bishops supported the English Ministry, but Privy Council and Parliament remonstrated against Wood's scheme, and the Chancellor and the Archbishop of Dublin opposed it. An irresistible attraction

[1] *Gulliver's Travels*, p. 177.　　[2] *Prose Works*, vi. 113, 115.

drew all sections of the English colony together in opposition to the Government. Archbishop Boulter, the Primate, told the Duke of Newcastle 'that the people of every religion, country, and party here, are alike set against *Wood's* halfpence, and that their agreement in this has had a very unhappy influence on the state of this nation, by bringing on intimacies between Papists and Jacobites, and the Whigs, who before had no correspondence with them'. He doubted whether Protestant justices of the peace would be strict in disarming Papists, and urged the English Government not to 'take any angry steps' against the offending Protestants, because 'no great damage can be done them, without sensibly hurting *England*'.[1] In short, to borrow Swift's figurative phrase, 'the adamantine bottom' was cracked and in danger of falling off.[2]

Perhaps the most significant symptom of the crisis was the opposition of the Lord Chancellor of Ireland to Wood's patent. Alan Brodrick had been Lord Chancellor since 1714, and had been created first Baron and then Viscount Middleton. Three times in succession he had been one of the Lords Justices appointed to fill the place of the absent Viceroy (1717–19), and there was no stronger Whig in Ireland. However, he was honest, conscientious, and independent. Owing to his opposition in the English Parliament to the Peerage Bill he had been omitted from the list of the Lords Justices in 1722. Walpole believed he was the chief cause of the opposition to Wood's patent, and declared in October 1723 that the King was determined to remove him. Grafton, the Lord-Lieutenant, denounced him and urged his removal.[3] On the other hand, Middleton strongly repudiated the doctrine of the independency of Ireland asserted in the fourth of the

---

[1] *Letters written by Hugh Boulter* (1769), i. 8–9.
[2] *Gulliver's Travels*, p. 177.
[3] W. Coxe, *Robert Walpole* (1798), ii. 276, 281, 355, 363.

Drapier's Letters, and subsequently refused to allow the collected edition to be dedicated to him.[1] His opposition did not go beyond what was decent and legitimate. 'Whatever the event may be,' he wrote to his brother, 'I have the comfort to know that I fall a sacrifice to the opposition I gave to Wood's Halfpence, and I had rather fall for these with my country.'[2] His brother told him that 'the honest part he had acted in reference to the patent was, he might be assured, a mortal sin, not to be forgiven'. Convinced by too many proofs that he would be removed, he preferred to tender his resignation.[3]

It is probable that the character of Munodi in the fourth chapter of the Voyage to Laputa is intended to suggest Middleton. 'This Lord Munodi', says Gulliver, 'was a person of the first rank, and had been for some years Governor of Lagado; but by a cabal of ministers was discharged for insufficiency.' He was too conservative, 'content to go on in the old forms', for which he was regarded as 'old, and wilful, and weak', and unsuccessful projectors laid 'the blame entirely upon him'.[4]

The final touches to the account of Laputa in Chapters III and IV can only have been added when Wood's patent had been cancelled and the surrender of the Government announced (Sept. 1725). It was natural that Swift, while representing under the veil of allegory the story of the struggle, should allude also to the chief opponent of the patent amongst Irish statesmen. But it had to be done in a guarded way; so Swift added, altered, and suppressed a few circumstances in order that the resemblance between the real and the fictitious personage might be perceived, but the identity incapable of proof.

---

[1] Ibid. 395, 437.　　　　　[2] Dec. 28, 1723.
[3] March 18, 1725, Coxe, ii. 417, 434; Torrens, i. 263, 334.
[4] *Gulliver's Travels*, pp. 182–4.

Seeking to explain the hints, parallels, and characters in *Gulliver's Travels*, I have followed Swift's own advice, 'to consult annals and compare dates'. The history of the years 1713–26 gives the events which might be reflected in Swift's romance. The other writings of Swift show which of those events interested him. If at a given time his pamphlets, his sermons, his verses, and his letters are all full of one idea it will not be absent from his mind when he depicts imaginary countries. *Gulliver's Travels* show plainly that when Swift began to write them England and English politics filled his mind, and that when he completed them Ireland and Irish affairs were his absorbing interest. As he passed from one subject to another his tone altered, his satire ceased to be playful and became serious and bitter.

Satire was not to him merely a literary exercise: it was an instrument with which he sought to effect a definite practical end. He had the restless temperament of the reformer. 'My notion is', he wrote in 1714, 'that if a man cannot mend the public he should mend old shoes if he can do no better.'[1] He described himself in the *Modest Proposal* as 'wearied out for many years with offering vain, idle, visionary thoughts, and at length utterly despairing of success'.[2] In *Gulliver's Travels* he denounced projectors, but confessed that he had been himself 'a sort of projector' in his younger days. It was folly, he said now, and of all projectors those were most irrational who proposed schemes for teaching ministers to consult the public good and princes to know their true interest.[3] In his later letters he spoke with some scorn of his own 'foolish zeal in endeavouring to save this wretched island',[4] and disclaimed any right to the title of patriot: 'What I do is owing to perfect rage and resentment, and the mortify-

[1] *Correspondence*, ii. 265.   [2] *Prose Works*, vii. 215.
[3] *Gulliver's Travels*, pp. 185, 195.   [4] *Correspondence*, iv. 331.

ing sight of slavery, folly, and baseness.'[1] And again: 'What I did for this country was from perfect hatred at tyranny and oppression. . . . We are slaves, and knaves, and fools.'[2] Thus he raged on paper, but in reality he was a charitable and public-spirited misanthropist who, in spite of ingratitude and disappointment,

. . . kept the tenor of his mind,
To merit well of human kind.[3]

[1] Ibid. iv. 34.   [2] Ibid. v. 64.   [3] *Poems*, i. 259.

INDEX